JuMBo

Puzzle

Book

Word searches, hidden pictures,
and wild, wacky puzzles!

Beth L. Blair

Adams Media
Avon, Massachusetts

Published by
Adams Media, an F+W Publications Company
57 Littlefield Street, Avon, MA 02322. U.S.A.
www.adamsmedia.com

ISBN 10: 1-59869-048-5
ISBN 13: 978-1-59869-048-4

Printed in the United States of America.

J I H G F E D C B

**Library of Congress Cataloging-in-Publication Data
available from publisher**

This publication is designed to provide accurate and authoritative information with regard to the subject matter covered. It is sold with the understanding that the publisher is not engaged in rendering legal, accounting, or other professional advice. If legal advice or other expert assistance is required, the services of a competent professional person should be sought.
     —From a *Declaration of Principles* jointly adopted by a Committee of the American Bar Association and a Committee of Publishers and Associations

Many of the designations used by manufacturers and sellers to distinguish their product are claimed as trademarks. Where those designations appear in this book and Adams Media was aware of a trademark claim, the designations have been printed with initial capital letters.

Interior Illustrations by Kurt Dolber

*This book is available at quantity discounts for bulk purchases.
For information, please call 1-800-289-0963.*

Contents

Introduction

Ready to laugh out loud, stretch your brain, and most of all, have fun? You can do all this and more with the *Jumbo Puzzle Book!* More than just a regular activity book, you'll find every mind-bending game you can think of.

In the first section of our book, you'll find Crazy Puzzles. Packed with word searches, hidden pictures, and wacky riddles, these puzzles will live up to their name. From Funny Food, Spazzy Sports, and Tricky Travels, this section has puzzles for every category, and they're all crazy!

Get ready to test your number skills in our second section—Math Puzzles. Forget the idea that math can't be fun. Chapters include Radical Reasoning, Brain Benders, and Geometry Games. Packed with brain teasers, games, and riddles, our Math Puzzles section is sure to make you laugh out loud and—uh oh!—learn something.

In the final part of our book, you'll find Super Puzzles. We dare you to think of a type of puzzle you won't find here. Mazes, jokes, and funny facts are on every page of chapters like Piles of Pets, Pizza Party, and Creepy Crawlies. There is even a "What a Great Idea!" section!

So get your pencil ready, and enjoy the *Jumbo Puzzle Book!*

Introduction to Crazy Puzzles

In the Crazy Puzzles section, you'll find word searches and hidden pictures, mazes and math puzzles, scrambles and crisscrosses, and much, much more. All these puzzles look at things that you're familiar with—friendship, hobbies, family, nature, food, travel, parties, and sports—but look at them in a fun and funny way.

Here's an example:

Lots of people run and bike and hike to give their body exercise. But how often do you exercise your face? Why not give it a workout by having a funny face contest with your friends?

Look closely at the picture on the next page. Find the hidden letters on each kid. Put them in order on the lines provided to create the two-word answer to this crazy riddle.

What is yours, but other people use it more than you do?

If you thought that puzzle was fun, flip open the book and try a few more. There are enough peculiar puzzles and ridiculous riddles here to keep you busy and laughing for hours and hours.

Happy puzzling!

Funny Faces

_ _ _ _ _ _ _ _!

Chapter 1

Humorous
Houses

Houses in Houses

Have you ever thought about all the things in your house that can be found inside something else? See if you can figure out the names of all of the "housemates" listed below. Then fit the names into their proper place in the crisscross grid. We left you a few H-O-U-S-E-S to help!

I live in a frame. _____

I live in a piggybank. _____

I live in a vase. _____

I live in a carton. _____

I live in a tube. _____

I live in a deck. _____

I live in a trashcan. _____

I live in a book. _____

I live in a tank. _____

I live in a jar. _____

I live in a lamp. _____

I live in a box. _____

I live in a hamper. _____

I live in a clock. _____

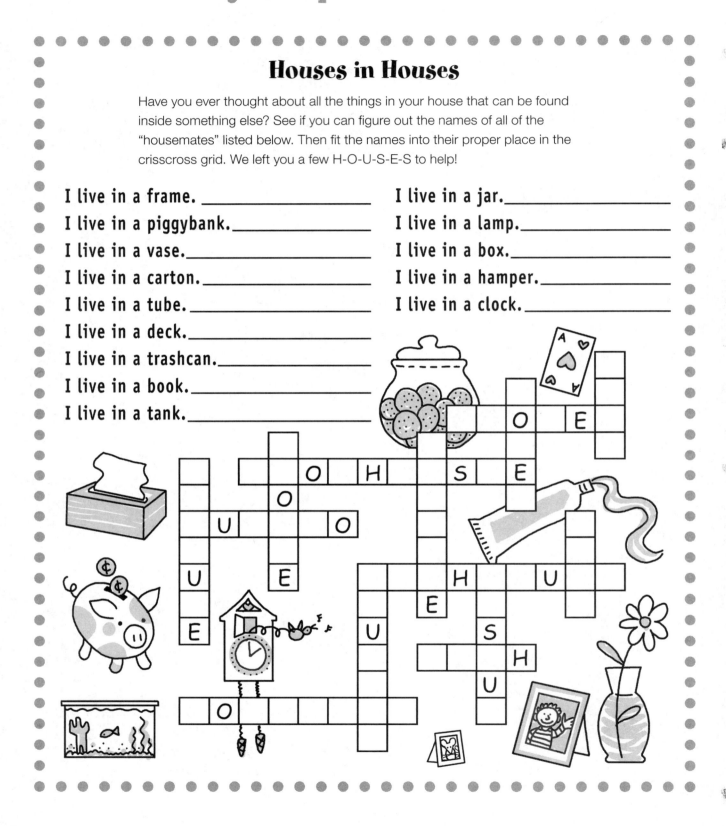

Knock, Knock!

Who's there? To find out, collect all the words with the same number from the grid and write them in their numbered door. Rearrange the words to get the answer to each door's joke.

1
Knock, knock.
Who's there?
Anita.
Anita who?

5 own	2 play?	4 with	2 come	4 you.
3 it's	4 tell	1 minute	3 out	3 up,
1 to	5 name?	4 Ketchup	2 out	5 your
4 I'll	5 know	3 here!	3 Harry	1 over.
2 and	3 cold	1 Anita	4 and	5 Don't
1 think	2 Canoe	5 you	1 it	4 me

2
Knock, knock.
Who's there?
Canoe.
Canoe who?

3
Knock, knock.
Who's there?
Harry.
Harry who?

4
Knock, knock.
Who's there?
Ketchup.
Ketchup who?

5
Knock, knock.
Who's there?
Me.
Me who?

No Way!

Pamela has gotten stuck crawling through the fence around her backyard. Her brother says he can't help to get her out. Why? Break the wingding code to find out the reason!

It's impossible!

Silly Sand

Can you find the 11 differences between these two sand castles?

HINT: It doesn't count that they are mirror images.

Muddy Madness

Mom is not happy—there is mud all over her clean kitchen floor! Look carefully at the list of suspects. Can you figure out who made the four sets of tracks?

Next time, WIPE YOUR FEET!

SUSPECTS

hamster
turtle
cat
snake
kangaroo
chicken
goose
dog
elephant
mouse

Name Game

The people in this family have normal names, but they sure have a strange way of acting out what they are! Match each name in the list to the correct family member.

Alexis   José   Angelina   Matt   Noah
Art   Carol   Abigail   Mark   Isaac

Dog in the House

These words are all missing a few letters. Figure out which letters to add so that you end up with the names of eight different places in which you might live!

EXTRA FUN: Collect the letters you added. Use them to spell the name of a familiar small and curly dog. Write this pet's name on the lines below.

_ _ _ _ _ _ _ _ _ _

_ _ _ _ _ _

H _ U S _

B _ A T

_ R A _ L E R

A _ A _ T _ E _ T

H O T _ _

C _ B _ N

_ _ P L E X

Shy Pets

Can you find the 12 animals hidden in these sentences? Look carefully—some of these animals are not normally found in a house!

HINT: We circled the first pets for you.

Can't you catch me?
We allow lots of oxygen here.
The sad ogre ate chili on toast.
I wish arks were floating in my pond.
"Woof" is how Max says hello.
Please grab bits of drab earth.
Caspar rotated the extra tires on his car.

That's Different!

Put the missing words from each rhyme into the proper spaces. Then connect the dots to see what kind of unusual houses you have built!

travel
straight
base
ground
skins
sticks
apart

I come _____ so I can _____.
I'm covered with_____ that
won't unravel. I'm built on
_____stuck in the_____ —
the sticks are _____, but
my _____ is round!

found
blocks   below
shape
warm
cold
walls

I'm icy _____ and made of
snow. Outside my_____
it's 10_____! I'm built
from _____, but my
_____ is round.
Where it's_____,
I won't be_____!

Tidy Cat

Answer as many clues as you can and fill the letters into the grid. Work back and forth between the box and the clues to find the answer to the crazy question.

A. The ninth letter

$\overline{7}$

B. Holds up pants

$\overline{12}$ $\overline{5}$ $\overline{6}$ $\overline{3}$

C. The way out

$\overline{10}$ $\overline{14}$ $\overline{1}$ $\overline{9}$

D. Opposite of south

$\overline{2}$ $\overline{13}$ $\overline{11}$ $\overline{8}$ $\overline{4}$

Where does a crazy house cat hide the family's garbage?

1C	2D		3B	4D	5B	
6B	7A	8D	9C	10C	11D	
12B	13D	14C		!		

EXTRA FUN: Look for the following 10 items hiding in the trash: banana, glove, capital letter H, fried egg, hanger, cat, fish, umbrella, fish hook, and Mervin, of course!

Who Lives Where?

Unscramble the list of five rather unusual places to live. Then put the number of each house next to the crazy character who lives there!

EXTRA FUN: Fill in all the squares with a dot in the upper right-hand corner to see where the last crazy character lives.

1. HILGT HOUSE

2. RBID HOUSE

3. ARCD HOUSE

4. ETAHUND HOUSE

5. ERGBREGADIN HOUSE

The Ha-Ha House

Match a number with a letter to get a joke and its answer!

END

A The outside!

3 How can paint make a cold house warmer?

2 "Our next door neighbor is on the phone."

B It was having windowpanes!

1 Does a snake's house have a big cellar?

1 ___
2 ___
3 ___
4 ___
5 ___
6 ___

4 If people live in condos, where do ducks live?

C Put on two coats!

5 What side of a house gets the most rain?

D Pondos!

Find Mervin's path from START to END.

START

6 Why did the old house go to the doctor?

E "That's a close call!"

F No, just a crawl space!

Chapter 2

Fritzy Friends

Autograph Fun

Some clever friends have signed this page with rebus autographs.
Can you figure out these silly sentiments?

Loony Language

Aidan and Nadia are best friends with their own special language. Can you figure out what they are saying? **HINT:** Think opposites!

Goodbye, Nadia.
What are me down to?

Goodbye, Aidan. You just got in of school.

Did I have a bad night?

Yes! You had too few tests.

That's too good.
Yesterday will be
the same.

You hope not!

Well, you have
to stay. Hello!

Hello!

Goodbye! How are I?

You am bad!

Friendly Hink Pinks

The answers to Hink Pinks are rhyming words with the same number of syllables. Think of words that mean the same as "friend," and see if you can figure these out.

A girl friend

_ _ _

_ _ _

A dirty friend

_ _ _ _ _

_ _ _ _ _

A wonderful friend

_ _ _ _ _

_ _ _ _ _

A sad friend

_ _ _ _ _

_ _ _ _

Almost Twins

Mary and Myra are such good friends that they wish they were twins. Many days they try to dress exactly alike. Today, they do look very similar, but there are 10 things that are different about their outfits. Can you find them all?

Looks the Same, But . . .

Can you think of two different ways to pronounce each of these words?

bass   lead   wind

bow   sewer   tear

Bead Buddies

Ivy and Lilly made friendship bracelets out of lettered beads. Only they know what the letters spell out when they are read in the correct order! Start at the bead with the dot. Move clockwise around the bracelet picking up every third letter. Write the letters on the lines to learn what these two friends always say to each other.

_ _ _ _ _ _ _ _ _ _ _ _

_ _ _ _ _ _ _ _ _

Just Friends

This is weird—Josh has 21 friends and all their names start with the letter J! Can you find them in this word search? How many are boys? How many are girls?

J	E	R	E	M	I	A	H	O	O	J	J	U	Y
O	I	R	E	F	I	N	N	E	J	U	O	W	D
H	O	O	J	O	L	O	J	U	O	W	A	L	U
N	U	J	I	J	I	J	I	J	S	O	N	I	J

			U	J	U	L	I	E
			J	I	L	I	N	W
			A	N	J	J	O	E
			N	J	O	A	O	L
			N	I	T	S	U	J
			A	G	I	O	A	E
			U	I	J	N	N	S

S	J	O				O	J	U	O	U	S	
E	O	D	J			J	I	I	U	J	E	
M	W	E	I	X		I	L	J	G	L	N	O
A	I	J	A	C	K	U	O	A	E	J	L	O
J	J	G	W	L	O	Y	O	C	L	A	N	J
	G	E	D	A	J	I	J	O	S	I	E	
	E	I	U	U	G	O	B	G	N	O		
	J	A	N	E	T	I	O	J				

19

Get your lemonade here!

1 SIZE - 35¢ LEMONADE

Pucker Up!

Josie and Arlo have lemonade stands across the street from each other. If they both sell all of their cups of lemonade, who will make the most money?

ICE COLD LEMONADE!

Lemonade large 50¢ small 25¢

Crazy Keyboard

Kayla is e-mailing a funny joke to all of her friends, but her keyboard is acting weird. The letters she types are not the letters that appear on the screen! Can you crack the code to see what joke will make Kayla's friends LOL (Laugh Out Loud)?

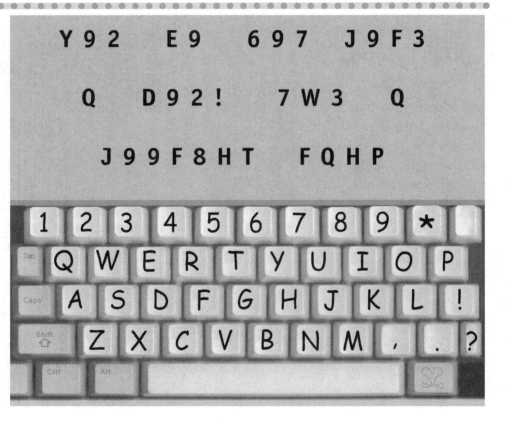

Y 9 2   E 9   6 9 7   J 9 F 3

Q   D 9 2 !   7 W 3   Q

J 9 9 F 8 H T   F Q H P

Tough for Two

There are many games that are impossible to play with only one other friend.
The names of these games have been broken in two. After you have matched
up the two halves, fit the name into its proper place in the crisscross. We've left
you some G-A-M-E-S to get you started.

Silly Sleepover

Missy and Chrissy have chosen a very odd place to have their sleepover! Follow the directions to find out where they are.

Find box 1-A and copy it into square 1-A in the grid.

Find box 1-B and copy it into square 1-B in the grid.

Continue doing this until you have copied all the boxes into the grid.

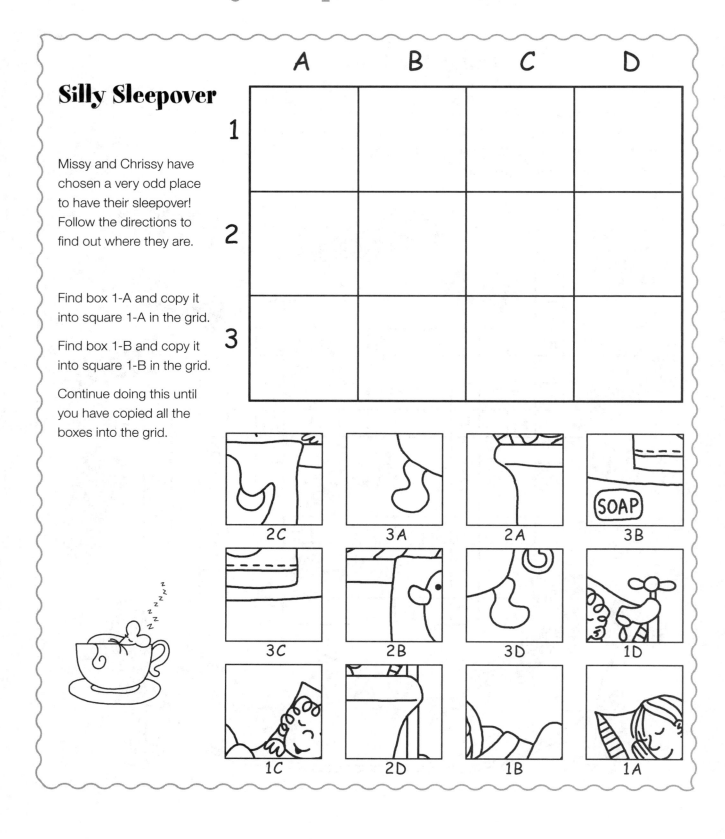

Pass It On

Parker tried to pass this funny joke to Toshi during math class. When he got caught, Parker ripped up the note. Can you piece it back together so you can have a good laugh, too? Write the fixed-up joke on the blank piece of paper.

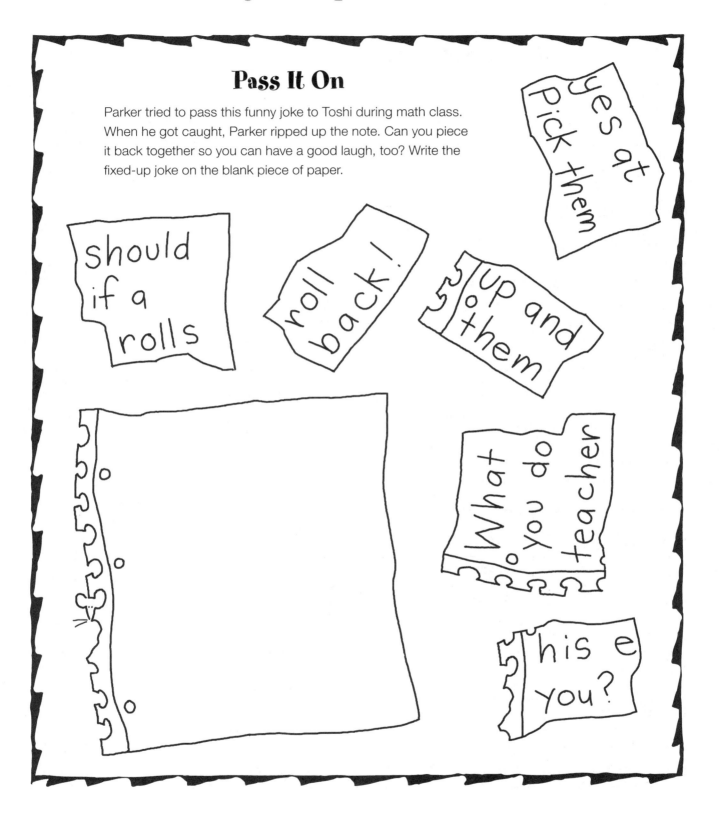

yes at
pick them

should
if a
rolls

roll
back!

up and
them

What
you do
teacher

his e
you?

Ready, Set, Go!

Griffin and Aubrey are racing to the library. Griffin can hop only on odd-numbered squares that touch each other. Aubrey can glide only on even-numbered squares that touch! The race starts at Griffin's house. Who will use the fewest squares to get to the library?

HINT: Enter buildings at the white triangles.

Tasty Pastry	Bud's Florist	Home Run Sports	38	8	16	12	40	10	22	Harry's Pottery

The board game grid contains the following:

Top rows: Tasty Pastry, Bud's Florist, Home Run Sports, 38, 8, 16, 12, 40, 10, 22, Harry's Pottery

4, Hair Flair, 13, Post Office, 18

84, 7, 114, 26, 32, 12, 13, 51, 22, 20, 8, 6, 44

75, 17, Movieland, 20, Pete's Pets, 14, Park

93, Library, 62, 12, 41, 6, 100, 12

9, 43, 31, 40, 23, 21, 13, 11, 37, 42, Deep Blue Computer Store, 4

8, Doh Nuts, 53, All-Nite Diner, 19, Lots o' Pizza, 33, Renta Movie, 11, 48

21, 17, 7, 17, 12, 2

42, 11, 19, 15, 22, 339, 71, 9, 37, 3, START

83, 47, 217, 3, Fire Station #9, Shop n' Shop Grocery, 4, Griffin's House

Parkside Elem. School, 13

26

In the Shadows

Mieko and Harry are making shadow puppets on the wall. Can you find the pattern that exactly matches the picture to the right?

Friends to the End

Milo, Soozie, and Caspar have found words that all contain the word END. Figure out each word from the clue given. The first one has been done for you!

<u>F</u> <u>R</u> <u>I</u> <u>E</u> <u>N</u> <u>D</u> = a person you like who likes you

_ <u>E</u> <u>N</u> <u>D</u> = to let a person borrow something

_ _ <u>E</u> <u>N</u> <u>D</u> = to mix together completely

_ _ <u>E</u> <u>N</u> <u>D</u> = to pay money

_ _ _ <u>E</u> <u>N</u> <u>D</u> _ _ = pale purple

_ <u>E</u> <u>N</u> <u>D</u> = to fix or repair

_ <u>E</u> <u>N</u> <u>D</u> _ _ = kind or loving

_ _ <u>E</u> <u>N</u> <u>D</u> _ = a list of things to be done

_ _ _ <u>E</u> <u>N</u> <u>D</u> = to protect against danger

_ _ _ <u>E</u> <u>N</u> <u>D</u> = to make longer

_ _ _ <u>E</u> <u>N</u> <u>D</u> = story told for many years

_ _ _ <u>E</u> <u>N</u> <u>D</u> = to cause to be angry

<u>E</u> <u>N</u> <u>D</u> _ _ _ _ = never stopping

_ _ <u>E</u> <u>N</u> <u>D</u> _ _ = long and thin

_ _ _ <u>E</u> <u>N</u> <u>D</u> _ _ = info at the end of a book

_ _ _ <u>E</u> <u>N</u> <u>D</u> _ _ = place to write special dates

_ _ _ <u>E</u> <u>N</u> <u>D</u> _ _ = really awesome

_ <u>E</u> <u>N</u> <u>D</u> _ _ = metal piece over a bike's wheel

Chapter 3

Peculiar Parties

Birthday Bowling

Nayib is celebrating his birthday at the bowling alley. How old do you think he is?

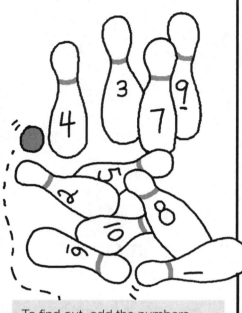

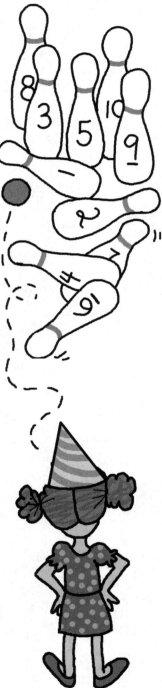

To find out, add the numbers on all the pins left standing, then subtract the numbers on all the pins knocked down.

Happy Half

Something is wrong with Hunter's instant camera. Only one half of each picture comes out! Can you help him by drawing in the rest of each party picture?

Peculiari-tea

Tanika invited four friends to a tea party, but each guest wanted something different to drink! Break the code on each cup to see what kind of drinks Tanika made for her guests.

Hink Pinks

The answers to these riddles are two single-syllable words that rhyme. Can you figure out these party hink pinks?

A quick present = _ _ _ _ _ _   _ _ _ _

A not real dessert = _ _ _ _   _ _ _ _

A dumb party activity = _ _ _ _ _   _ _ _ _ _

Kooky Carnival

How many weird or wacky things can you find at this backyard carnival?

Cake-o-licious

Everyone has their favorite kind of cake. What sort of cake do you think each of these characters likes best? When you have decided, see if you can fit the cake names into the puzzle grid. We left you a B-I-T-E of I-C-I-N-G to get you started!

Why Do Candles . . .

Drop the letters into their proper place in the grid. The letters in each column fit in the spaces directly underneath that column, but they may be scrambled. Once you have them in their correct spots, you will know the answer to this silly riddle:

Why do candles go on top of a birthday cake?

What Should You . . .

The four words that make up the answer to this riddle are hiding in this picture. Once you find them, put them in the correct order and write the answer in the colored box.

What should you do if your birthday cake tastes burnt and crunchy?

You're Invited!

Hannah is having a party and sent this eccentric invitation to all of her friends. Can you read the invitation, and figure out what kind of party Hannah is having?

EXTRA FUN: Guess why Hannah chose this kind of party!

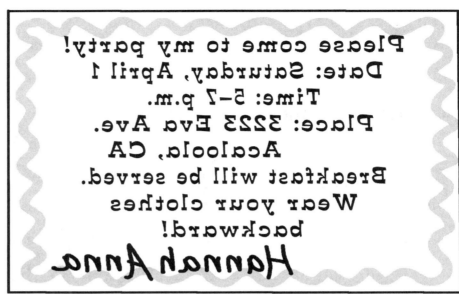

Please come to my party!
Date: Saturday, April 1
Time: 5–7 p.m.
Place: 3223 Eva Ave.
Acaloola, CA
Breakfast will be served.
Wear your clothes backward!
Hannah Anna

Goofy Guests

Hannah is addressing her invitations, but has only written each guest's last name! Finish each envelope by using the names and initials scattered on the table.
HINT: Each correct name is silly!

Crazy Costume

Chloe is having a hard time deciding what to wear to Zoe's costume party. Use the clues to figure out what Chloe finally decided to wear. Circle her choices.

HINT: The party has an "ocean" theme!

She did not wear boots or clogs.

She did wear a dress, but it did not have polka dots.

She did wear something on her head, but it wasn't a hat.

She did wear something around her neck, but it wasn't a scarf.

She did carry something, but it wasn't an umbrella.

Silly Song

It is traditional to sing to a person on his or her birthday. Use the note decoder to figure out some loony lyrics that you might like to try at your next birthday party!

Balls of String

There's an extra letter hiding several times in each row. Take it out, and you will leave behind the name of a classic party game! Write each hidden letter on the blank line for that row. Read down the letters to answer this riddle:

Two balls of string ran a race. Which one won?

___ mtutsicatl cthatirts
___ bhlhihnd mhahn's hbhlufhf
___ esiemoen esaeyes
___ byinygyo
___ cwhawrawdes
___ feolleow thee eleeaeder
___ rrerd lrigrht rgreren rlrigrht
___ eleeaepferog
___ thot ptotattot
___ iduick diuicki goiosie
___ heidee eande eseeke
___ dstatdudes

Find Your Way

from balloon to cake!

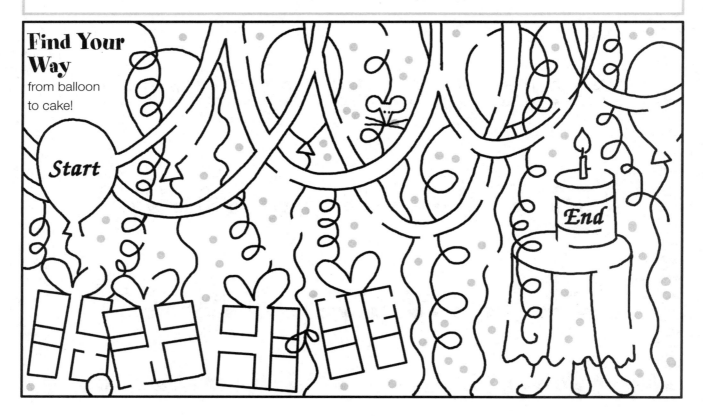

Start

End

36

Looking for Loot

This band of party pirates is looking for treasure. Start at number 1 and connect the dots in order to see where they finally found their goodie bags.

EXTRA FUN: After you have connected the dots, use a green crayon or marker to add some important details to finish the picture!

jumbo puzzle book

Tons of Fun

You can plan a party around any theme or for any occasion! Can you find all 50 party ideas hidden in this word search?

```
S R U A S O N I D H I P P I E L G N U J
W M M A C A R N I V A L X P A J A M A S
I Y A B H C E O X A E S E H T R E D N U
M S E C R E T A G E N T S P I Z Z A O S
M T R P I B S S D B E G N I T A K S T T
I E C R S A R T S A N D C R A F T S R H
N R E I T R E R E L I H W A S O E I A G
G Y C N M B T O I L T I S T W S D L V I
G N I C A E N P V E N P E E H Y L L E N
N E D E S C I S O R E P X S X O O Y L K
I E W S D U W S M I L Y A D H T R I B D
V W C S B E A C H N A C I G A M A S E N
I O O R O L A F A A V D A N C I N G E A
G L O E S R D W W S H A N U K K A H C S
S L K T S O E C A P S R E T U O S I A N
K A I S O C O M I C B O O K S L R X M O
N H E A D X W W I L D W E S T C L D P G
A T S E I F E D A L S X L B U G S W I A
H S L L O D M O N S T E R S U O S X N R
T S E O R E H R E P U S F I S H I N G D
```

arts and crafts
barbecue
beach
fiesta
Hawaiian
jungle
monsters
mystery
pirates
pizza
swimming
secret agents
Thanksgiving
outer space
birthday
circus
camping
dragons and knights
Christmas
cookies

Wild West	Hanukkah	horses	dancing	princess	travel
ballerinas	under the sea	comic books	skating	fishing	silly
dinosaurs	Valentine	movies	Halloween	toys	ice cream
Easter	carnival	cars	winter	hippie	magic
superheroes	sports	pets	pajamas	bugs	dolls

38

Chapter 4

Funny Food

Soup's On!

It seems some very strange items have fallen into each of these pots of soup. Can you cross out the ingredients you would NEVER find in soup? Then look at the remaining ingredients and see if you can tell what kind of soup is in each pot.

Kind of Soup

onions	dry sand
clams	pepper
flour	milk
bathing suit	pebbles
plastic shovel	parsley
potatoes	sunscreen
clam shells	butter
salt	

Kind of Soup

water	onion
chicken	chicken feed
chicken wire	carrots
pepper	grit
celery	noodles
straw	salt
egg carton	feathers

Kind of Soup

onion	water
celery	watering can
carrots	salt
zucchini	pepper
potatoes	fertilizer
glove	basil
tomatoes	dirt
green beans	

Instant Soup

How quickly can you find 10 three-letter words hiding in the word CHOWDER?

What a Mouthful

Is this a secret code? No, each food is simply listed by its dictionary pronunciation! Write the more familiar spelling of each name in the empty spaces.

ap´ əl sôs
_____

kū´ kum bər
_____

sī´ dər
_____

bə nan´ ə
_____

kô´ lə flou´ ər
_____

brok´ ə lē
_____

cher´ ē
_____

säl´ sə
_____

sə lä´ mē
_____

av´ ə kä´ dō
_____

bā´ ken
_____

Berry Good

Each berry in this garden uses two sets of letters. Can you match the letter sets to find all the berries? Be careful—there's one extra letter set!

_ _ _ _ _ _ BERRY

_ _ _ _ BERRY

_ _ _ _ _ BERRY

_ _ _ _ BERRY

_ _ _ _ BERRY

_ _ _ _ _ BERRY

BL

CR

CK

RA

STR GO BLA

HU

SP

OSE

UE

AN AW

Put a different letter from the list into each empty box to make a familiar cooking word. The empty box might be at the beginning, the middle, or the end of the mystery word. **HINT:** Each letter in the list will be used only once.

When you are done, read down the shaded boxes to discover the answer to this curious cooking question:

Where should you go if you are a really, really bad cook?

K N E		D L E
A S F		Y T E
B A K		S A N
S I M		T I R
D I S		E W C
A R O		S T S
C E C		T E N
O N B		O I L
U T O		S T Y
B L E		D I X
M E L		A R D

A R T T E S A R U
A T T A S A N R N

Dizzy Donuts

The Kruller family bought a baker's dozen donuts. Can you tell, by using the following clues, how many donuts each person ate? **HINT:** A baker's dozen = 13.

- **Dad ate twice as many donuts as Mom.**
- **Brooke ate fewer donuts than everyone else.**
- **Austin and Caleb ate the same number of donuts**

EXTRA FUN: Someone has taken a bite—and a letter—out of each of these donuts! Can you figure out what kinds of donuts were tasted?

Splash!

The ship's cook dropped dinner in the drink! Can you help him find his soggy supper? Look for a piece of cheese on a cracker, orange slice, apple, bowl of spaghetti, bowl of salad, slice of bread, stick of butter, glass of water, ice-cream cone, salt shaker, knife, fork, spoon, and teacup.

Second Helpings

Each food name in this puzzle has a double letter in it. Some names have two sets of double letters! Write the answer to each clue in the crossword grid on the next page. We left the double letters to give you a hand.

ACROSS

3 Smooth and creamy dessert served in a bowl

5 Hot tomato and cheese pie served in triangles

7 Breakfast food covered with little squares

8 Sometimes this is inside a roast chicken

11 Creamy drink made in a blender from milk, fruit, and ice

12 This gets sliced on pizza, or tossed in salads

15 Fluffy, sweet and golden bread made with many eggs

17 Italian pasta you twirl on a fork

19 Prickly golden fruit with stiff green leaves on top

24 Small, round fruits that grow on bushes

25 Leafy vegetable used to make salads

26 A sweet treat eaten after a meal

27 Dark colored soda that's not cola

28 Fragrant spice often used in Christmas cookies

DOWN

1 Tasty dip made from chickpeas

2 Long, flat pasta made from flour and egg

4 Hard, golden candy made from butter, sugar, and cream

6 These long, green vegetables grow like crazy in the summer

9 Sweet treats made on a stick

10 Mexican flat bread used to wrap around food

12 Small breakfast cakes

13 Cooked spheres of hamburger, egg, and spices

14 Round, flat, baked treats

16 Mervin loves this dairy product that's sometimes sliced and sometimes stretchy.

18 Crunchy Chinese "tube" filled with vegetables and meat

20 Vegetable that looks like a tree

21 Dairy product you can melt or spread

22 Round, red vegetables that grow underground

23 Small, round, red fruits with long stems

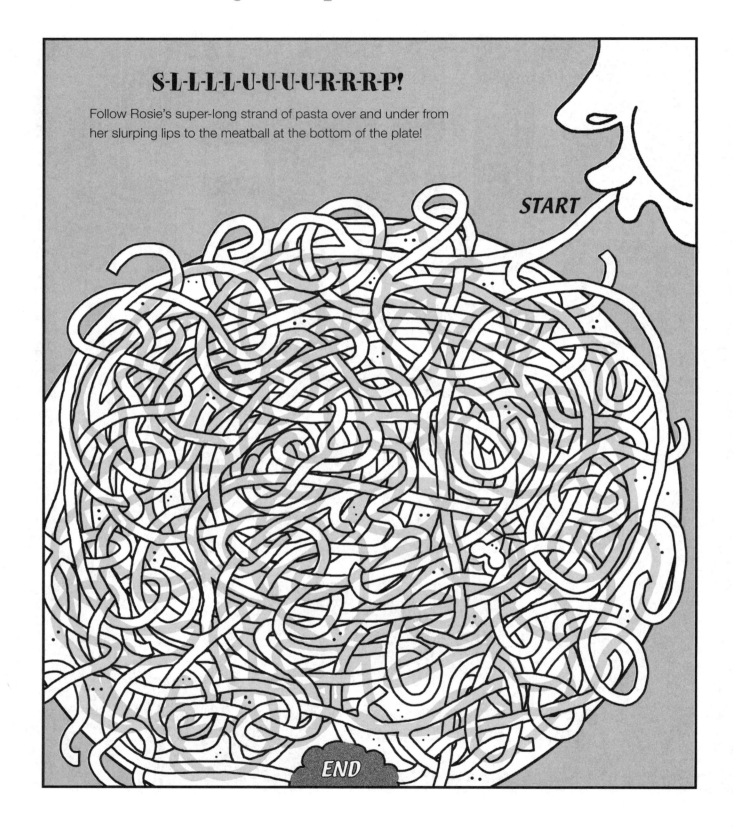

S-L-L-L-L-U-U-U-U-R-R-R-P!

Follow Rosie's super-long strand of pasta over and under from her slurping lips to the meatball at the bottom of the plate!

START

END

How Do You Make . . .

The new kid working at the snack bar is still learning his job. Look closely at the menu. Can you find the answer to his question?

How do you make a hotdog roll?

hoT dog   YOgurt   chiPs

Ice cream   hambURger   grilLed cheese

miLk   sAlad

Tuna fish   Taco

                     french friEs

Fill 'er Up!

The average person in America eats about 29 bowls of this tasty treat every year! Fill in all the shapes that have the letter C, R, U, N, C, or H to find the name of this popular snack.

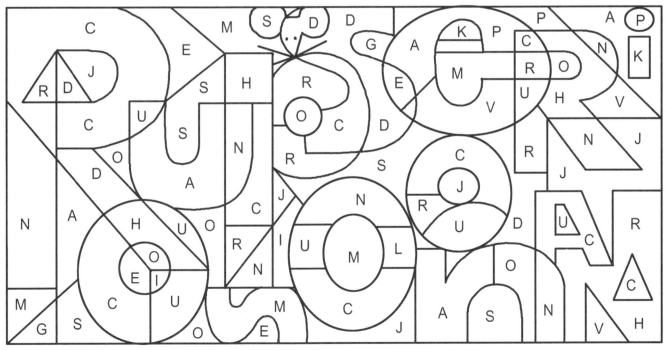

Scrambled Eggs

Each of these character's favorite meal has been broken into three pieces and scrambled around the page. Can you match up the parts and make silly-sounding breakfasts for everyone? Write your answers on the empty lines.

OF
LEGS
AND
WHEAT
BACON
SCREAM
LES
OF
WO

Leftovers

Write a word from the shaded column next to a word in the left column to make the name of a familiar food. There may be more than one way to match up all the words—just make sure there are no leftovers!

I've got my part!

I have my part, too!

CUP _____
STRAW _____
POTATO _____
PEANUT _____
POP _____
CORN _____
COLE _____
HOT _____
HAM _____
FRENCH _____
TUNA _____
APPLE _____
EGG _____

FRIES
MELT
SAUCE
ROLL
BURGER
BERRY
CORN
BUTTER
CAKE
SALAD
SLAW
CHIPS
DOG

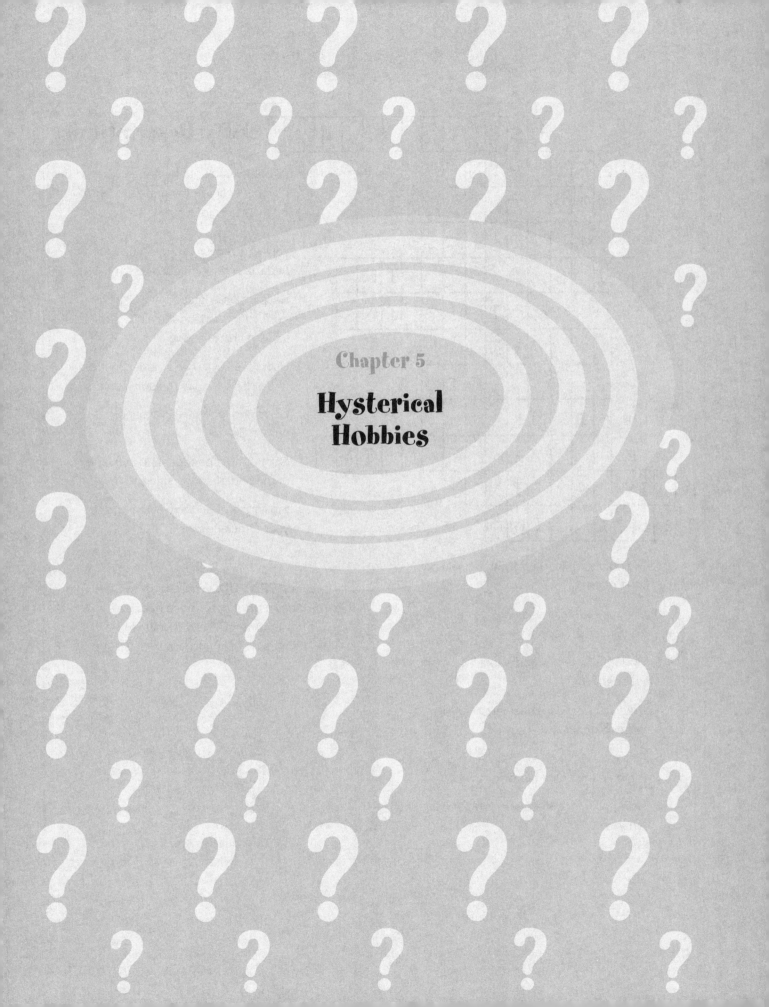

Chapter 5

Hysterical Hobbies

jumbo puzzle book

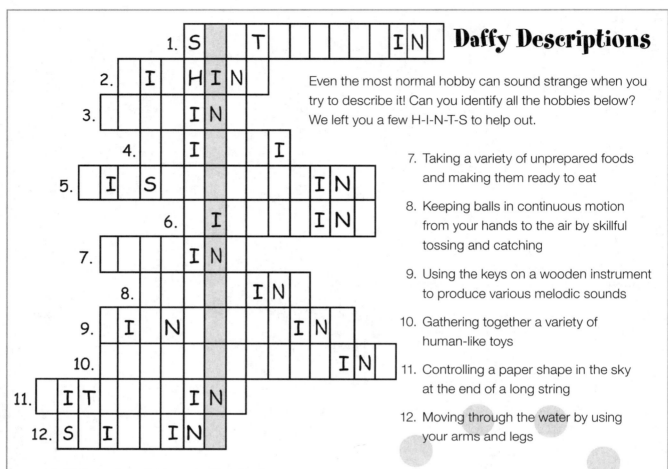

Daffy Descriptions

Even the most normal hobby can sound strange when you try to describe it! Can you identify all the hobbies below? We left you a few H-I-N-T-S to help out.

7. Taking a variety of unprepared foods and making them ready to eat

8. Keeping balls in continuous motion from your hands to the air by skillful tossing and catching

9. Using the keys on a wooden instrument to produce various melodic sounds

10. Gathering together a variety of human-like toys

11. Controlling a paper shape in the sky at the end of a long string

12. Moving through the water by using your arms and legs

EXTRA FUN: What would you call a giant ape whose hobby is table tennis? Read down the shaded column to find out!

1. Riding a low, flat board with wheels on the bottom

2. Using a rod, reel, and hook to catch aquatic creatures

3. Rolling a large ball and knocking down wooden pins

4. Practicing the Japanese art of folding paper to make small sculptures

5. Fitting together small pieces of a picture to recreate the entire big picture

6. Using your legs to power a vehicle with two wheels

Take a Hike

A riddle and its answer were put into the large grid, and then cut into seven pieces. See if you can figure out where each piece goes, and write the letters in their proper places. When you have filled the grid in correctly, you will be able to read the puzzle from left to right, and top to bottom. **HINT:** The black boxes stand for the spaces between words.

Tacky Ties

Dad has some pretty tacky ties in his collection. Today he is hunting for one in particular. Can you help him find it? Look for the tie that has all of the following:

- dark diamonds
- light background
- skinny horizontal stripes
- same-sized polka dots

Too Much Fun

This person has a LOT of hobbies! Can you tell how many he is trying to do at the same time?

Cool Collections

Can you find nine things in this word search that you might want to collect, and nine things that you would probably never collect?

```
S T A M P S H O V E G
F O O S H B I N G P O
F L O C O I N S C A L
X J E L L Y F I S H O
T Y P E S H E L L S H
O K R O W E M O H T A
M A R B L E S M I L E
B A N A T I S S U E S
F O H A T S D U S K Y
S L L O D L P E A S N
O P A L G R E E N Q U
L I G H T B U L B S P
R U N T R R O C K S I
Q S T A P L E S A N D
N O T S E L D O O N O
O V E R D U C A R D S
C O T T O N C A N D Y
S K O O B W O R M S T
```

Might Collect:

Would Never Collect:

Absurd Authors

Levi loves to read—especially about his hobbies!
Write each author's number next to the book they wrote.

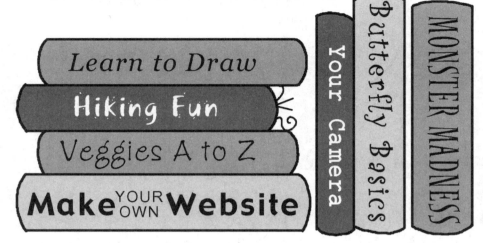

Authors:
1. Rocky Slopes
2. Dot Comm
3. Annette N. Ajar
4. Brock O. Lee
5. U. Ken Klick
6. Frank N. Stein
7. Art X. Ibit

Camera Chaos

Bryant's new hobby is photography. He tried to take pictures of his visit to the zoo, but he only got part of the animal in each of his shots. What were the animals he was trying to capture on film?

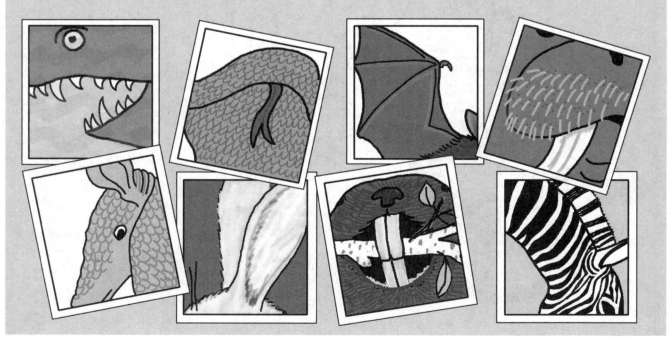

Movie Night

First answer all the clues. After you fill the answers in the numbered grid, collect the letters in the shaded boxes. Unscramble them to find out what movie Kristen and her friends went to see!

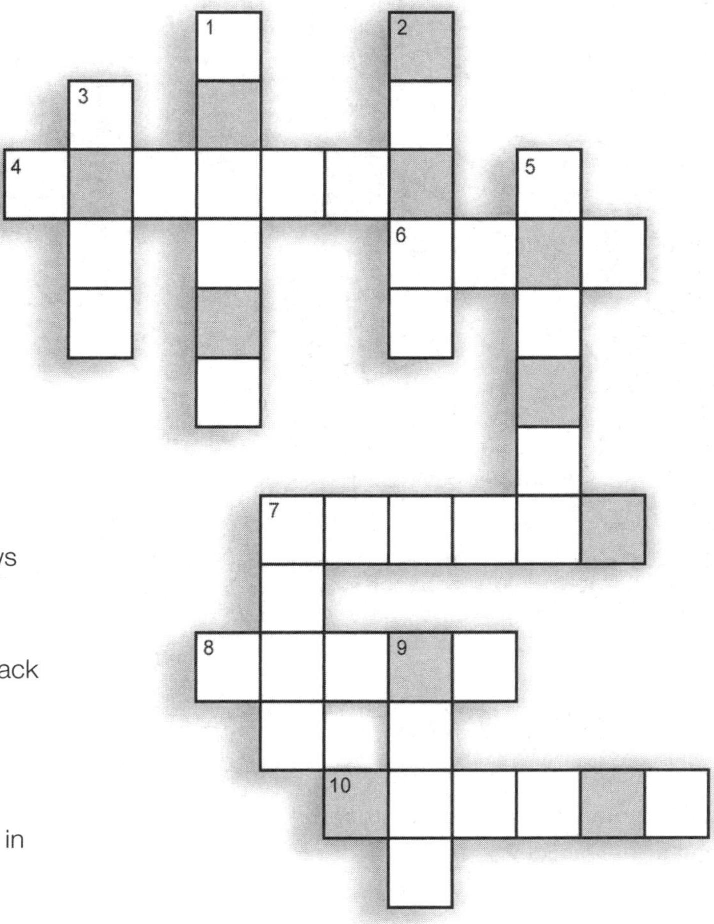

ACROSS

4   White, fluffy kernels served with butter and salt

6   The way out

7   Surface on which the movie shows

8   Sweet treats

10   A person you like who likes you back

DOWN

1   Small piece of paper that lets you in

2   You pay with this to get in

3   A sweet and fizzy drink

5   A little laugh

7   Where you sit in the theater

9   What it is when the lights go out

EXTRA FUN: After doing this puzzle, can you guess what Kristen and her friend's three hobbies are?

Whittle Away

Wally's hobby is carving tiny sculptures from bars of soap! See if you can find the four different items that Wally plans to create.

EXTRA FUN: Can you find the letters S, O, A, and P hiding in these bars?

Totally Tiles

Tanika's hobby is creating pictures made from tiny colored tiles glued onto a board. This is called making a mosaic (mo-zay-ik). Color in all the squares marked with the letters T-I-L-E-S and you will see Tanika's latest project!

EXTRA FUN: To finish the picture, connect the dots A, B, and C in order. Then connect the dots 1, 2, and 3 in order.

D	F	G	K	J	F	J	F	M	P	F	G	F	D	K	F
F	T	I	L	N	G	N	G	N	R	G	M	T	I	E	G
G	E	F	T	S	M	R	J	D	U	J	S	L	F	I	J
J	S	M	F	R	T	X	K	O	V	E	P	D	K	L	K
F	T	L	I	X	D	I	M	P	L	K	V	T	E	S	M
K	G	P	O	T	P	S	N	D	S	M	E	K	O	G	N
M	J	D	U	K	I	T	O	V	E	S	J	O	U	D	O
F	K	V	G	O	T	L	I	E	L	L	N	U	G	M	P
N	M	J	M	E	Z	O	P	X	P	N	I	G	D	P	R
O	N	F	S	U	H	I	R	F	L	O	R	T	M	V	U
A	O	N	L	J	F	B	U	G	R	P	X	I	P	F	1
F	P	R	I	N	K	S	L	T	S	R	D	L	V	K	X
K	R	X	T	R	O	B	I	E	2	U	F	E	J	O	V
C	U	F	E	X	U	P	V	J	U	V	K	S	N	U	3
U	V	K	P	T	B	D	X	K	V	D	T	M	R	G	F
V	W	F	V	O	I	E	L	T	S	I	O	P	X	M	G
D	X	O	U	D	N	Q	F	M	X	F	D	V	F	D	J

Milo's Magic

Connect the dots to see what Milo has learned to pull out of his magic hat! To finish the picture, put a dime on each of the dots without numbers, and trace around them.

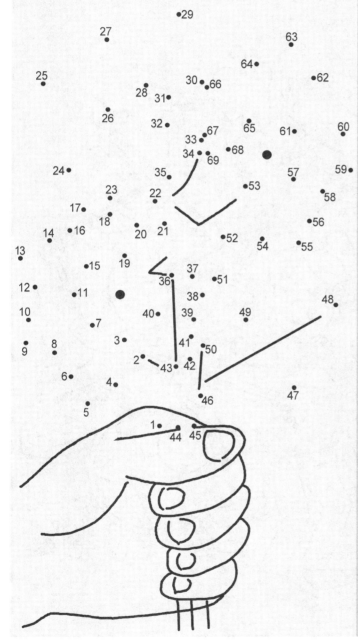

Go Fly a Kite

Kaity's hobby is flying kites. She's not alone—kite flying is popular all over the world! See if you can fit all of the words into this story about Kaity and her kite. **HINT:** Each word gets used only once!

—WORDS—
sight • delight • tight
bright • might • right
height • fright • white • kite

Kaity's kite was red and _____.

To her _____, it flew to a

great _____. She hung on

_____ with all her _____,

but the kite veered sharply to

the _____. Snap went the

string! "Oh, no!" Kaity cried with

_____, as her _____

new _____ flew out of

_____.

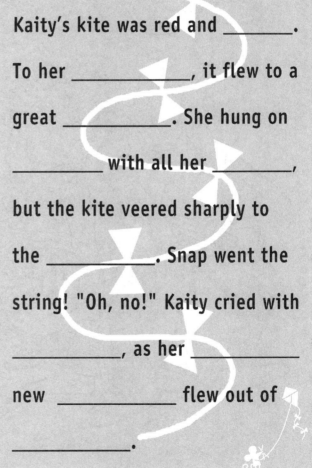

Loony Tunes

Curtis invited his musical friends to come play their instruments at his house for the afternoon. But what is wrong with this picture? Can you find the 15 things that are definitely very strange?

Sticky Stamps

Artie dropped his stamp collection and needs help resorting them!
See if you can answer the following questions:

1. Are there more patriotic stamps or stamps with birds?

2. What kind of creature is featured on the most stamps?

3. There are four stamps that are almost identical. What object is on each one?

4. What stamp has the most postage?

59

Is camping your hobby? Then you know that each camper going on a trip needs to bring some of the gear. But who brings what? Use the multiplying code to find out the answer!

What do you ask an octopus to bring on camping trips?

80 32 56 80 - 8 24 48 32 72

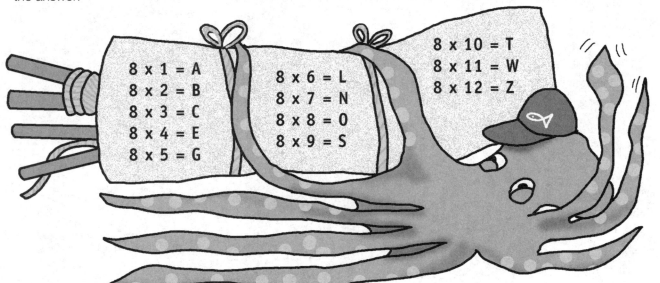

8 x 1 = A
8 x 2 = B
8 x 3 = C
8 x 4 = E
8 x 5 = G

8 x 6 = L
8 x 7 = N
8 x 8 = O
8 x 9 = S

8 x 10 = T
8 x 11 = W
8 x 12 = Z

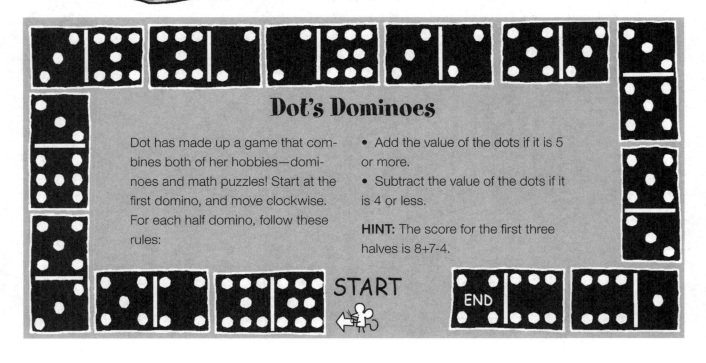

Dot's Dominoes

Dot has made up a game that combines both of her hobbies—dominoes and math puzzles! Start at the first domino, and move clockwise. For each half domino, follow these rules:

- Add the value of the dots if it is 5 or more.
- Subtract the value of the dots if it is 4 or less.

HINT: The score for the first three halves is 8+7-4.

START

END

Chapter 6

Spazzy Sports

Loopy Hoops

These teams have just finished a close game. Who won? Add the numbers on each team's shirts plus the numbers hiding on each team's players, to find out. In this crazy game, it is the team with the least number of points that wins!

DARK SHIRTS:

LIGHT SHIRTS:

Happy Camper

This camper went without sleep for seven days and was never tired. How did he do that? To find out, answer the clues below and enter the letters into the grid.

1D	2B		3A	4C	5D	6A	7C	
	8A	9B		10B	11C	12A	13B	14C

A. Spaces where something is missing __ __ __ __
                                      12 8 6 3

B. Opposite of now __ __ __ __
                    9 13 2 10

C. To make crooked __ __ __ __
                    14 11 4 7

D. Opposite of she __ __
                    1 5

Color in all the following kinds of letters:
- last letter of READY
- first letter of SET
- both letters of GO

Then read the uncolored letters to get the answer to the crazy riddle!

What should you put on before you get dressed to be in a relay race?

YOSRGUGYO
NYOSGYSOG
SGDYOOEYG
SSGOYSGOY
OROYSWGYE
OSYAGORYO

Why does everyone want spiders on their baseball team?

Pick up letters as you find the correct way through the web and around the bases from HIT to HOME RUN. Write them down in order and you will learn the answer to this riddle!

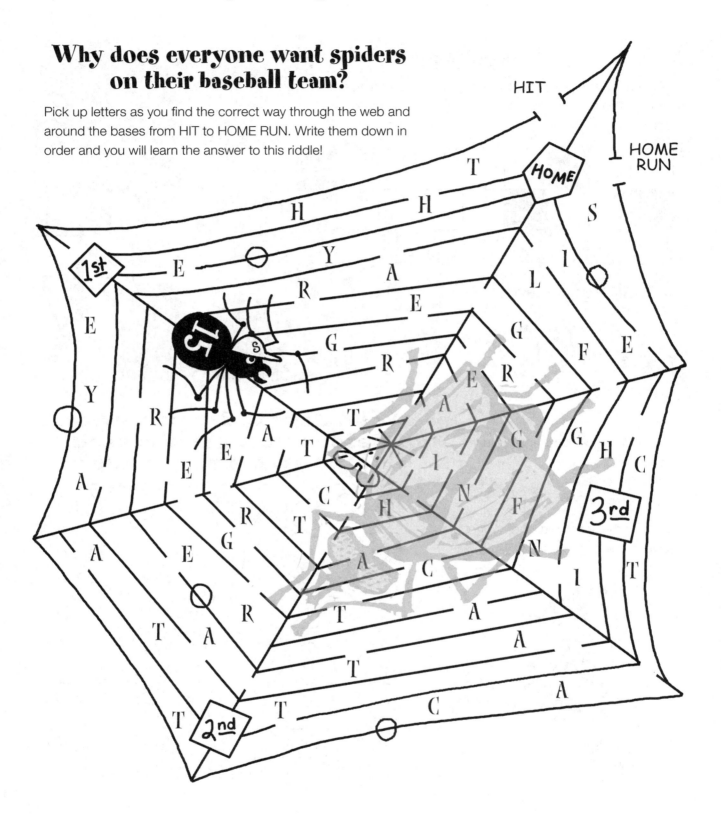

Which ghost cheers the loudest at the high school football games?

To find out, unscramble these common football terms. Write the words in the spaces at the end of each line. Finally, read the letters in the white boxes from top to bottom.

1. Player wears this on his head = METHEL
_ _ _ _ _ _

2. Score! = CHDOTOUWN
_ _ _ _ _ _ _ _

3. To handle clumsily = LEBMUF
_ _ _ _ _ _

4. To bring a player to the ground = CAKTEL
_ _ _ _ _ _

5. Shirt with a number on it = SERJYE
_ _ _ _ _ _

6. To receive the ball = CHATC
_ _ _ _ _

7. Midway through the game = METIHAFL
_ _ _ _ _ _ _ _

8. Important January game = PRUES LOWB
_ _ _ _ _ _ _ _ _

9. Throw ball to another player = SAPS
_ _ _ _

10. Catch ball meant for other team = CEPTERINT
_ _ _ _ _ _ _ _ _

11. Three feet = DAYR
_ _ _ _

12. The game is played on this = LEDIF
_ _ _ _ _

13. He leads the team = TRAQUEBRACK
_ _ _ _ _ _ _ _ _ _ _

What is the hardest thing about learning to skate?

This skater has invented a new sport—spelling out words with the blades of her skates! Connect the dots to learn the answer to this important question:

HINT: Try to connect the dots with swooping, curved lines—as if you were skating!

jumbo puzzle book

Go Team!

These fans want to show that they are crazy for a certain sport! Follow the directions below to see their message.

1. Fill in all the blocks on the left side of signs 1, 2, 3, 6, 7, 9, 11, 12, 15, 21

2. Fill in all the top squares on signs 2, 3, 5, 6, 9, 11, 15, 16, 21

3. Fill in all the bottom squares of signs 1, 2, 3, 9, 11, 12, 16

4. Fill in all the right squares of signs 1, 6, 11, 12

5. Fill in all the squares down the middle of signs 5 and 8

6. Fill in the very middle square of signs 1, 6, 7, 16, 21

7. Fill in the square just below the middle square of sign 1

8. Copy sign 9 onto sign 18 and 19

9. Copy sign 5 onto sign 13

10. Copy sign 7 onto sign 10

11. Copy sign 2 onto sign 4 and 20

12. Copy sign 11 onto sign 14 and 17

Why do soccer players do well in school?

Use this soccer ball decoder to find out.

Archery Addition

Archibald, Annibelle, and Ace are all shooting at the same target! Can you figure out who is shooting which arrows?

Then, count the points each archer has scored using these rules:

— Add the value of each ring an arrow has stuck into

— Subtract 10 points for any arrow that is on the ground

BONUS: If all of an archer's arrows have stuck in the target, that person gets 5 extra points!

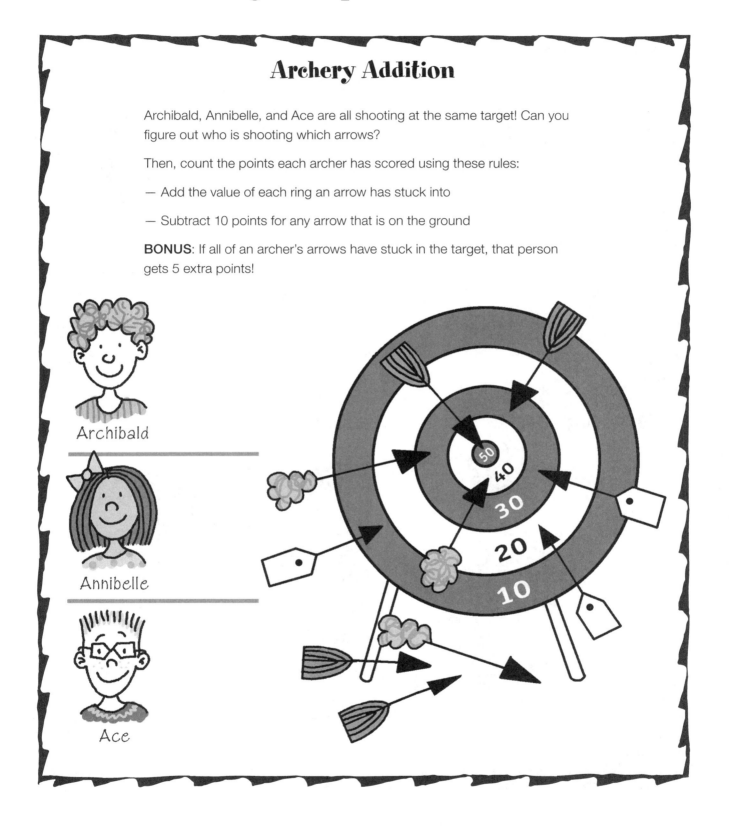

X-treme Sports

Decipher the picture puzzles to find the names of four wild-and-crazy sports!

On Your Mark!

Find the 14 reasons why these kids would be crazy to go swimming!

Goofy Golf

Giorgio loves to play goofy golf. You will, too!
Here are the rules:

- You must go to every hole.
- Count the dots you hit along each path.
  Each dot is worth 5 points.
- Add the value of the hole.
- You get a 20-point bonus on any hole with
  an even-numbered score.

Snake

Windmill

Penguin

Flamingo

71

Crazy Coach

Coach Wazoo has invented some new and crazy sports! Fill in the letter that matches each new sport with its description.

Which two familiar sports did Coach Wazoo combine to create each crazy sport?

__ **Bassocketcerball**

__ **Gymtennasnistics**

__ **Icefootskatballing**

__ **Tracycckling**

__ **Golarcherfy**

A. Throwing a ball while skating on a frozen field.

B. Using a club to hit small, hard, white balls into a target.

C. Tumbling while hitting a small, fuzzy ball with a racquet.

D. Players kick a black and white ball into an overhead net.

E. Running alongside your bike many times around a track.

Now this is fun!

Shadow Race

Can you find the shadow pattern that exactly matches this picture of Coach Wazoo?

Chapter 7

Natural Nonsense

To the Top!

There is only one correct way to hike to the top of this crazy mountain. Starting at the bottom, add the value of two neighboring trees. You may only move to the next level where the tree above has a value that matches the sum.

What is a tornado's favorite party game?

To find out, start at the dot at the top of the tornado. Twist your way down to the ground, picking up every third letter as you go.

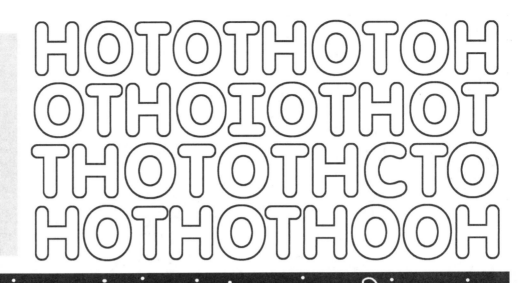

Not Hot!

What are the two coldest letters in the alphabet? Fill in all the H-O-Ts and say the two remaining letters out loud.

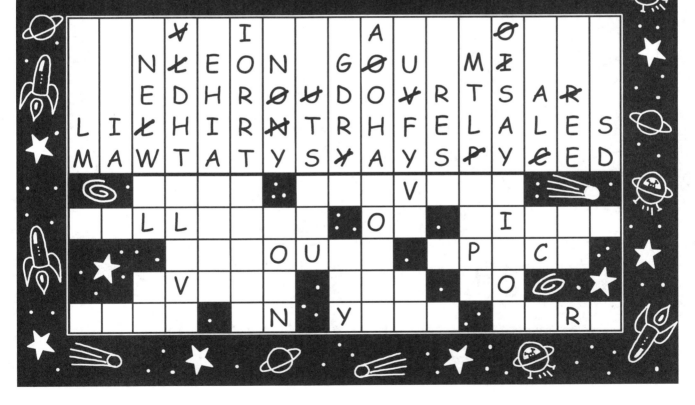

The Silly Answer Is "Sunlight"!

What's the silly question? To find out, put each of the letters below in its proper place in the grid. The letters all fit in spaces under their own column, but maybe not in the same order!

Whoooosh!

Hurricane Harriet scattered Pat's Hat Shop! Can you help put it together again? Start here and find a path that collects the sign, roof, awning, and door. Return them here to the store.

EXTRA: See if you can find the 35 hats that Pat lost!

Wacky Weather

March has all kinds of weather going on! Use these clues to make a picture history. Draw the correct weather symbol on each day.

1. It rained every day that could be evenly divided by 6.

2. A cloudy day always came before a rainy day.

3. There was a snowstorm for two days in the middle of the month, starting on a Saturday.

4. There was only one windy day, exactly in the middle of the month.

5. All the rest of the days were sunny.

CLOUDY

SNOWY

SUNNY

RAINY

WINDY

March

Sun.	Mon.	Tues.	Wed.	Thurs.	Fri.	Sat.
		1	2	3	4	5
6	7	8	9	10	11	12
13	14	15	16	17	18	19
20	21	22	23	24	25	26
27	28	29	30	31	Notes:	

What Is a Tree's Favorite Drink?

Fill in all shapes marked with the letters G-U-L-P to find out!

Hide-and-Seek

Put the animal names scattered on this page into the proper blanks to form new words. **HINT:** Some names can be used more than once, and one won't be used at all!

BEAR
FLY
PIG
BIRD
COW
ANT
DOG
CAT
LION

1. _ _ _ WOOD
2. S _ _ _ L
3. MIL _ _ _ _
4. _ _ _ EON
5. S _ _ _ TER
6. _ _ _ _ HOUSE
7. _ _ _ BOY
8. STIF _ _ _
9. S _ _ _ OT
10. _ _ _ _ DS

Animal Addition

How do you make a baby frog? Add the answers to each definition and you will create a baby frog—and five other animals, too!

word for soil _____

+ word for pig _____

= a woodchuck _____

breathe quickly _____

+ opposite of him _____

= dark leopard _____

pet you ride _____

+ foot covering _____

+ cranky person _____

= seashore animal _____

role in a play _____

+ chain of hills _____

= game bird _____

pull slowly _____

+ atop = _____

+ move through the air _____

= long, thin insect _____

a small boy _____

+ long, thin piece of wood _____

= baby frog _____

The Silly Answer Is "You"!

What's the silly question? To find out, see if you can figure out where each puzzle piece goes in the empty grid. Then, write the letters in their proper places.

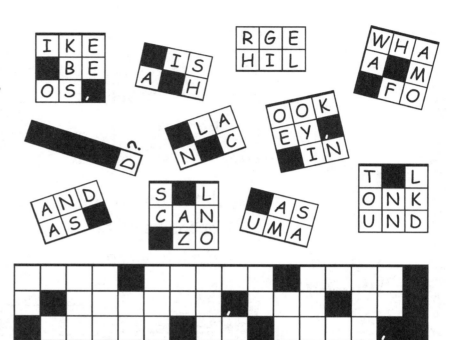

Where's the Weather?

There are 13 weather words hiding in these sentences. Can you find them all?

How independent Kevin is now!

I certainly hope the river runs under our house.

Kami stole the cobra in Concord.

The twins were both under the bed.

Two gruff ogres hum identical tunes.

The Earth ails when recycling fails.

Winston scolds Eric loudly.

The aisle Ethan walked down was skinny.

WORD LIST

fog	humid
cold	hail
ice	cloud
sun	sleet
mist	thunder
rain	wind
snow	

Rain Man, Sun Man

No one wants poor Rain Man at the beach! Can you help him move through the maze until he turns into a sunny day? Make a path that alternates between rain and sun. You can move up and down, or side-to-side, but not diagonally. If you hit a cloudy day, you are going the wrong way!

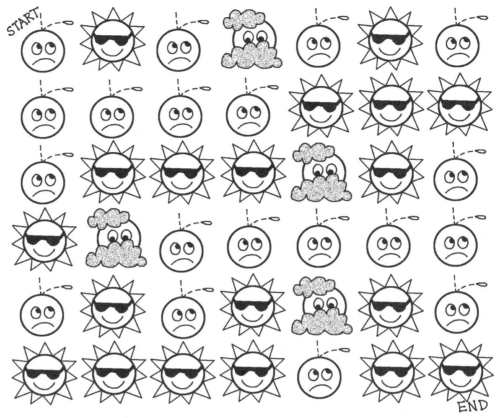

What nickname do weather forecasters call their baby boys?

Use a simple number substitution code (A=1, B=2, C=3 . . .) to find out!

Secret Garden

Gwendolyn's garden is missing a secret ingredient. To complete each word in the grid, add letters from the word E-A-R-T-H. We've given you some hints, but they are not in the same order as the answers! Can you write the number of each hint by its answer?

1. gets cut in summer
2. smells nice
3. falls in Fall
4. freezes in Winter
5. makes walls
6. grows from seeds
7. blooms in Spring
8. grows in pods
9. running water
10. sips flowers
11. eats dirt

EXTRA FUN:
Read down the shaded column to get the answer to this riddle:

What do you use to fix a broken tomato?

The Silly Answer Is "Water"!

What's the silly question? To find out, use the directions to cross words out of the grid. Read the remaining words from left to right and top to bottom!

Cross out all words that . . .

. . . start with the letter O

. . . rhyme with the word "fair"

. . . are bodies of water

. . . have U in the middle and N at the end

. . . have three letters and no T

CARE	WAS	WIN
ONCE	RUN	WHAT
OCEAN	RUNS	SUN
MAN	WEAR	BEAR
AIR	ONLY	STARE
POND	BUT	FUN
NEVER	BUN	LAKE
CAR	OKAY	WALKS

Zany Rainy

Ramona and Celeste are twins who do everything together, even jumping in puddles! Can you find the 10 differences between the pictures of the girls enjoying a rainy day?

83

Dark Shadows

The sun was low on the horizon late this afternoon. Can you tell what it is causing to cast these six long, strange shadows? We've given you a few hints, but be careful. There are more hints than shadows!

car   boat   bike   wheelchair   giraffe   rabbit   dog

boy on a ladder   cat in a wagon   bird on a branch

rocking chair   Mervin   watering can   bottle   TV

Chapter 8

Tricky Travels

What Do You Call It . . .

What do you call it when tourists go out dancing in the hot, tropical sun?

Think of words that mean the same thing as each of the words below.
Fill them in the blanks; then read the shaded letters from top to bottom.
HINT: All the words you need rhyme with "quake."

meat = _ _ _ _ _

pain = _ _ _ _ _

cook = _ _ _ _ _

snow = _ _ _ _ _ _

tool = _ _ _ _ _

phony = _ _ _ _

reptile = _ _ _ _ _ _

male duck = _ _ _ _ _ _

damage = _ _ _ _ _ _

dessert = _ _ _ _ _

error = _ _ _ _ _ _ _

alert = _ _ _ _ _ _

Go! Go! Go!

See how quickly you can travel through this list
to fit all the letter sets into their correct spaces!

Not silver = <u>G</u> <u>O</u> _ _

Long dress = <u>G</u> <u>O</u> _ _

Turkey noise = <u>G</u> <u>O</u> _ _ _ _

Large ape = <u>G</u> <u>O</u> _ _ _ _ _

Not hello = <u>G</u> <u>O</u> _ _ _ _ _

A cart = _ _ <u>G</u> <u>O</u> _

Fairytale lizard = _ _ _ <u>G</u> <u>O</u> _

Didn't remember = _ _ _ <u>G</u> <u>O</u> _

Western state = _ _ _ <u>G</u> <u>O</u> _

Spanish friend = _ _ _ <u>G</u> <u>O</u>

Deep blue = _ _ _ _ <u>G</u> <u>O</u>

City in Illinois = _ _ _ _ _ <u>G</u> <u>O</u>

BYE	LD	IN
N	WN	N
DI	AMI	CA
N	LE	BB
FOR	RIL	DRA
T	LA	CHI
ORE	OD	WA

EXTRA FUN:

All these travelers are go, go,
going somewhere! Can you find
the two cars that are exactly alike?
It doesn't matter that the cars are
going in different directions.

Peculiar Passport

This passport is strange—all of the country names are written in rebus form! Figure them out and write the real name underneath each country's stamp.

EXTRA STRANGE:

It would be impossible to get your passport stamped in one of these countries today. Do you know which one, and why?

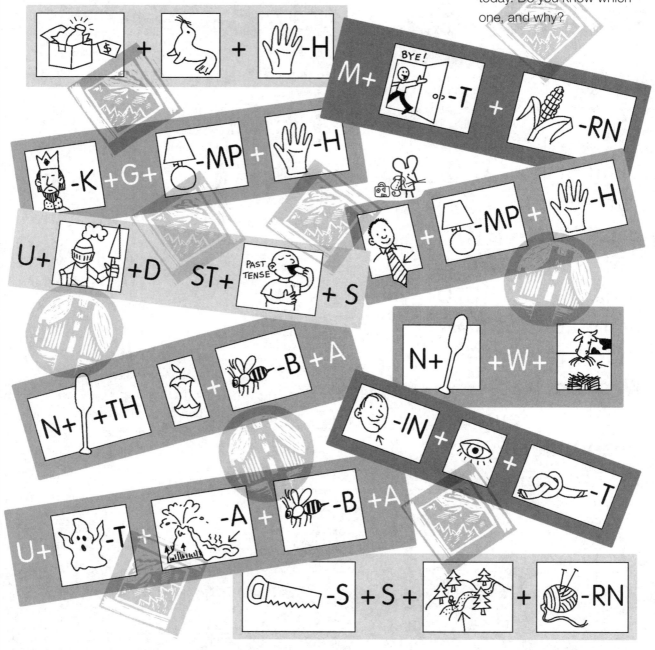

USA, ABC

Three consecutive letters are needed to finish each name of these famous national monuments and parks.

National Monuments

FO_T _UM_ER

_OU_T RUSHM_RE

__AT_E OF LIBERTY

_ASA GRAN__

National Parks

G_EAT _MOKEY MOUN_AINS

VALL_Y _OR_E

C_RLS_AD _AVERNS

PET_IFIED FORE__

Amazing Liberty

Find your way through the Statue of Liberty from START to END.

END

START

Potholes

Each of these sets of words is missing one travel word that will make them into compound words.

_____hog   _____go

_____map   _____pet

_____way   _____fare

_____runner   _____pool

_____side   _____sick

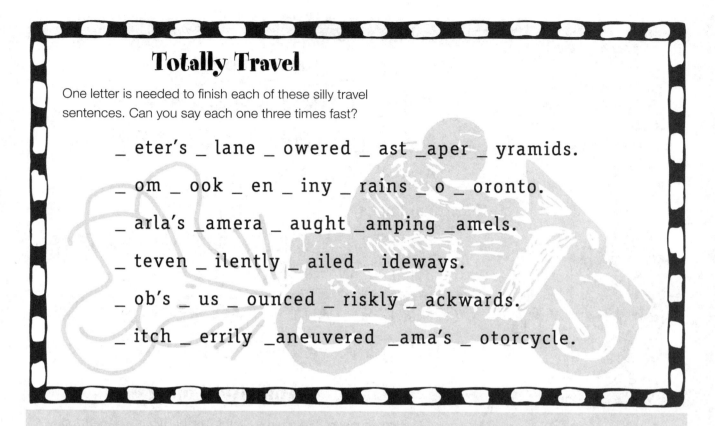

Totally Travel

One letter is needed to finish each of these silly travel sentences. Can you say each one three times fast?

_ eter's _ lane _ owered _ ast _aper _ yramids.

_ om _ ook _ en _ iny _ rains _ o _ oronto.

_ arla's _amera _ aught _amping _amels.

_ teven _ ilently _ ailed _ ideways.

_ ob's _ us _ ounced _ riskly _ ackwards.

_ itch _ errily _aneuvered _ama's _ otorcycle.

Hi-Ho Hink Pinks

Hink Pinks are two single-syllable words that rhyme. Can you come up with the hink pinks that fit these transportation explanations?

Undecorated track-rider = _ _ _ _ _   _ _ _ _ _

Celebrity vehicle = _ _ _ _   _ _ _

Commotion on public transport = _ _ _   _ _ _ _

Not-crazy flying vehicle = _ _ _ _   _ _ _ _ _

Long trip on two-wheeler = _ _ _ _   _ _ _ _

Jacket for floating vehicle = _ _ _ _   _ _ _ _

Big vehicle for chickens = _ _ _ _ _   _ _ _ _

Huge car for hire = _ _ _ _   _ _ _ _

An intelligent, small wagon = _ _ _ _ _   _ _ _ _

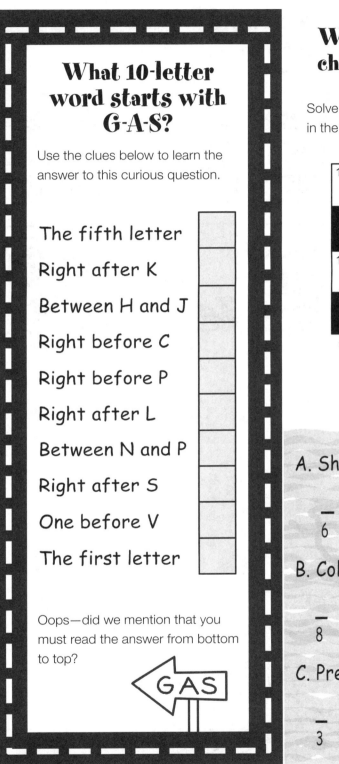

What 10-letter word starts with G-A-S?

Use the clues below to learn the answer to this curious question.

The fifth letter

Right after K

Between H and J

Right before C

Right before P

Right after L

Between N and P

Right after S

One before V

The first letter

Oops—did we mention that you must read the answer from bottom to top?

GAS

Why is traveling by boat the cheapest way to get around?

Solve the clues and put the letters in their proper place in the grid until you have the answer to this riddle.

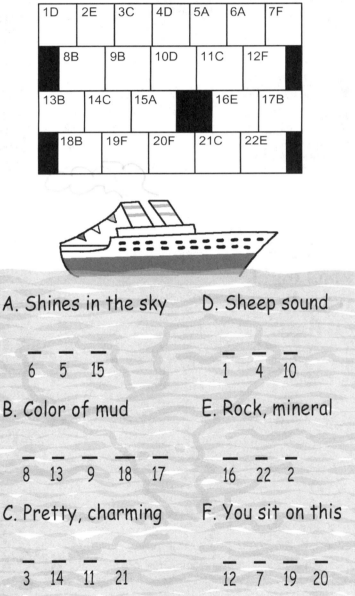

1D	2E	3C	4D	5A	6A	7F
	8B	9B	10D	11C	12F	
13B	14C	15A		16E	17B	
	18B	19F	20F	21C	22E	

A. Shines in the sky

‾ ‾ ‾
6 5 15

B. Color of mud

‾ ‾ ‾ ‾ ‾
8 13 9 18 17

C. Pretty, charming

‾ ‾ ‾ ‾
3 14 11 21

D. Sheep sound

‾ ‾ ‾
1 4 10

E. Rock, mineral

‾ ‾ ‾
16 22 2

F. You sit on this

‾ ‾ ‾ ‾
12 7 19 20

Out the Window

Malena is looking out the window of the train. She watches the following events roll past. Can you put the pictures in the right sequence so that they make sense?

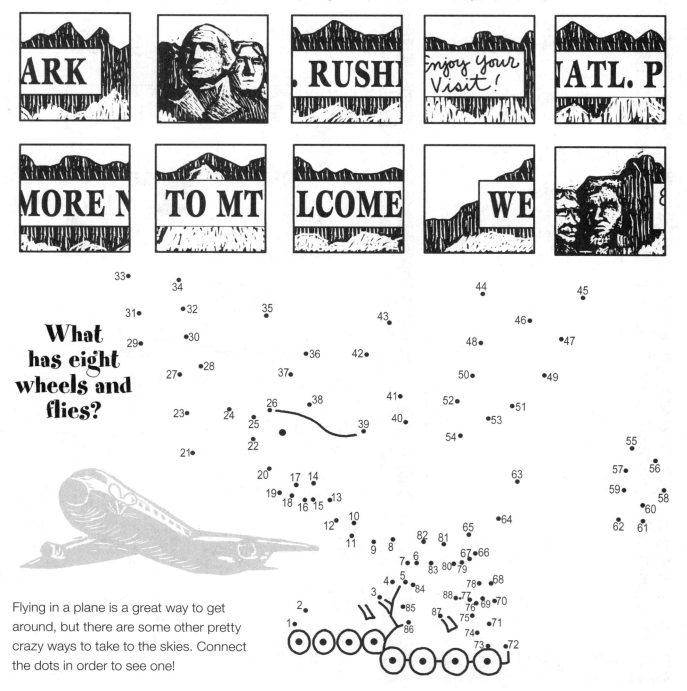

What has eight wheels and flies?

Flying in a plane is a great way to get around, but there are some other pretty crazy ways to take to the skies. Connect the dots in order to see one!

This tropical tourist spot holds a lot more than monkeys and toucans. Look for a bow tie, mitten, ski hat, crown, teacup, kite, eyeglasses, banana, sock, scissors, bunny, spoon, heart, fork, and umbrella!

Hidden Jungle

Time to Get Up!

The Avion family have to get up early to catch a plane. They don't want to oversleep, so everyone sets an alarm clock! Unfortunately, only one clock is set to go off at the correct time. Find the pattern in all the clock times, below. The correct time is halfway between the earliest time and the latest time.

What is the correct time for the Avion family to get up?

Time to Leave!

Catching a plane on time takes a lot of math! Use this information to figure out when you would have to leave for the airport if your plane is at 9:15 A.M.

- 45 minutes to drive to the airport.
- 20 minutes to park and check bags.
- 10 minutes to walk to the gate.
- You need to be at the gate 1 hour before the plane leaves.
- Add an extra 30 minutes, just in case!

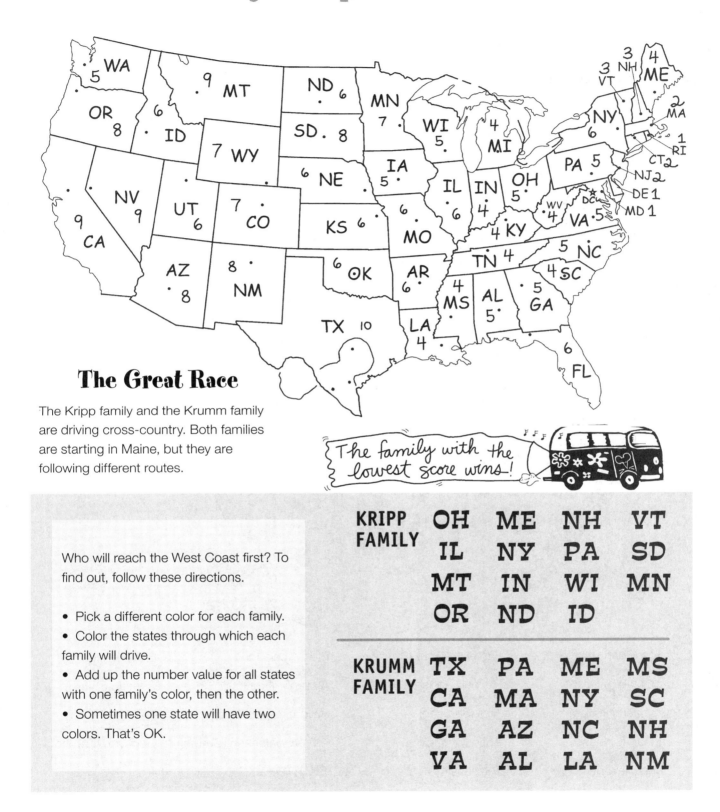

The Great Race

The Kripp family and the Krumm family are driving cross-country. Both families are starting in Maine, but they are following different routes.

The family with the lowest score wins!

Who will reach the West Coast first? To find out, follow these directions.

- Pick a different color for each family.
- Color the states through which each family will drive.
- Add up the number value for all states with one family's color, then the other.
- Sometimes one state will have two colors. That's OK.

KRIPP FAMILY	OH	ME	NH	VT
	IL	NY	PA	SD
	MT	IN	WI	MN
	OR	ND	ID	

KRUMM FAMILY	TX	PA	ME	MS
	CA	MA	NY	SC
	GA	AZ	NC	NH
	VA	AL	LA	NM

See You Later

No matter where you travel, sooner or later it is time to say goodbye. Can you find each of the following farewells in this around-the-world word search?

```
            C I A O
        S E S H A L O M G E
      Y O U L E T O F A O A T
    E R Z A L E L H I T O S G A
    T K W A H E R I A O U D A A R I
    N A W I H I I L E C S B Y N R O
    C O D I J E A O S E E C Y O T Y O U
    A U F W I E D E R S E H E N I B L A
    T E R S A A I L L H I G A A O L T O
    W T T F N R O I N E A F A R V E L W
    H I L E C S R O J C O D A I S L
    T O T Z I E N S H E S E E Y S O
    U L A R R I V E D E R C I A
    T E R A L L J I F A T O
    R A U R E V O I R I
        N A W H
```

Adiós (Spanish)	Farvel (Danish)	Bless (Icelandic)	Shalom (Hebrew)
Ciao (Italian)	Hej hej (Danish)	Au revoir (French)	Cheerio (British)
Arrivederci (Italian)	Tofa (Samoan)	Sayonara (Japanese)	Kwaheri (Swahili)
Zai Jian (Chinese)	Antio (Greek)	Auf Wiedersehen (German)	Goodbye (English)
Aloha (Hawaiian)	Tot ziens (Dutch)	Tusch (German)	

Chapter 9

Nutty
Notations

DREAM

SOME

RIGHT

MADE

OFF

OUT

HOME

ENGLISH

Wanda Wonders

Wanda should be studying, but she has let her mind wander. See if you can follow Wanda's thoughts by figuring out the best word to put in each blank. Follow these directions:

• Start at Wanda and work your way up the word string. Yes, you'll be writing upside-down part of the time!

• The word you add must work with the word on either side of it to form a common phrase or compound.

HINT: Not all of the words are used, and one of them is used twice!

WORD LIST

RUN	**TIME**
UP	**DAY**
PUT	**FLY**
HAND	**WORK**

13
16
15
14
12
17
11
18
9
10
19
8
21
7
22
20
6
3
23
37
5
25
26
4
31
36
38
2
27
35
24
32
1
30
28
39
29
33
34

Wish Upon a Star

Use a white gel pen or white pencil to connect the dots in order to see what Cassandra is wishing for.

Gnop Gnip

What makes this silly noise? See if you can figure out how to read the amazing answer to this ridiculous riddle!

A PING-PONG BALL BOUNCING BACKWARDS!

Gobbledygook

This looks like crazy talk, but these sentences actually make sense! Read each one aloud until you can figure out what it really says.

1. Vat ary ewe due ing?

2. We aris da pahrtty?

3. Eye kan tsea yu enew ear!

4. Vatis yoa rphav o aret kollar?

5. Hoo isy oarb ist fre nde?

Eye ill bet chew can treed iss!

pocketbook into
medical person
to

baked dessert
into garden tool
to

what you read into
curved metal hanger
to

middle of your face
into a flower
to

finger jewelry into
male royalty
to

bird's home into
a sleeveless sweater
to

baby bear into
bathtime place
to

long, soft seat into
a drawstring bag
to

penny into
portable shelter
to

feline pet into
baseball stick
to

dotted cubes into
small rodents
to

street into
cousin of a frog
ROAD to TOAD

teddy into fruit
to

Imagine That!

You can change one thing into another
just by using your imagination! Imagine a
different first letter of each word to get a
completely different thing.

TABLE

PAPER

POT

STAMP

KEY

PAN

PENCIL

SHOE

SOCK

COMB

HIDE

Hand in Glove

Some words always seem to go together—like bacon and eggs! We have collected 12 word pairs for you. Pick a word from a hand and match it to one in a glove. Cross off pairs as you go.

NOW

THREAD

ENVELOPE

SEEK

CHAIR

BRUSH

NAIL

NEEDLE

HAMMER

FORK

THEN

LOCK

SPOON

102

Noble Knight

Hubert likes to imagine he is a knight in shining armor. Five "knightly qualities" are hiding in the letter grid. To find them, pick one letter from each column moving from left to right. Each letter can be used only once. The first has been done for you!

H̶	A	U	Ø	R̶
T	E	N̶	R	K
H	Ø	L	T	T
V	P	A	N	H
S	R	U	O	R

1. HONOR
2. _____
3. _____
4. _____
5. _____

Creative Cook

Francesca can cook everything from soup to nuts! Can you help her? Work from top to bottom. Use the clues to help you decide which one letter in the word to change on each step.

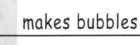
SOUP

_____ makes bubbles

_____ to fly up high

_____ used to row boats

_____ cereal grains

_____ big rodents

_____ grooves in the ground

NUTS

Hopping Harry

Harry hops everywhere he goes, but he will only hop on odd numbers. Help Harry hop down to his friend, Horatio. Harry can hop up, down, left, right, but not diagonally.

START

8	22	40	25	9	43	66	19
90	39	7	53	32	81	14	51
46	3	18	64	6	77	95	3
12	49	27	17	35	58	12	34
2	10	82	70	19	4	86	27
7	23	41	96	1	18	54	9
11	16	9	44	65	33	17	45
5	38	55	13	3	76	8	20
7	22	12	8	6	13	10	3

END

Curious Question:

Can you hop higher than an elephant?

Lotsa Lists

Lyle loves to make lists, but he always abbreviates them!
Using the clues to help, can you write out his complete lists?

Holidays: NY. V. E .4J. H .T. H. C.

_____

Weather: S. C. R. F. W. S.

_____

Pets: C. D. B. F. G. H. S.

_____

Colors: R. Y. B. G. O. P. B. W.

_____

Vehicles: C. B .T. B. P. M. B.

_____

Quick Catalog

To "catalog" a collection is to make a detailed list of everything that's in it. How quickly can you catalog the 11 three-letter words hiding in the word C-A-T-A-L-O-G?

CATALOG

Triple Triangles

Use the bottom word of each triangle as your letter list. Starting at the top, add one letter at a time to create new words as you move down the triangle.

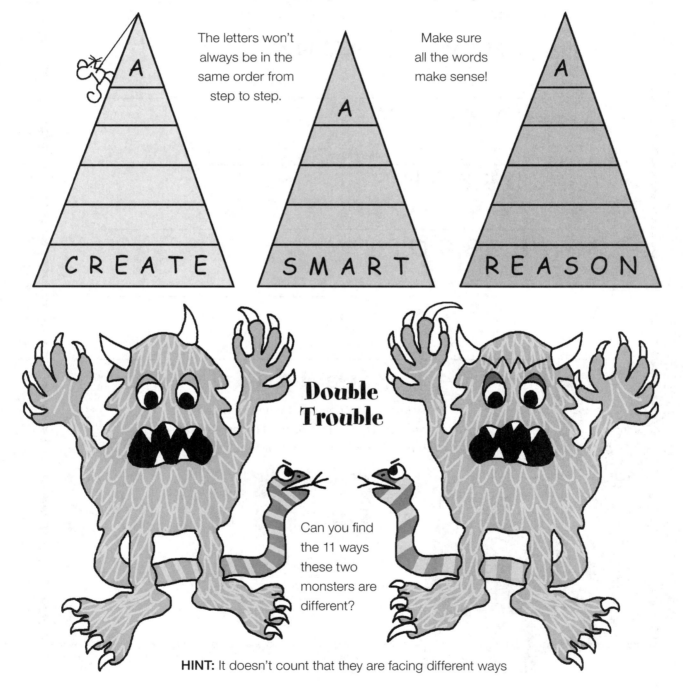

The letters won't always be in the same order from step to step.

Make sure all the words make sense!

A

A

A

C R E A T E

S M A R T

R E A S O N

Double Trouble

Can you find the 11 ways these two monsters are different?

HINT: It doesn't count that they are facing different ways

Crossed Creatures

Use the hints below to come up with the names of 14 magical or monstrous creatures. Then see if you can fit them into their proper places in the criss-cross. We left you some M-A-G-I-C and a little M-O-N-S-T-E-R to help out.

Tinkerbell was one

Small, magical helper

Hides under bridges

Sings in the sea

Howls at the moon

Half eagle, half lion

Half man, half horse

Half man, half goat

Tolkien's tree creature

Sleeps all day

Fire breather

Big and tall

One white horn

Lives in gardens

Black or White?

Can you find the figure that is the EXACT opposite of each figure in the box below?
Draw a line to match the pairs.

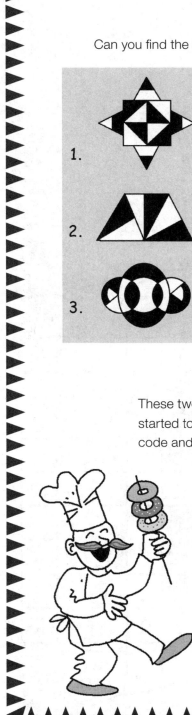

1.

2.

3.

Who's Crazy Now?

These two men have worked together for so long that they have started to speak their own special language. Can you break the code and figure out what they are laughing about?

**WHEEHHEEAHOTHO
DHAOHA   YHEEOHEEUHO
CHOAHALHALHEE   AHEE
CHORHOAHAZHAYHEE
BHEEAHOKHOEHARHA?**

**AHEE   DHEEOHOUHOGHAHHA
NHEEUHEETHO!**

Introduction to Math Puzzles

Although we certainly understand that math comes more easily to some than to others, we believe anyone can "get it" and should get it. It's very important that all kids learn math because it will be an essential skill in the twenty-first century. The puzzles in this book will help kids develop skills in arithmetic, geometry, number sense, logical thinking, and problem solving, which form the foundation of mathematical understanding.

Math is more than just a collection of math facts and vocabulary (although those are important). Math should also be a way of thinking about and solving real problems. You can be an absolute whiz at the multiplication tables, but you won't find them very useful if you are unsure when you should be multiplying and when you should be dividing. Here is a simple everyday-life problem: There are forty-five fifth-graders going on a class trip to the Museum of Math Puzzles. Parent volunteers with minivans are driving; each van can carry six students. The teachers plan to have enough cookies on the trip for each student to get four. How many cookies do the parents need to prepare and how many vans should they take? If your answer is eight vans and 180 cookies, your field trip will be a success.

Math puzzles are both fun and rewarding—we are confident that any child will enjoy doing the puzzles in this book, and knowing that you've solved a challenging puzzle is definitely rewarding. Beyond simple enjoyment and satisfaction, puzzles also provide wonderful opportunities for learning. Challenging puzzles offer children a chance to practice skills they already know and also to stretch their minds and extend their knowledge by discovering new ideas.

Chapter 10

Number Notions

A VERY BRIEF HISTORY OF NUMBERS

"uhn"

"uhn uhn"

No one knows who invented numbers, but it's fun to think that some early caveman named Oog did it when he said "uhn," "uhn uhn," and "uuuuuuhhhn," which meant "one," "two," and "lots."

Tallying

The earliest written numbers were most likely **tallies**—simple lines that each represent one object. You have probably used them yourself to keep score in a game with a friend:

> **Counting Sticks**
>
> Tallies were found carved on pieces of animal bone about 50,000 years old. What do you think those people were counting?

You: / / / / /
Friend: / / / / / /

Roman Numerals

The Roman numerals, invented by—yes, you guessed it!—the Romans, served many people over many centuries, and have not been forgotten today. Can you think of how they might be used?

ROMAN NUMERALS	
number	Roman numeral
1	I
5	V
10	X
50	L
100	C
500	D
1,000	M
5,000	$\overline{V}$
10,000	$\overline{X}$

FUN FACT

It's about Time!

Today, Roman numerals are most often used to show time (see if you have a clock in your house that uses Roman numerals) and dates (try to find Roman numerals on old buildings and also in movies and videos).

HEE HEE HEE

The rules for reading the Roman numerals sound difficult but are actually very simple, once you get the hang of it:

I.   When a symbol is followed by a smaller symbol or symbols, you add up their values.

For example: VI = 6; CXXIII = 123; DII = 502.

II.   When a symbol or symbols are followed by a larger-value symbol, you subtract their values:

For example: IV = 4; CMXL = 940; CDII = 402.

What do you call a person who can't stop doing sums?

An add-ict !

Figure This Out

Which face would you see on a grandfather

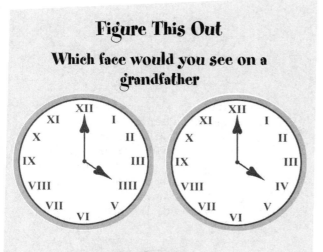

clock?

Grandfather clocks use Roman numerals for each hour, but with a surprise: Four o'clock is represented with IIII instead of IV! See if you can find a watch with Roman numerals on its face and check out four o'clock.

Try This

Read All about It!

Want to practice your Roman numerals? How about counting a thousand squealing pigs? Just grab *Roman Numerals I to MM* by Arthur Geisert (Houghton Mifflin Company, 1996) and let the fun begin. We'll bet you never knew there could be so many pigs in one picture!

When in Rome

Question:
What would you use to count organic apples?

First, take a look at these Roman numerals and see if you can figure out what numbers they represent.

a	b	e	l	m
XIV	XXIX	VIII	LXI	CDXI

n	r	s	t	u
CXLIX	MDCVI	DCCLI	MMDCLX	CMXXII

Now, place the letter for each Roman numeral under the corresponding Arabic number to find the answer to the puzzle.

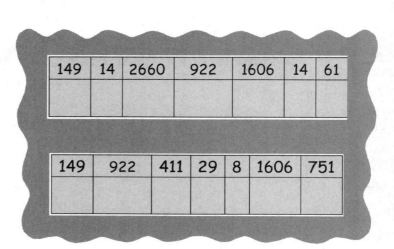

149	14	2660	922	1606	14	61

149	922	411	29	8	1606	751

Adding and subtracting with Roman numerals is not easy; and multiplication and division are nearly impossible.

XLIII + XXIV = _____

XCII - XXVI = _____

XV × IV = _____

XVIII ÷ III = _____

Arabic Numerals

To simplify things, people eventually gave up Roman numerals in favor of the Arabic system, which relies on ten digits—0, 1, 2, 3, 4, 5, 6, 7, 8, and 9.

WORDS 2 KNOW

digit: A number—but also a word for "finger." Coincidence? We think not. It's very likely that the first people to start counting used their fingers—just as little kids continue to do today.

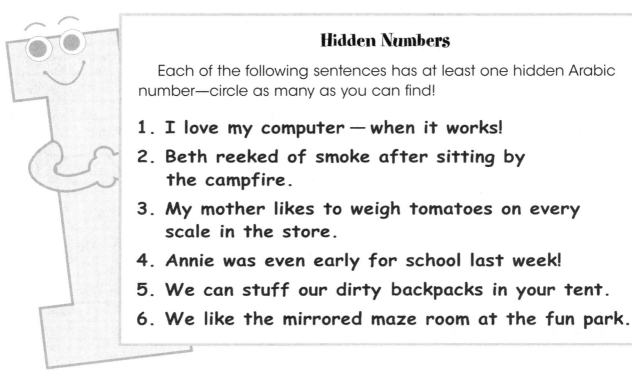

Hidden Numbers

Each of the following sentences has at least one hidden Arabic number—circle as many as you can find!

1. I love my computer — when it works!
2. Beth reeked of smoke after sitting by the campfire.
3. My mother likes to weigh tomatoes on every scale in the store.
4. Annie was even early for school last week!
5. We can stuff our dirty backpacks in your tent.
6. We like the mirrored maze room at the fun park.

Practice Your Digits

Get from START to END by moving around the square either vertically (up or down) or horizontally (left or right), moving the number of squares given by the number you are on. (For example, if you are standing on 3, you can move three spaces up, down, left, or right.)

START				
3	3	4	2	3
4	1	1	2	2
2	4	3	1	4
2	3	1	4	3
4	2	1	2	END E

START					
4	2	1	2	3	4
3	3	4	2	3	4
4	2	4	2	4	3
3	2	1	3	2	4
2	2	4	2	3	4
4	1	4	1	2	END E

THE IMPORTANCE OF ZERO

How important is "nothing"? Sometimes, it's very important. But we humans didn't always understand what exactly "nothing" is.

We need zero for several reasons. For one-thing, how can you tell what's 15 – 15? Furthermore, we need zero as a placeholder. Otherwise, how would you tell the difference between 5-and 50, or between 25 and 205?

Counting Sheep

Numbers were invented to count things. For example, an early herdsman might have wanted to know how many sheep he had. If he had no sheep, he wouldn't have wasted his time counting them, so he didn't need a number for them—that's why people didn't need zero for a long time!

"You're just nothing without me!"

"You're worth ten times as much when you're with me!"

What's 10 + 8 - 3 + 12 - 7 - 5 - 15 ?

"A whole lot of work for nothing!"

ALL YOU NEED IS 0 AND 1

What does math really fast and always gets the right answer? No, it's not that smart kid at school—it's the computer.

Computers don't have anything like fingers. Instead, early computers had simple circuits that act sort of like ordinary light switches—they turn on (1) and off (0). So computers do all their math by just using zeros and ones. This is known as a binary system.

How does the binary system work? Well, it's all about the number placement and the powers of 2. Each place **n** in the sequence that is "turned on" (marked with 1) stands for a 2 raised to the power **n**:

Binary System	
binary number	Arabic numeral
0	0
1	1
10	2
11	3
100	4
101	5
110	6
111	7
1000	8
1001	9
1010	10

$$1\ (2^0)\quad 2\ (2^1)\quad 4\ (2^2)\quad 8\ (2^3)\quad 16\ (2^4)\quad 32\ (2^5)\quad 64\ (2^6)\quad 128\ (2^7)\ldots$$

So, a binary number 110 is actually $2^2 + 2^1 + 0$, or $4 + 2 = 6$.

On or Off?

What time is it when the math teacher goes to the dentist? Convert the binary numbers to find out.

Number Decoder

H	6
I	3
O	8
R	2
T	7
Y	10

111 1000 1000 111 110   -

___ ___ ___ ___ ___   -

111 110   11   10   111 1010

___ ___ ___ ___ ___ ___

Making Sense of the Irrational

The value of π has fascinated people for centuries. Mathematicians and ordinary people alike have spent years looking for patterns in the digits. Do some digits appear more frequently than others? **Count up how many times each digit appears below and see if you can detect a-pattern.**

Here are the first 201 digits of π:

3.1415926535..8979323846.... 2643383279

5028841971.....6939937510.... 5820974944

5923078164....0628620899.... 8628034825

3421170679 ...8214808651.... 3282306647

0938446095.....5058223172.... 5359408128

4811174502....8410270193.... 8521105559

6446229489.....5493038196

digit	tallies	total
0		
1		
2		
3		
4		
5		
6		
7		
8		
9		

Now, you can graph the results on the facing page to see if a pattern emerges.

DIGIT VALUE

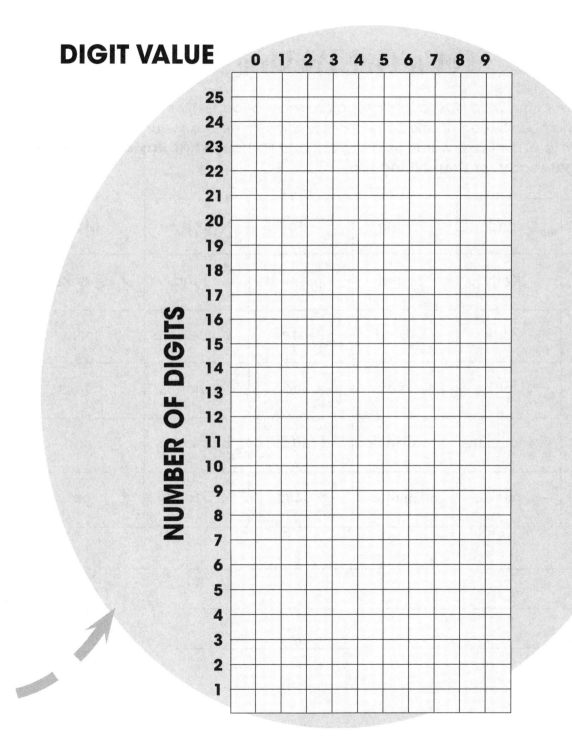

NUMBER OF DIGITS

Let's Get Packing

In the space next to the word box (or on a separate sheet of paper) list all the words in the boxes with the number 1. Then do the same for the words in the boxes numbered 2, 3, 4, 5, and 6. Finally, write each list of words as a sentence to find out **what Kayla and Dustin had to do to get ready for their hiking trip.**

1 Call	**4** and	**2** bug	**1** to	**5** extra	**2** block
4 bottles,	**1** Kelly	**5** and	**3** flashlight	**6** Find	**4** snacks,
2 Buy	**5** Pack	**6** bird	**4** water	**1** directions	**2** spray.
3 the	**4** Fill	**1** for	**6** and	**5** ponchos	**6** books.
1 Short	**6** binoculars	**3** Check	**2** sun	**3** batteries.	**2** and
4 chocolate!	**1** park.	**4** make	**5** socks.	**1** State	**4** get

1. _____

2. _____

3. _____

4. _____

5. _____

6. _____

See What I Mean?

You usually add and subtract by writing numbers on a piece of paper, or using a calculator. But there are other ways to talk about numbers. For example, people who know **American Sign Language** can use hand signals! Study the chart below. Then write the answer to each sign language equation in number form. **See if you can sign the answer, too.**

1 **2** **3** **4** **5**

6 **7** **8** **9** **10**
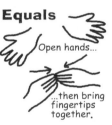
Wag thumb back and forth.

Divide
Sweep hands down.

Add
Bring fingertips together.

Subtract
Pull downward.

Multiply
Make two V's and cross them in front of you.

Equals
Open hands...

...then bring fingertips together.

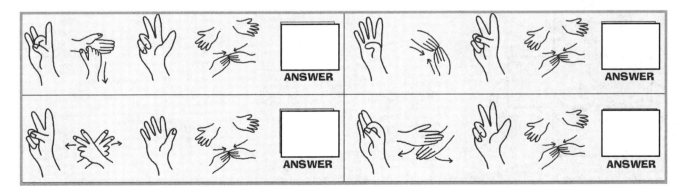

121

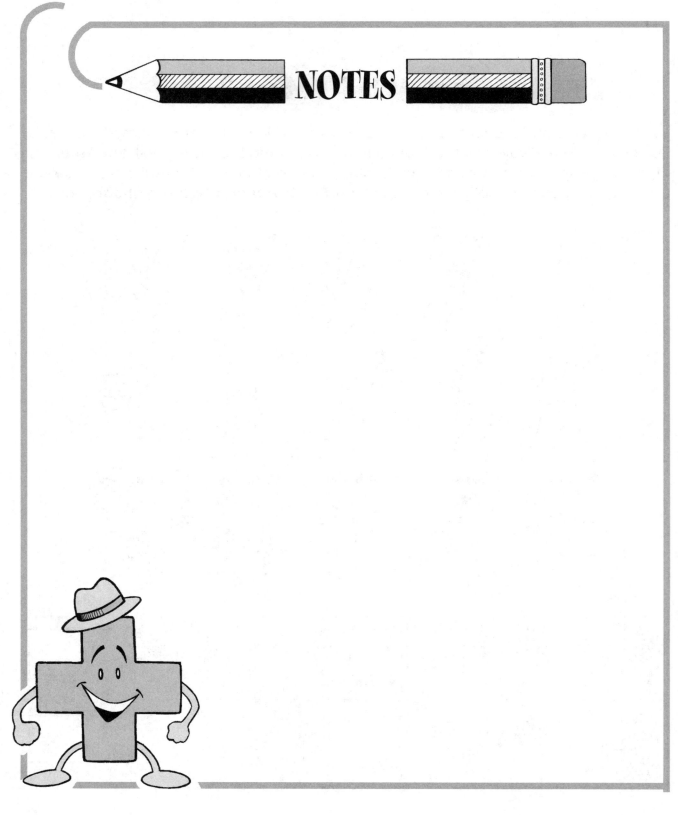

NOTES

Chapter 11

Plus or Minus a Puzzle

ARITHMETIC ACTIVITIES

Arithmetic is doing calculations with numbers, especially addition, subtraction, multiplication, and division. If you already know most of your basic arithmetic facts, you are ready to try the following activities and puzzles.

Clock Math

Arithmetic is full of surprises! Don't believe it? Try this question on a friend: When does **10 + 4 = 2?** He'll probably think you are crazy, but you're not. This question has a perfectly sensible and important answer: **When it is 4 hours after ten o'clock.**

Adding and subtracting on a clock doesn't always work the same way as adding and subtracting regular numbers. Use the clock to solve the following problems. Then use the decoder and the numbers in the shaded boxes to figure out the answer to this riddle:

What time did the math teacher go to the dentist?

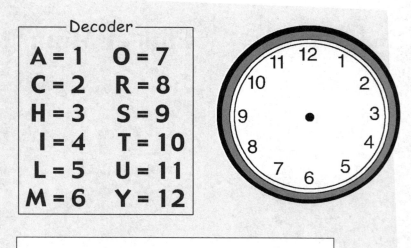

Decoder

A = 1	O = 7
C = 2	R = 8
H = 3	S = 9
I = 4	T = 10
L = 5	U = 11
M = 6	Y = 12

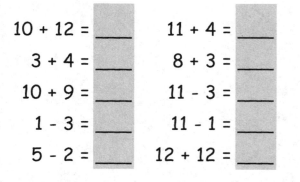

10 + 12 = ____   11 + 4 = ____

3 + 4 = ____   8 + 3 = ____

10 + 9 = ____   11 - 3 = ____

1 - 3 = ____   11 - 1 = ____

5 - 2 = ____   12 + 12 = ____

Calendar Math

Here is another practical arithmetic problem. When does 5 + 3 = 1? Three days after the fifth day of the week: from Thursday (5) to Sunday (1).

It doesn't really make sense to say "Thursday + 3 = Sunday," but if you give each day of the week a number, then you can do calendar arithmetic exactly as you did clock arithmetic. The trick is, if your result is over 7, just subtract it from the total. In our example, 3 + 5 = 8; 8 – 7 = 1. Now, what day is 12 days after a Wednesday? 4 + 12 = 16; 16 – 7 = 9; 9 – 7 = 2. This means that 12 days after Wednesday is a Monday—two weeks from then.

Sunday = 1
Monday = 2
Tuesday = 3
Wednesday = 4
Thursday = 5
Friday = 6
Saturday = 7

"The different branches of Arithmetic—Ambition, Distraction, Uglification, and Derision."

–Lewis Carroll, Through the Looking Glass

When Numbers Don't Obey

Why don't hours of the day and days of the week work the same way as "normal" numbers? Maybe it has to do with limits. Normally, numbers go up as far as infinity, so you never have to start over. With defined terms like the day (which can never have more than twenty-four hours) or the week (which can never have more than seven days), you can't go on forever and therefore need to start over, which messes up the calculation. Can you think of any other instances when numbers don't behave normally?

MAGIC SQUARES

Magic squares have been popular math puzzles for over 3,000 years, and once were thought to have mystical powers. Follow these simple rules to complete your own magic square:

1. Use each number only once.
2. Each row, column, and diagonal must add up to the same answer.

For this first magic square, use the numbers from 1 to 9. HINT: Each column, row, and diagonal adds up to 15.

Try again, but this time use only the EVEN numbers from 2 to 16 (2, 4, 6, and so forth). HINT: Each column, row, and diagonal adds up to 30.

Try again, but this time use only the ODD numbers from 1 to 17 (1, 3, 5, and so forth). HINT: Each column, row, and diagonal adds up to 27.

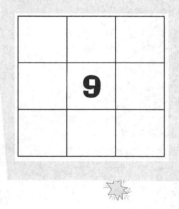

jumbo puzzle book

Now, let's make things more difficult. In the following magic square, some of the numbers are negative—you need to use every number from –4 to 4. HINT: Each column, row,

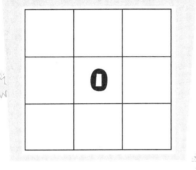

and diagonal adds up to 0.
Here is another magic square. This time, use the numbers from 3 to 5.
HINT: Each column, row, and diagonal adds up to 3.

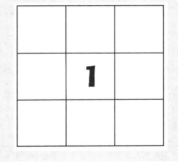

How Big Can You Go?

If you think the 4-by-4 square is hard, you'll really be impressed by Ben Franklin, a scientist, inventor, statesman, printer, philosopher, musician, and economist (a jack of all trades!), famous for flying a kite during a lightning storm. In addition to all his other jobs and hobbies, Ben liked to solve math puzzles. One of his mathematical achievements was to solve an 8-by-8 and 16-by-16 magic square. That's humongous! Visit *www.pasles.org/Franklin.html* to take a closer look at Ben's magic squares.

So, now you think you are a magic square pro? Not so fast! Let's make the magic square larger and see if you can still solve the puzzle. For the following square, use the numbers from 1 to 16. HINT: Each column, row, and diagonal adds up to 34.

16			13
4			1

GAME OF 15

Here is another **add**ictive game you can play! All you need is another player, a piece of paper, and a pen.
First, write down the numbers 1 through 9 on a sheet of paper, like this:

1 2 3 4 5 6 7 8 9

Then, you and another player take turns selecting numbers. When a number is selected, the player who chose it crosses it off the list and it can no longer be taken. The first person to get *any* 3 numbers that add up to exactly 15 wins!

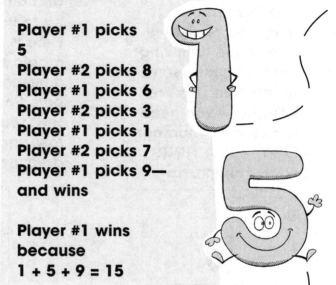

For example:

Player #1 picks 5
Player #2 picks 8
Player #1 picks 6
Player #2 picks 3
Player #1 picks 1
Player #2 picks 7
Player #1 picks 9— and wins

Player #1 wins because
1 + 5 + 9 = 15

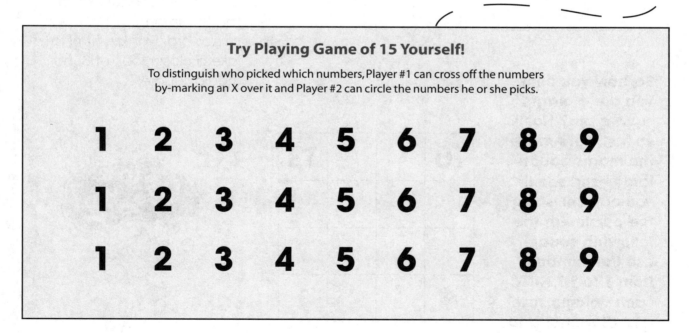

Try Playing Game of 15 Yourself!

To distinguish who picked which numbers, Player #1 can cross off the numbers by-marking an X over it and Player #2 can circle the numbers he or she picks.

1 2 3 4 5 6 7 8 9

1 2 3 4 5 6 7 8 9

1 2 3 4 5 6 7 8 9

SOLVE A CROSS-NUMBER PUZZLE

You have probably seen crossword puzzles, and it's possible that you have even solved one or two yourself. But what about cross-number puzzles? Does it sound like something you'd like to try? The cross-number puzzle in this chapter is special. In order to solve it, you have to read the following story for clues, so pay attention!

The Camping Trip

There was an old lady who lived in a shoe. She had so many children she didn't know what to do.

Well, one day, she just couldn't stand it anymore. Jamie was fighting with Orville, Wilbur wanted a snack, Oscar and Ophelia were drawing crayon pictures on the walls, and Hortense was crying because Delphinia had stolen her *Jumbo Puzzles Math Book*. And it was just seven o'clock in the morning.

"Enough already!" shouted their mother, "I-need some peace and quiet. All of you, play-outside for the rest of the day. Better yet, canoe over to Mystery Island and play there. Even better, make it a camping trip! Yes, everybody go camping on Mystery Island. Don't come back until Christmas."

At first this seemed rather harsh but then everybody remembered that Christmas was just two days away. This got the children, who had been quiet for just a moment, all excited again. "Out!" yelled the mother.

The children immediately began preparations. With three kids to a canoe, they needed a dozen canoes and two paddles for each canoe. Each kid grabbed clean underwear, two extra pairs of socks, exactly four pounds of food and fifteen pounds of equipment (bowls, cups, silverware, sleeping bags, flashlights, handheld video games; Hortense took along her *Jumbo Puzzle Book*).

At eight o'clock in the morning, they piled into the canoes and paddled out to Mystery Island. The trip took just three-quarters of an hour and was uneventful until they had almost reached the island. Jamie was leaning out over the edge of her canoe when she said, "Hey, we're in canoe number 29."

"No, you're not," laughed Gertrude from another canoe. "You're reading it upside down!"

"I am?" asked Jamie, and tried to twist around to see it right and promptly fell in the lake. "Yeow!" she shrieked, while splashing hurriedly to shore, "this water is FREEZING!"

Jamie quickly got out of her wet clothes and crawled into her sleeping bag from where she could supervise the setting up of the tents. Originally, the kids wanted to sleep three to a tent, but they didn't have enough tents so they crowded in four to a tent. Five of the tents were just enough for the boys, the others were for the girls. Unfortunately, no one had remembered to bring tent pegs, so the rest of the morning was spent scrounging up pieces of wood until there was enough for twelve pegs for each tent. The kids then ate a hearty lunch of chocolate-chip cookies.

The next order of business was to build a fire, which wasn't easy because so much of the available wood had been used for tent pegs. Things weren't looking too hot until Rupert brought over a big piece of wood, broke it in half, and fed it to the fire that immediately started burning much better. All the kids cheered except Dominic who yelled, "Rupert, you dodo, that was a canoe paddle!"

The afternoon was spent exploring the island, playing games, fishing, and talking about what everyone hoped to get for Christmas. Jamie stayed in her sleeping bag all afternoon, playing solitaire and waiting for her clothes to dry by the fire. She didn't win many solitaire games after the wind blew her cards around and the Seven of Hearts landed in the fire.

Dinner was more cookies, toasted over the fire this time; after that, the children all sat around telling ghost stories. This was great fun until Mabel, with big eyes, said quietly, "Uh, guys, I-think I hear something creeping around in the woods!" Instantly, everyone was quiet and all ears were listening for noises. After a few minutes, they all heard a distinct "whooo-oo-oo." Immediately, everyone ran for the tents and dove into their sleeping bags and didn't come out until morning.

The next day, Lysander got a length of rope and tied knots in it every seven feet to make it easier to hold on to. He ended up with nine knots, including one at each end. The children spent the morning making up different teams and waging tug-of-wars with Lysander's rope until it broke. Later in the day, some of them held a fishing contest. Maxwell won by catching the most fish. Penelope caught half as many as Maxwell, Guineviere caught a third as many as Penelope did, and Baxter caught one-quarter as many as Guineviere. Baxter's fish was so small that he let it go. No one else caught anything. That night, they had a fish feast.

The next morning, all the children were up early and eager to get home. But they were short one canoe paddle and no one was sure what to do about it until Xavier suggested they tie all the canoes together end to end and make a big "supercanoe." The canoes were each eight feet long and when they were all tied together bow to stern they were hard to control. The supercanoe was veering left and right, like a huge water snake, as the kids tried to cross the lake. Nevertheless, the kids made it home in one hour, arriving at 8 o'clock in the morning. Their mother, well rested, was delighted to see them back and they all celebrated a great Christmas. (Except their neighbor Fergus, who insisted for many years after that he had seen a sea serpent on the lake that Christmas morning.)

Now you can try to solve this crossword puzzle using the-clues you read in the story . . .

Across

1. Number of campers on the trip
3. Date on which they returned home
5. Total length of the supercanoe
6. Total number of canoes plus tents
8. How many minutes it took to get home
9. Total number of hours the trip lasted
10. Number of paddles on way home
11. Total number of fish caught during the contest
12. Length of Lysander's rope (before it broke)
13. Total weight of food and equipment in-each canoe (pounds)
15. Number of hours from noon to midnight

Down

1. Water temperature, according to Jamie
2. Jamie's canoe number
3. Number of girls on the trip
4. JAMIE on the telephone
7. Total number of tent pegs needed
10. Total number of socks on the trip
11. Number of minutes it took to get to the island
13. Number of cards left in Jamie's deck
14. Number of ears that listened for ghosts

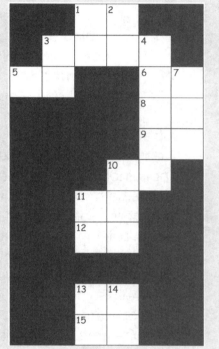

A Puzzle of Your Own

Did you like the story and the cross-number puzzle? Maybe you can create one for your friends or family to solve. You can be as inventive as you like—to provide clues, make up a story, provide word problems, or simply give clues that the puzzle solver is likely to know.

Cross Sums

You must figure out what combination of numbers to use-so-that-each column or row adds up to the totals shown in the white numbers. The white arrows show you in which direction you will be adding, and we have left you some numbers as hints. Better sharpen your pencil! Here are a few simple rules:

- You are only adding the numbers in any set of white boxes that are touching each other.
- Use only the numbers 1 through 9. Each number can only be used *once* in each set.

Remember, you need to think ahead a little bit. Each number has to be correct both across and down!

WORDS 2 KNOW

Fibonacci series: A series of numbers that begin with 1, 1, 2, 3, 5, 8, 13, and so on, where the two first numbers add up to the third (1+1=2), the second and third numbers add up to the fourth (1+2=3), and so on. This sequence was devised by Leonardo Pisano (Fibonacci), a mathematician who lived in Pisa, Italy, between 1170 and 1250.

Solve each of the following problems. Watch the signs carefully! Shade each answer on the number grid to discover the hidden message. HINT: When there's an equation with parentheses ( ) around two numbers, do the part of the problem inside the parentheses first.

HIDDEN MESSAGE:

Professor Proof's bumper sticker tells about his favorite kind of calculation.

1	2	3	4	5	6	7	8	9	10	11	12	13	14	15	16	17	18
19	20	21	22	23	24	25	26	27	28	29	30	31	32	33	34	35	36
37	38	39	40	41	42	43	44	45	46	47	48	49	50	51	52	53	54
55	56	57	58	59	60	61	62	63	64	65	66	67	68	69	70	71	72
73	74	75	76	77	78	79	80	81	82	83	84	85	86	87	88	89	90

1 x 1 = _____

2 + 1 = _____

2 + 2 = _____

12 - 6 = _____

3 + 3 + 1 = _____

5 x 2 = _____

22 - 11 = _____

22 - 11 + 5 = _____

7 + 7 + 7 = _____

25 - 2 = _____

25 x 1 = _____

18 + 9 = _____

15 + 15 = _____

(15 x 2) + 4 = _____

(18 + 18) + 1 = _____

(14 x 3) - 3 = _____

(12 x 4) - 5 = _____

(12 x 4) - 1 = _____

25 x 2 = _____

52 - 1 = _____

(25 x 2) + 2 = _____

(17 x 3) + 2 = _____

(17 x 3) + 3 = _____

5 x 11 = _____

29 x 2 = _____

(60 x 2) - 60 = _____

16 + 16 + 16 + 16 = __

80 - 10 = _____

(10 x 7) + 3 = _____

(10 x 7) + 7 = _____

(10 x 8) + 1 = _____

41 + 41 = _____

41 + 41 + 1 = _____

(84 x 2) - 84 = _____

(10 x 8) + 8 = _____

Chapter 12
Multiplied and Divided

MIGHTY MULTIPLICATION

Multiplication is nothing more than a shortcut to addition. Let's say you have five baskets with apples, and each basket contains seven apples. If all you know is addition, you will have to do the following problem: 7 + 7 + 7 + 7 + 7. Or, if you know how to multiply, you can just do 7 × 5. Either way, you will get the same number of apples: 35.

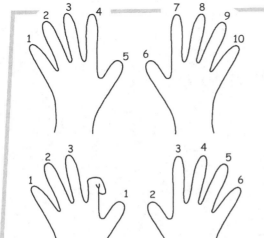

Multiplying on Your Fingers

Here's a trick you can try with your friends—show them how to multiply by nine on your fingers. Hold your hands out in front of you. Then follow the following example.

To multiply 4 × 9, bend down the fourth finger from the left. The number of fingers to the left of the bent finger represent the "tens" digit and the number of fingers to the right represent the "ones" digit, so the answer is 36. This trick works up to 9 × 9 = 81.

To Multiply 9 by Any Digit

Can you figure out how the finger multiplication trick works? Here is another way to look at it—try to multiply 9 × 6:

The "tens" digit: 6 – 1 = 5
The "ones" digit: 9 – 5 = 4

Therefore, 9 × 6 = 54. Right?

Play Five in a Row

Improve your multiplication skills by playing Five in a Row, a game of multiplication tic-tac-toe, at *http://nu.fi. ruu.nl/wisweb/en/applets/html/ 00023/welcome.html*.

Positive and Negative Numbers

Previously, you learned how to add and subtract positive and negative numbers. But what about multiplication? Do the same rules apply? Actually, they don't. In fact, the number line method doesn't work for multiplication. Instead, it might be helpful to imagine a video of a person who is walking backward and forward. People can walk backward and forward, and the video can be played forward or rewound:

Walking forward is a positive action.
Walking backward is a negative action.
Film running forward is positive.
Film running backward is negative.

Imagine that you videotape your friend walking forward. If you watch it on video played forward, you will see your friend walking forward. This represents multiplying two positive numbers: $(+) \times (+) = +$. Now, if you rewind the tape, your friend will seem to be walking backward: $(+) \times (-) = -$.

Now imagine you videotape your friend walking backward and then play the video forward. On the screen, you will see your friend walking backward: $(-) \times (+) = -$. But what if you took that same film and played it backward? It would appear that your friend is actually walking forward: $(-) \times (-) = +$.

FUN FACT

To Make a Long Story Short

The nice thing is that these exact same rules work for division, so you needn't learn any more new rules. In fact, these four rules are usually shortened to make them easier to remember: For multiplication and division, if the signs are the same, the answer is positive. If the signs are opposite, the answer is negative.

HEE
HEE
HEE

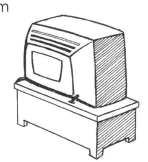

Multiplication Boxes

Now you are ready for some fun with multiplication boxes. A multiplication box has six multiplying problems: Each row and each column are separate problems; the first two numbers are multiplied to get the third number.

The following multiplication box is filled out for you, with explanations on the side and bottom.

-3	4	-12
2	-6	-12
-6	-24	144

-3 x 4 = -12

2 x -6 = -12

-6 x -24 = 144

| -3 x 2 = -6 | 4 x -6 = -24 | -12 x -12 = 144 |

Now, complete each of the following multiplication boxes:

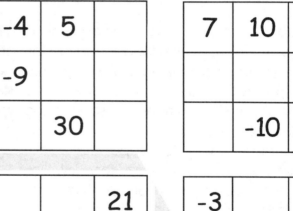

-4	5	
-9		
	30	

7	10	
		-11
	-10	

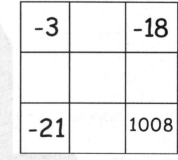

		21
-5		10
	-6	

-3		-18
-21		1008

DAUNTING DIVISION

Which arithmetic operation is the most difficult? Most people think it's division. Problems like 42 ÷ 7 = 6 are not too bad; you just memorize them. Hopefully, you already have your division facts memorized or maybe you are working on them now in school. Problems like 542 ÷ 7 are harder. You have to learn how to solve them.

One of the things that makes division difficult is that unlike addition and multiplication, even when you start with two whole numbers, the answer is not always a **whole number**; it may be a **decimal** (for example, 43 ÷ 8 = 5.375). This is different from adding or multiplying. When you add or multiply any two whole numbers, your answer is always another whole number—no exceptions. Mathematicians say that whole numbers are **closed** for addition and multiplication.

Musical Math

Use division to complete the ten problems. Then cross off the answers in the box below. The remaining letters will spell out the answer to the following riddle:

What comes before a tuba?

Y	A	U	O	R	N	Y	M
31	45	47	16	19	12	21	29
R	E	B	R	M	G	A	W
44	13	15	33	25	18	22	14

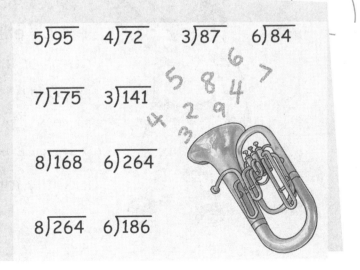

$5\overline{)95}$ $4\overline{)72}$ $3\overline{)87}$ $6\overline{)84}$

$7\overline{)175}$ $3\overline{)141}$

$8\overline{)168}$ $6\overline{)264}$

$8\overline{)264}$ $6\overline{)186}$

PRIME NUMBERS

Let's see. Prime beef is the best beef, so prime numbers must be the best numbers, right? Well, maybe prime numbers are not the best, but they are very important.

You can probably figure out the first several prime numbers in your head. But as the numbers get bigger, it gets harder to know if they are prime (quick, is 91 a prime number?). For thousands of years, people have been curious about ways to find prime numbers. **The Greek mathematician Eratosthenes invented one such way more than two thousand years ago.**

WORDS 2 KNOW

prime number: A number that is divisible by just two different numbers, 1 and itself. Seven is prime because it can only be divided by 1 and 7. Eight is not a prime number because besides 1 and 8, it is also divisible by 2 and 4. The word **prime** comes from *primus,* the Latin word for "first."

Is 1 a Prime Number?

Most mathematicians do not consider 1-to be either a prime or a composite number. It is a special number in multiplication because you can multiply any number by 1 and the answer is the same. Because of this property, 1 is called an **identity for multiplication.**

The Sieve of Eratosthenes

The Sieve of Eratosthenes is a method for finding prime numbers on a number grid, and you can try it yourself by working with a number grid. •-First, circle the 2, then cross out all the numbers that are multiples of 2. •-Then, circle the next number not crossed out, 3, and cross out all numbers that are multiples of that number. •-Continue to circle the number closest to the beginning and cross out all its multiples until all the numbers are circled or crossed out. •-When you are done, the circled numbers are **prime** numbers and the crossed-out numbers are **composite** numbers.

Who's That?

Eratosthenes (276–194 b.c.) was born in Cyrene, North Africa (now Libya), and died in Alexandria, Egypt. He was a well-rounded scholar who investigated many areas of math and science. He estimated the circumference of the Earth to be about 24,400 miles. Now we know it's about 24,900 miles—Eratosthenes was remarkably accurate for his time.

	2	3	4	5	6	7	8	9	10
11	12	13	14	15	16	17	18	19	20
21	22	23	24	25	26	27	28	29	30
31	32	33	34	35	36	37	38	39	40
41	42	43	44	45	46	47	48	49	50
51	52	53	54	55	56	57	58	59	60
61	62	63	64	65	66	67	68	69	70
71	72	73	74	75	76	77	78	79	80
81	82	83	84	85	86	87	88	89	90
91	92	93	94	95	96	97	98	99	100

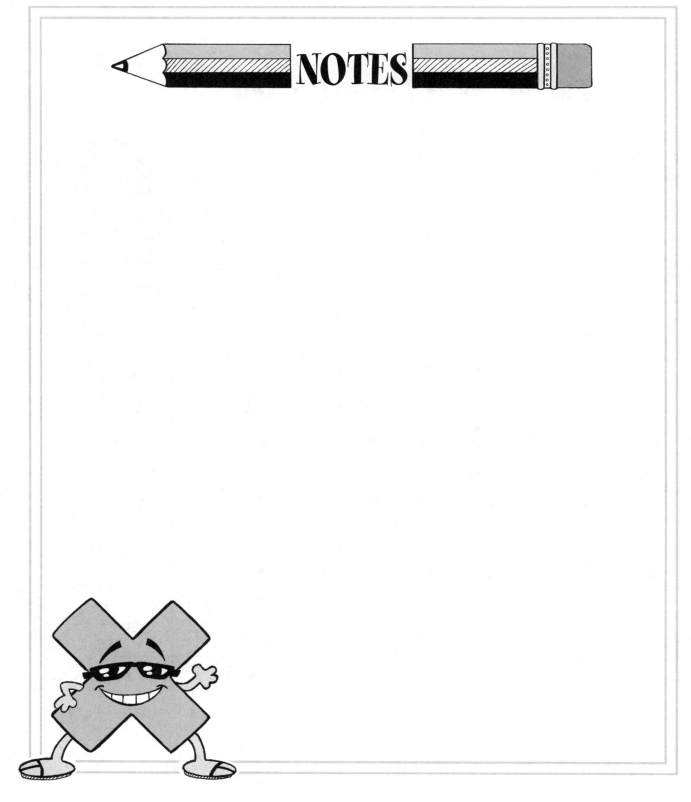

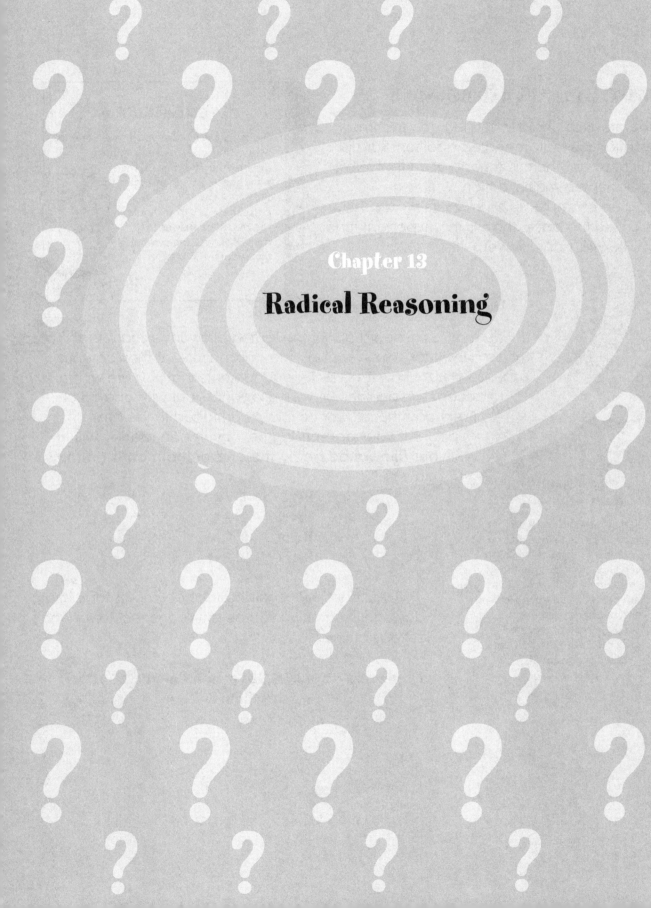

Chapter 13

Radical Reasoning

GROWING BY LEAPS AND BOUNDS

In the previous chapter, you learned that multiplication is simply repeated addition. But did you know that there is an operation that substitutes for repeated multiplication?

Here is an example: $3 \times 3 \times 3 \times 3 \times 3 = 3^5 = 243$. The **3** here is called the **base**, the **5** is the **exponent**, and the answer, **243**, is the **power**.

A Calculator Tip

On many calculators, you use exponents by pressing a key marked x^y. Put in the base number first, 3, then press the x^y key, then press the exponent value, 5, then press the = key. You should see 243 as the answer. (A few calculators use the symbol ^ instead of the x^y key.)

The Allowance Scam

You may have heard about the famed allowance scam that made a few lucky math-wiz kids into millionaires—at their parents' expense. Here is how it works: Tell your parents that you are willing to accept two pennies for your allowance, but with one catch. Every day, the allowance should be raised to the next power. **If your parents agree, how much money will your allowance be by the end of the month (in thirty days)?**

Day 1	$2^1 = 2$
Day 2	$2^2 = 4$
Day 3	$2^3 = 8$
Day 4	$2^4 = 16$

If you continue receiving your payments for thirty days, how much will you be entitled to receive on the last day of the month?

2^{30} **pennies = 1,073,741,824 pennies or \$10,737,418.24 —over ten million dollars!**

It's Growing and Multiplying!

As you may have noticed with the allowance example, exponents on whole numbers can quickly lead to some very large answers. Many things in both nature and people's lives (though probably not your allowance) grow by repeated multiplication instead of repeated addition. Such growth is called **exponential growth**.

SQUARES AND RADICALS

Square numbers are numbers that are the result of multiplying the same number twice. In other words, they can all be written with the exponent 2:

$1^2 = 1, 2^2 = 4, 3^2 = 9, 4^2 = 16, 5^2 = 25, 6^2 = 36, \ldots$

You can see what square numbers look like when you look at floor tiles, like the ones you probably have on the bathroom floor.

$1 \times 1 = 1^2 = 1$ $2 \times 2 = 2^2 = 4$ $3 \times 3 = 3^2 = 9$ $4 \times 4 = 4^2 = 16$

Complete the table to find more square numbers.

5^2	=	25	13^2	=
6^2	=		14^2	=
7^2	=		15^2	=
8^2	=		16^2	=
9^2	=		17^2	=
10^2	=		18^2	=
11^2	=		19^2	=
12^2	=		20^2	=

Goofy Gardener

Use the decoder to figure out the answer to this riddle:

WHY DID THE MATHEMATICIAN PLANT HIS GARDEN IN MILK CARTONS?

A Radical Sign

You know that subtraction is the opposite of addition and division is the opposite of multiplication. The operation called **squaring** also has an opposite, called the **square root.** A square root of a number is written using a **radical sign:** $\sqrt{36}$ means "What number must I square (multiply by itself) to get 36?" If you know your multiplication facts, you should be able to find an answer fairly easily—it's 6, because 6 × 6 = 36. Now that you know what a square root means, finish filling in the following table.

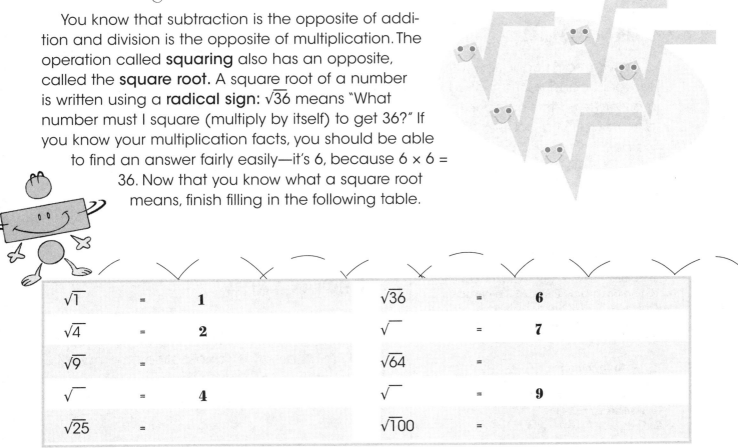

$\sqrt{1}$	=	1	$\sqrt{36}$	=	6
$\sqrt{4}$	=	2	$\sqrt{}$	=	7
$\sqrt{9}$	=		$\sqrt{64}$	=	
$\sqrt{}$	=	4	$\sqrt{}$	=	9
$\sqrt{25}$	=		$\sqrt{100}$	=	

The Square Root's Double

Did you know that $\sqrt{36}$ has another square root in addition to 6? Can you think of what it is? What other two identical numbers can you multiply to get to 36? How about –6 × –6? All positive numbers really have two square roots that are opposites of each other, one positive and the other negative.

147

On Your Mark!

Answer each equation with a number between 1 and 10. Then read the phrases in order (read the number, too!) from least to most to find a popular way to count to the beginning of a race!

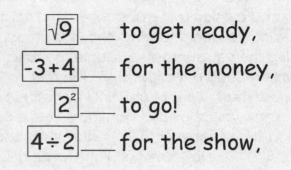

$\sqrt{9}$ ____ to get ready,

$-3+4$ ____ for the money,

2^2 ____ to go!

$4 \div 2$ ____ for the show,

FUN FACT

Drawkcab (Backward) Numbers

Palindromes are words that read the same forward and backward. "Racecar" is a palindrome. Numbers can be palindromes if they are the same forward and backward, like 121. Here's how to make your own palindrome numbers:

- Start with any number: 49
- Reverse it: 94
- Add the two: 49 + 94 = 143
- Reverse the sum: 341
- Add again: 143 + 341 = 484

Presto! You've got a palindrome number: 484.

THREE IN A ROW

This is a game for two players. The goal of the game is to identify square, triangular (divisible by 3), and palindrome numbers and be the first player to get three of your markers in a row. To play, you will need:

- A paper clip
- A pencil
- Two sets of different place markers (such-as coins, buttons, or small candies)

Use the point of a pencil to hold one end of a paper clip at the center of the spinner and spin the paper clip.

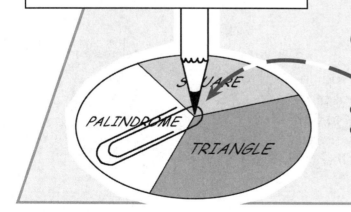

How Four Can You Go?

Four is a very powerful number. With exactly four fours (4 4 4 4), you can make lots of other numbers. Using addition, subtraction, multiplication, division, and square roots, as well as some parentheses (to show what to do first), see if you can come up with the numbers from 1 to 15. We've done 1 as an example, but feel free to do it again—most of these can be done more than one way.

1 = **EXAMPLE:** $4 \div 4 + 4 - 4 = 1$

2 =

3 =

4 =

5 =

6 =

7 =

8 =

9 =

10 =

11 =

12 =

13 =

14 =

15 =

HINT: Stumped? Don't forget that $\sqrt{4} = 2$!

Your Number's Up

See how many common phrases or familiar objects you can think of that relate to the following numbers. Can you fill in all the blanks? We did a few to get you started.

1

2

3   **LITTLE PIGS**

4

5

6

7

8

9

10   **FINGERS OR TOES**

11

12

13

14

15

16

17

18

19

20

21

22

23

24   **HOURS IN A DAY**

25

50

100

If you are stumped, you can check the answer key, but don't be surprised if your answers are different than ours!

Chapter 14

Geometry Games

AN ANCIENT MATH

You may recall that numbers were invented to count things—for example, a herdsman needed to keep track of how many sheep he had. Well, that same herdsman may also have been interested in measuring how much land his sheep had to graze on. This and other problems like it evolved into one of the earliest and most important branches of mathematics: geometry.

For thousands of years, many people from around the world have known the importance of geometry. The Chinese in the Far East, the Greeks in the Mediterranean, and the Inca and Maya in the

WORDS 2 KNOW

geometry: A study of physical shapes. Literally, **geometry** means "to measure the Earth."

Shape Changers

These are the shape-change codes for the puzzle you are about to solve.

Notice that each letter is found in a unique shape. To send a message, draw the outline of the shape each letter is in, including the dot, if there is one. For example, here is how to send the message LOOK AT THAT!:

Now use the decoder to figure out the answer to this riddle: What do geometry teachers like to eat?

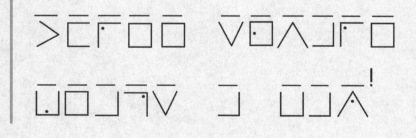

BASIC GEOMETRY

Understanding geometry requires learning lots of words that are used to describe geometric figures and properties. Some of them you will encounter here. Although you won't begin your studies in geometry until high school, you already know a lot of geometrical concepts. You can tell the difference between a long line and a short line or between a square and a circle, and you already know about π.

Six-Sided Math

Here are four big hexagons that share some edges with each other. Use the numbers from 1 to 9 to fill in the empty spaces. When the puzzle is finished, the six numbers around every big hexagon should add up to 30.

WORDS 2 KNOW

polygon: A geometrical figure with three or more sides. The term **polygon** is from the Greek roots *poli* (many) and *gonus* (knees). Greeks thought of a polygon as a shape of many angles, which look like bent knees.

Q: Why did the cube cross from the second to the third dimension?

A: The second dimension was too square.

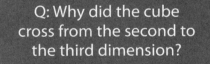

Hide in Plain Sight

See if you can find this list of basic geometry terms hidden in the letter grid.

HINT: The words in the grid will be "acting out" their meaning. For example, if you were searching for the word CIRCLE, expect to find the letters in a circular pattern, not a straight line! This means that some of the words will appear more than once in the puzzle, even if they only appear once in the list!

EXTRA CREDIT: Use bright-colored markers to run a line through each word you find. If you use a different color for each word, the patterns will be easier to see.

Words to Search For

Parallel
Parallel lines are always the same distance apart. They never meet or cross over each other.

Right Angle
A 90° angle, like the corner of a book, or the capital letter L.

Perpendicular
Straight up and down; at right angles to the surface (a telephone pole is usually perpendicular to the road).

Congruent
Exactly equal in shape and area.

Line
The path made by a moving point, sometimes straight, sometimes curved.

Rays
A group of lines coming from a center.

Bisect
To part into equal halves.

Rectangle
A figure with four sides that has four right angles.

```
V W M O B V H J K C W F I H F
A T H G I R O P G R U M L O C
N W M V S F J E N H E Z E H M
G J V / / / V R O H N C N F O
L F K Z E H O P C — T F I P L
E O W M C F W E M V J O L A E
C H J K T O V N F R E C E R L
S O C S J H S D V L E T N A L
J Y K Y L Y K I O G N A I L A
M J A A A Z M C J K O H L L R
S Y A R A Y S U G R U K E E A
O C A A A K J L N H E O N L P
F Y J Y H Y K A O H N F I O C
S O F S O J S R C — T V L M O
V P E R P E N D I C U L A R J
```

PAPER FOLDING

Origami is the art of folding paper. You can make lots of intricate figures with origami; in fact, you may have seen an origami crane—one of the most popular origami animals.

The paper cranes are so well known because of Sadako, a Japanese girl who was dying of leukemia. Sadako heard an old legend: If a sick person folds one thousand origami cranes, the gods will grant her wish and make her healthy again. And so, she set out on a quest to fold one thousand cranes. Unfortunately, Sadako died before completing her project. Ever since then, people have been making origami cranes in memory of-this bright girl.

Sadako and Her Paper Cranes

Learn how to make paper cranes in memory of Sadako. Visit www.personal. umich.edu/~adysart/origami/crane/ to learn how to make these paper creatures.

Life of the Party

Match each name to its geometric shape, numbering each shape as you go. Then, take the letter in each shape and place it in the corresponding box to get an old saying.

1. Triangle
2. Circle
3. Rectangle
4. Trapezoid
5. Rhombus
6. Ellipse
7. Pentagon
8. Hexagon
9. Octagon

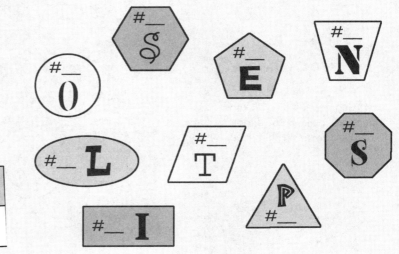

Without geometry, life would be:

1	2	3	4	5	6	7	8	9

CIRCULAR REASONING

You have already learned something about circles. Circles are certainly mysterious. The center of the circle is exactly the same distance to any point on the circle; that distance is known as the **radius.** Because circles cannot be measured by a ruler, you can't really divide them into inches or feet—but we can divide them into degrees.

A circle by any other name is just as round!

Compasses travel in the best circles!

Ho Ho Ho

FUN FACT

360 Circles

A circle is divided into 360 degrees. But did you know that a golf ball has 360 dimples? Coincidence? We think not!

HEE HEE HEE

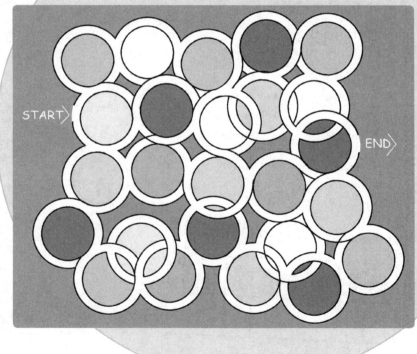

Going Around in Circles

Find your way around the circles from start to end.

START

END

TAMPERING WITH TRIANGLES

What could be simpler than a triangle? It's a shape with three interconnected sides of any length. But actually, there are all kinds of triangles. Triangles may vary by the **length of their sides:**

Triangles with three sides of equal length are equilateral triangles.

Triangles with two sides of equal length are isosceles triangles.

Triangles with three different sides are scalene triangles.

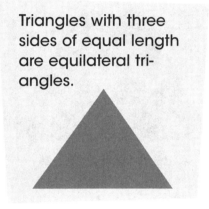

But that's not all! Triangles can also be sorted by their **angles:**

A triangle is equiangular (and, therefore, equilateral) if all its angles are congruent (same).

A triangle is a right triangle if one of its angles measures 90 degrees (and two of its sides are perpendicular to each other).

A triangle is obtuse if one of its angles is larger than 90 degrees.

A triangle is acute if all three of its angles are smaller than 90 degrees.

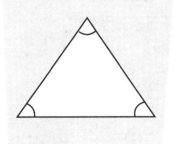
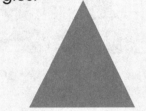
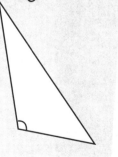
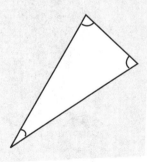

Triangle Numbers

Triangular numbers are found in the number of dots that can be used to make an equilateral triangle (triangle with three equal sides). The following illustrations represent 3, 6, 10, and 15.

Can you see a pattern here?

1+ 2 = 3   1 + 2 + 3 = 6   1 + 2 + 3 + 4 = 10   1 + 2 + 3 + 4 + 5 = 15

Draw a picture or add numbers to find the next three triangular numbers.

The next three numbers are 21, 28, and 36.

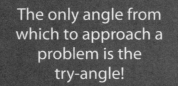

The only angle from which to approach a problem is the try-angle!

Ho Ho Ho

The Last Straw

If you take three drinking straws, you can easily arrange them into one triangle that has three equal sides. Now, suppose you have six drinking straws. Can you arrange them into FOUR triangles, all with equal sides?

HINT:-You may need some tape!

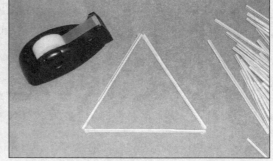

Get to the Point!

Color every triangle in this puzzle to
find the answer to the following riddle:

If you have ten cats in a box and one
jumps out, how many are left?

ON A TREASURE HUNT

The not-so-famous outlaw Cash Steele hid all the money he stole somewhere in or near the town of Nowhere, Nevada. After he died, his daughter, Penny, went looking for the treasure.

She knew her father very well. After looking around town, she decided that there were ten possible places where he could have hidden his money:

1. Under the dirt floor of his cabin.
2. In the hayloft of his barn.
3. In the Steele family cemetery.
4. High up in the branches of the Lone Pine-Tree.
5. On top of Windy Hill.
6. In the cave to the east of Windy Hill.
7. In the old mine shaft.
8. At the top of the windmill.
9. In a pile of dinosaur bones.
10. Down at the bottom of the well.

Here is what else Penny knew:

1. Her father was afraid of ghosts and wouldn't want his money close to the cemetery.
2. Cash Steele did not like small dark places either.
3. If he buried the money, it would be to the north of his cabin.
4. If he hid it aboveground, it would be south of the cabin.
5. If he didn't hide it in the well, then he didn't hide it in the windmill, either.

That leaves one possible hiding place. What is it?

(See the answer on page 339 for an explanation.)

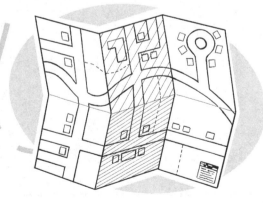

160

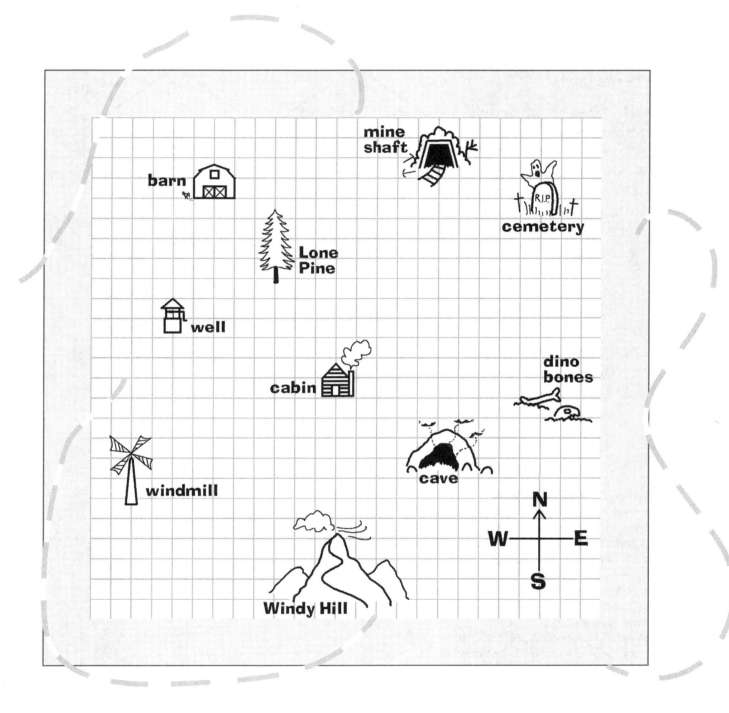

Magic Pentagrams

This puzzle is just for fun—there's no right or wrong answer!

Choose a number found on one of the points of a pentagram. Now, point to all the pentagrams on which this number can be found. Add the large number found in the center of those pentagrams. The sum will be the number that you chose!

Share the magic pentagram trick with a friend, or try making your own pentagram puzzle using different numbers.

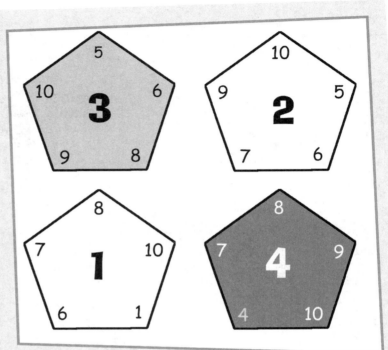

FUN FACT

Gargantuan Geometry

Did you know that one of the largest pentagons in the world is right here in the United States? That's right—the Pentagon building just outside Washington, D.C., which serves as the headquarters of the Department of Defense, is so big that the National Capitol could fit into any one of its five wedge-shaped sections. To get around inside, there are 17.5 miles of corridors! Want to know more fascinating facts about this prominent polygon? Check out *www.fortamerica.com/about-the-pentagon.html.*

SpiroGraphs

Create your own SpiroGraph design at *www.math.ucsd.edu/~dlittle/java/SpiroGraph.html.* There are suggestions for the different settings; try them all. Make the String of Pearls for someone special.

A Square Deal

Begin at the white number 4 that is in the dark box. Move up, down, or sideways four spaces in any direction. Add the numbers as you go and reach all four corners, but only one time each. **HINT: the pattern forms the outline of a letter of the alphabet.**

```
4 2 4 3 1 3 4 2 4
2 1 2 4 3 4 2 1 2
1 2 4 3 2 3 4 2 3
3 4 3 2 1 2 3 4 1
4 3 2 1 4 1 2 1 2
3 4 3 2 1 2 3 4 1
1 2 4 3 2 3 4 2 3
2 1 2 4 1 4 2 1 2
4 2 4 1 3 1 4 2 4
```

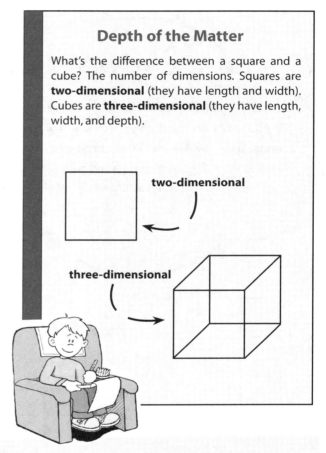

Depth of the Matter

What's the difference between a square and a cube? The number of dimensions. Squares are **two-dimensional** (they have length and width). Cubes are **three-dimensional** (they have length, width, and depth).

two-dimensional

three-dimensional

The Domino Effect

Do you know how to play dominoes? See if you can figure it out by filling in the missing squares. HINT: Each number, from 1 to 6, can only be used once.

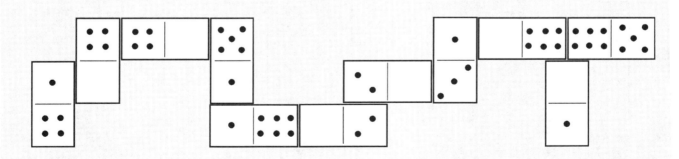

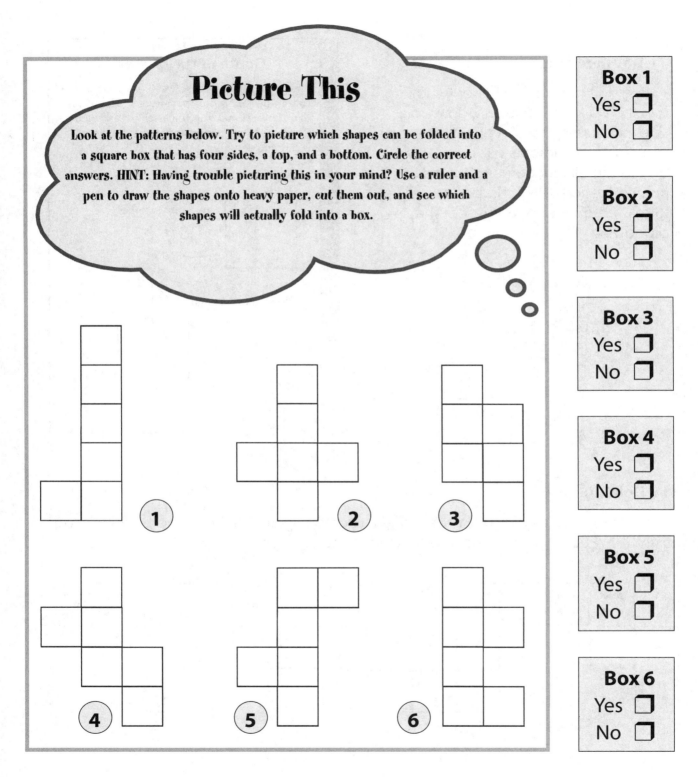

Picture This

Look at the patterns below. Try to picture which shapes can be folded into a square box that has four sides, a top, and a bottom. Circle the correct answers. HINT: Having trouble picturing this in your mind? Use a ruler and a pen to draw the shapes onto heavy paper, cut them out, and see which shapes will actually fold into a box.

Box 1
Yes ☐
No ☐

Box 2
Yes ☐
No ☐

Box 3
Yes ☐
No ☐

Box 4
Yes ☐
No ☐

Box 5
Yes ☐
No ☐

Box 6
Yes ☐
No ☐

Chapter 15

Measurement Mysteries

Answer the following questions and then fill in the answer key to find out which animal's tongue can grow up to 21 inches long–about as long as your arm. Slurp!

1. How long is a school bus?

   f) 6 feet
   g) 36 feet
   h) 160 feet
   i) 6 yards

2. How long is a twin bed?

   h) 6 inches
   i) 6 feet
   j) 60 inches
   k) 60 feet

3. How long is a football field?

   r) 360 feet
   s) 360 inches
   t) 36 miles
   u) 360 miles

4. How long is a dollar bill?

   a) 6 inches
   b) 60 centimeters
   c) 6 feet
   d) 6 millimeters

5. How long is a marathon?

   c) 26.2 meters
   d) 262 centimeters
   e) 262 kilometers
   f) 26.2 miles

6. How long is a blue whale?

   c) 10 meters
   d) 100 inches
   e) 100 feet
   f) 10 yards

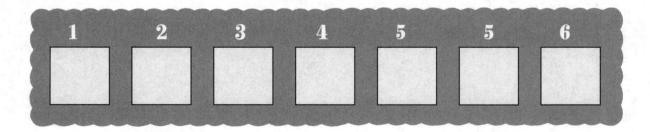

1	2	3	4	5	5	6

HINK PINKS

Each silly answer in the following Hink Pinks is made up of two words that rhyme. HINT: The first six are one-syllable words; the last Hink Pink is made up of words that are two syllables each.

1. Pile of games that weighs 2,000 lbs. _____

2. 5,280 foot grin _____

3. Two pastries that are each 12 inches long _____

4. Very difficult 3 feet _____

5. Rubber ball that weighs 16 ounces _____

6. 28.4 grams that jumps quickly _____

7. Urgent message that weighs 2.2 pounds _____

To St. Ives

As I was going to St. Ives
I met a man with seven wives.
Each wife had six sacks,
Each sack had five cats,
Each cat had four kits,
Each kit had three mice,
Each mouse had two pieces of cheese,
Each cheese had one toothpick.

How many toothpicks were there?

Math Online

Journey across 42 powers of 10 at *www.wordwizz.com/pwrsof10.htm*. These pictures show one image at the submolecular level enlarged to 10 times as big, over and over until you are looking at the entire known universe. Choose the smallest image and then keep clicking on the +1 button to increase the zoom by a factor of 10.

Star Power

Find the perfect center of this starry pattern.

START

FINISH

A WEIGHTY MATTER

It helps to know how much things weigh. We measure candy in ounces, fruit and vegetables in pounds, and elephants in tons. Here are the conversion tables for metric and English weight measurements.

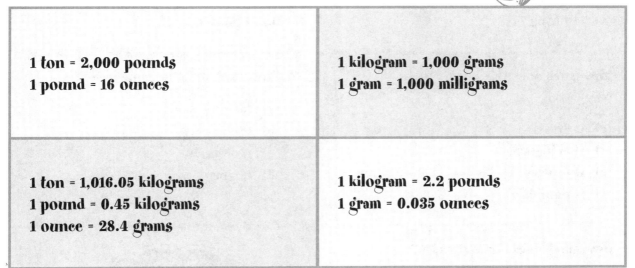

1 ton = 2,000 pounds 1 pound = 16 ounces	1 kilogram = 1,000 grams 1 gram = 1,000 milligrams
1 ton = 1,016.05 kilograms 1 pound = 0.45 kilograms 1 ounce = 28.4 grams	1 kilogram = 2.2 pounds 1 gram = 0.035 ounces

I am the world's largest animal. I can weigh 177 tons—that's 354,000 pounds. It would take more than 4,400 children averaging 80 pounds each to balance with-me!

1. How much does an average man weigh?	2. How much did a Tyrannosaurus rex weigh?
a) 172 ounces b) 172 pounds c) 172 grams d) 172 kilograms	j) 60 kilograms k) 60 pounds l) 6 tons m) 60 tons

continued on next page

3. How much does an adult polar bear weigh?

u) 1,400 pounds
v) 140 pounds
w) 14 kilograms
x) 140 tons

6. How much does an ant weigh?

h) 4 milligrams
i) 4 kilograms
j) 4 ounces
k) 4 pounds

4. How much does this book weigh?

c) 11 grams
d) 11 milligrams
e) 11 ounces
f) 11 pounds

7. How much does an apple weigh?

a) 160 grams
b) 160 ounces
c) 16 pounds
d) 16 grams

5. How much does a nickel weigh?

w) 5 grams
x) 0.05 ounces
y) 50 ounces
z) 50 grams

1	2	3	4	5	6	7	2	4

Measuring Your ZZZs

Write each letter in the space above the measurement that matches its place on the ruler. When you're finished, you will have the answer to the following riddle:

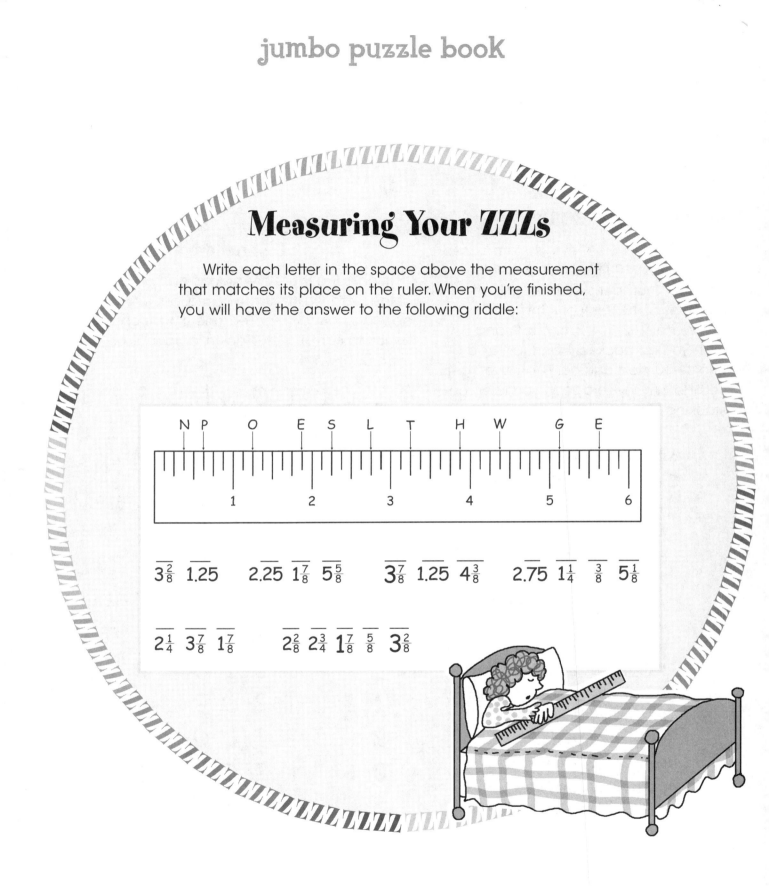

N P   O   E   S   L   T   H   W   G   E

1   2   3   4   5   6

$3\frac{2}{8}$ 1.25   2.25 $1\frac{7}{8}$ $5\frac{5}{8}$ $3\frac{7}{8}$ 1.25 $4\frac{3}{8}$ 2.75 $1\frac{1}{4}$ $\frac{3}{8}$ $5\frac{1}{8}$

$2\frac{1}{4}$ $3\frac{7}{8}$ $1\frac{7}{8}$ $2\frac{2}{8}$ $2\frac{3}{4}$ $1\frac{7}{8}$ $\frac{5}{8}$ $3\frac{2}{8}$

O O O O O O O O O O O O O O O

STACKING UP ZEROS

Why is the metric system based on 10? Because our entire number system is built on multiples of 10. Think of it this way: You've got 1, 2, 3, 4, 5, 6, 7, 8, 9, and then you go back to 1 and just add a 0 to it—10. Add another 0, and you get 100. How many zeros can you keep on stacking? Take a look here:

Number of Zeros	What you get
0	one
1	ten
2	hundred
3	thousand
4	ten thousand
5	hundred thousand
6	million
7	ten million
8	hundred million
9	billion
12	trillion
16	quadrillion
100	googol
googol	googolplex

Lost Billions

It looks like there are billions and billions of the word BILLIONS in this grid, but it only appears correctly spelled one time. It could be left to right, up and down, diagonal, or even backward.

```
B I L L I O N N S B B I
B I L S B S N O I L I B
I B S S N B I L L O N S
L S N N B O B I L L N O
L N I O I I I B B O B I
L O O I L B O L I B I L
I I L L O B S I L O B I
O L L L O N L B O I S L
N L I B I L I O B B I I
S I B L I B O B I L I B
I B L B B I L O O N S I
O B B I L I O O N S O L
```

Googols of Fun

A googol is a REALLY big number. If a ten has one zero (10), how many zeros do you think a googol has? Using a simple number substitution (A=1, B=2, C=3, etc.), see if you can break this number code.

1   7·15·15·7·15·12   8·1·19

—   — — — — — —   — — —

15·14·5   8·21·14·4·18·5·4

— — —   — — — — — — —

26·5·18·15·19

— — — — —

What's beyond Googolplex?

The rules of math say that you can keep counting for infinity. That means, that numbers keep going and going, and there is no such thing as the last or highest number. Infinity is not a number—it's a concept that is never-ending. Mathematicians use ∞ to represent infinity in mathematical calculations.

Counting Forever

The symbol ∞ has been around for more than two thousand years. The Romans used it to represent 1,000, a BIG number to them. Around the year 1650, an English mathematician, John Wallis, proposed that this symbol ∞ be used to represent infinity, and we have been doing just that ever since.

ON YOUR TOES

Use this fraction code to figure out the riddle.

CODE

The white part of each shape is empty.

The shaded part of each shape is filled. Estimate how much of each shape is full using the following rules:

HOW TO USE THE CODE

Look at the fraction or number below each blank. Using the shapes connected to each word box, pick the shape that is closest to that fraction or number. Write the letter of that shape on the blank.

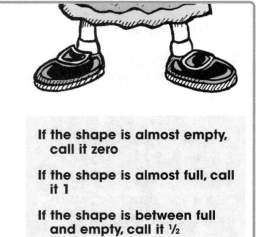

If the shape is almost empty, call it zero

If the shape is almost full, call it 1

If the shape is between full and empty, call it ½

RIDDLE: How does a math student make her shoes longer?

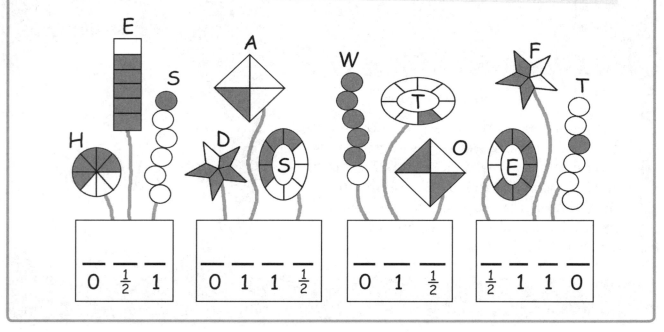

Chapter 16

Brain Benders

LOGICAL MATH

Most of us, when we think of math, think of numbers. But not all math involves numbers. You've already explored some geometry activities in Chapter 5 that involved lines and shapes. Another area of math that does not have to involve numbers is logic.

Go Figure!

1. You have two coins. Added together, they equal 15 cents—but one is not a nickel. How is that possible?

   ....
   ....
   ....

2. Can you take four nines (9, 9, 9, 9) and arrange them to make an equation that totals 100? You can use any math function, but you can only use each nine once.

   ....
   ....
   ....

3. What do you get if you divide 30 by half and add 10?

   ....
   ....
   ....

4. If there are five apples and you take away three, how many apples do you have?

....

....

5. What is the meaning of Faπrce?

....

....

6. What is the meaning of MILONELION?

....

....

7. What is the meaning of this phrase: ONE, ONE, ONE, ONE, ONE, ONE, ANOTHER, ANOTHER, ANOTHER, ANOTHER, ANOTHER, ANOTHER?

....

....

....

8. A clerk in a butcher shop is 6' 2" tall. What does he weigh?

....

....

....

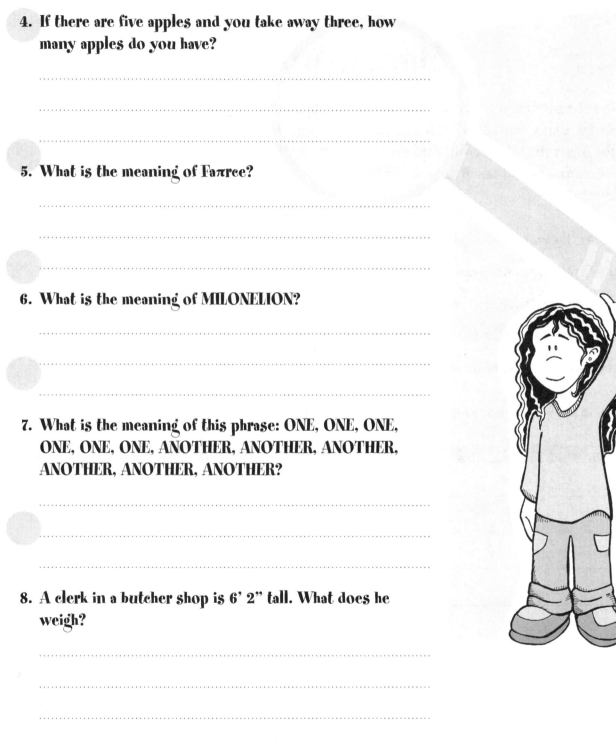

Moving Around

See if you can use logic to solve the puzzle about four fast friends: Gary, Harry, Larry, and Mary who lived in Los Angeles. One day, the four friends got news that they would be moving to four different cities: Atlanta, Boston, Chicago, and Dallas. By listening to their parents talk, the friends learned the following:

Gary's family was moving to either Boston or Dallas.

Harry's family was not moving to either Boston or Chicago.

Either Harry or Mary was moving to Atlanta.

If Harry moves to Atlanta, then Gary moves to Chicago.

If Larry moves to Chicago, then Gary does not move to Dallas.

Who is moving where? Use the table to figure out the answer.

	ATLANTA	BOSTON	CHICAGO	DALLAS
Gary				
Harry				
Larry				
Mary				

IN THE ENCHANTED KINGDOM

The logic puzzles on this page take place in an enchanted kingdom, at a castle inhabited by four princesses—Ruby, Sapphire, Jade, and Topaz—as well as their mother, Queen Diamond, and their four pet dragons.

Taming Dragons

These princesses don't need anyone to rescue them—they are dragon tamers and have four days to tame their four dragons. Every day, each one must work with a different dragon. On the **second day**, Ruby tamed Spitfire and Sapphire tamed Forktail. On the **third day,** Jade tamed Blaze and Topaz tamed Smokey. On the **fourth day,** Sapphire tamed Smokey and Topaz tamed Forktail. **Which dragon did each princess tame on each day?**

	Day 1	Day 2	Day 3	Day 4
Ruby				
Jade				
Sapphire				
Topaz				

The Marriage Proposal

Prince Pyrite came to the enchanted castle to ask for Princess Ruby's hand in marriage, but Ruby didn't like him. The Queen didn't want to offend Prince Pyrite, who was her guest, so she told him to go to her garden and put one black and one white pebble into his purse. If Ruby picks a **black** pebble, they will marry. If she picks a **white** one, the prince will have to go home alone.

As the prince went out to the garden, Ruby followed him and saw him put two black pebbles into the purse. At first, she's dismayed but then gets an idea. **How can Ruby trick the prince?**

IN THE LAND OF CONFUSION

All the people in the Land of Confusion are either sages or jesters. **Sages** are noted for their honesty—they always tell the truth. **Jesters,** however, are always kidding around and never tell the truth. Unfortunately, there is no way to tell one from the other just by looking at them.

Ima Visitor leaves her home in the Enchanted Kingdom and travels to the Land of Confusion. While there, she meets three men: Xavier, Yale, and Zachary. Ima asks, "How many of you are sages?"

Xavier says that he is not a jester.
Yale says that Xavier is lying.
Zachary adds, "Yale is lying."

Can you figure out who is a sage and who is a jester?

Two Kids in the Land of Confusion

Ima keeps on walking. Just as she approaches the emperor's palace, she finds a boy and a girl sitting on the steps, and hears three statements:

1. "I'm a boy," says the child with black hair.
2. "I'm a girl," says the child with red hair.
3. "Exactly one of us is a sage," says the boy.

Are the boy and girl sages and/or jesters, and what color hair does each one have?

A Boast?

Upon entering the emperor's palace, Ima overheard a man say, "If I am a sage, then so is my son."

What can you tell about him or his son?

You will find the answers in the Puzzle Answers section

Meeting the King

Inside the palace, Ima went looking for the King, and she met some sages. She asked them if the King is a sage or a jester, and they told her that they didn't know, but that according to their laws, he must be a citizen of the Land of Confusion, either a sage or a jester.

Just then, a man entered the hall wearing a crown and a beautiful purple cloak. The sages told Ima that it was the King, and that she could ask him whether he was a sage or a jester. To her question, the King responded, "I am a jester."

Immediately, the sages cried: "Imposter! Arrest that man!" Why?

Einstein's Math Troubles

"Do not worry too much about your difficulties in mathematics, I can assure you mine are still greater."

—Albert Einstein

Math Online

For fun math games, check out *www.mathispower.org*. **In particular, see if you can solve the code-breaker puzzle.**

Simple Symbols

Each symbol below equals one of the possible numbers in the box. Substitute the numbers for the symbols so that the subtraction problems work.

HINT: All numbers in the top row are greater than or equal to their corresponding place numbers in the bottom row. We have also left you two zeros to get you started.

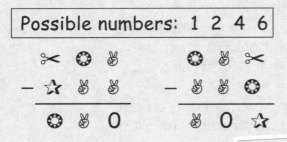

Possible numbers: 1 2 4 6

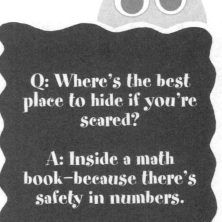

A Card Game

Two kids play five games of gin rummy. Each kid wins the same number of games, but there are no tied games. How is this possible?

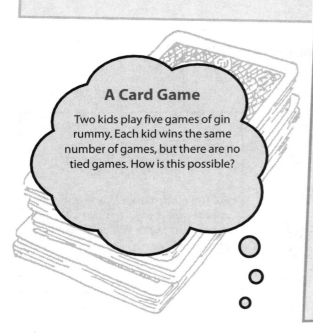

Buying Numbers

This conversation doesn't add up. Can you tell what's for sale?

Customer: How much is 1?

Salesman: 30 cents.

Customer: I'd like 14, please.

Salesman: That will be 60 cents.

Customer: Oops, I really need 114.

Salesman: No problem. That will be 90 cents.

I Can't Find It!

The numbers 1, 2, 3, 4, and 5 appear in a row only one time in this number grid! The answer can be up, down, side to side, or diagonal. Look extra carefully—the numbers might also appear backward!

1	2	2	1	3	1	2	3	5
2	2	3	3	1	2	1	4	1
1	2	1	2	5	2	2	1	2
2	3	1	4	3	1	4	2	5
1	2	3	4	2	3	3	4	4
4	1	5	2	1	2	1	3	3
5	3	4	1	2	4	4	5	5
1	2	2	1	3	4	5	1	2
3	1	1	2	4	3	3	2	1

I Found It!

Mr. Math asked four of his students to see how many math puzzle books they could find in the public library. How many books did each student find? Use the clues to complete the chart.

1. The four students found a total of 13 math puzzle books.
2. None of the students found more than 5-puzzle books.
3. None of the children found the same number of puzzle books.
4. Jasmine found 3 puzzle books.
5. Katlyn found fewer puzzle books than Jasmine.
6. Ethan found the most puzzle books.

Math Puzzles

Students	# of books each student found
Jasmine	
Katlyn	
Josh	
Ethan	
TOTAL number of puzzle books found	

NOTES

Chapter 17

Probability Puzzles

A PROBABLE CAUSE

You might be surprised to know that probability is a relatively new area of math. Probability began to be studied in the mid-1600s. That may seem like a long time ago, but remember that people have been doing geometry for thousands of years.

Probability is involved any time we do something where we can't know in advance what is going to happen. When we toss a coin in the air, we know it is going to come back down. However, we don't know if it will land as heads or tails. That is probability.

WORDS 2 KNOW

probability: The chances of something happening—actually, the ratio of the number of times it could happen compared to the number of possible things that could happen. For example, when you throw dice, you have 1/6 chances of getting each particular number.

Probability Scrabble

Can you guess how many other words you could make by using any of the eleven letters in the word PROBABILITY? Do you think you could make fifty words, or is the number closer to twenty? There is no way to know except by sitting down with paper and pencil and making a list. For each word, you can use each letter as many times as it appears in PROBABILITY. For example, you could spell BABY because there are two Bs, but you can't spell ROOT, because there is only one O.

A Coin Toss

The probability of getting a head or a tail in any coin toss is ½ heads and ½ tails. Do a simulated coin-toss experiment at *www.acs.ilstu.edu/faculty/bllim/java/progsinnotes/CoinToss.html.* First, try 25 tosses, then 100, and then 500. When we tried it, we got 10/15, 50/50, and 251/249.

PLAYING DICE

When you roll the die, you are playing with probability. With each roll, you are just as likely to get 1 as you are 2, 3, 4, 5, or 6. That means that you have one in six chances to get any number. And each time you throw the die, the probability of getting a particular number remains the same.

What If You Roll Two Dice?

Can you figure out what your probabilities are of getting a 1, 2, 3, 4, 5, or 6 if you roll two dice? Will your chances increase or decrease?

Prisoners Game

A Variation on the Prisoners Game

This time, each player picks where to put his or her prisoners. For example, Player 1 could put a prisoner in cells 1, 2, and 3 of the top row and cells 3, 4, and 5 of the bottom row. Each roll of the dice frees two prisoners at a time. After playing several rounds, who has the best strategy?

This is a game for two players. To play, you will need the following:

- **Five pennies and five nickels (or two sets of other markers)**
- **A pair of dice**
- **Paper and pencil for keeping score**

Players should each have five markers, which are prisoners. Player 1 places his or her five prisoners in each cell of the top row. Player 2 places prisoners in the bottom row. Players take turns rolling the dice and subtracting the smaller number from the larger. If the difference matches a cell number, the prisoner kept in that cell goes free (is taken off the board). **Whoever frees all the prisoners first, wins!**

Who Owns That Car?

A man came in to the motor vehicle department to register his new car. He requested a very special license plate with the numbers 337 31770. While signing the paperwork, the mysterious man said, "Now everyone will know that this car belongs to me!" **What was the man's name?**

337 31770

Let 'er Roll!

Unlike the Prisoners Game, this one offers equal chances of winning to all the players, and you can have as many as six people join the game. Here is what you will need to play:

- **Piece of paper and pencil for each player**

- **Pair of dice**

You also need to make a game card for each player. To do that, draw a five-squares-by-five-squares grid—you can use a ruler to make the lines straight, but it doesn't matter if they're wobbly.

Then, have one player read the following list of numbers:

1, 36, 9, 24, 18, 8, 6, 15, 30, 25, 10, 24, 18, 6, 3, 12, 2, 4, 12, 16, 9, 12, 16, 9, 12, 20, 6, 10

As each number is called out, each player should write it down in any one of the squares in the grid, until all the spaces are filled. Some numbers will appear twice.

Once you are done, the game can begin. Players take turn rolling the two dice, multiplying the two results, and then covering one number on the grid. **The first one to cover five squares in a row (in any direction) is the winner.**

Even and Odd

Here is a game that uses a principle similar to the Prisoners Game and Let'er Roll. To play, you will need two players: **Player E** (even) and **Player O** (odd), plus the following:

Let's see, 2 x 3 = 6. That's an even number, so I win!

- **Piece of paper**
- **Pencil**
- **Paper clip**

On the count of three, both players show each other one to five fingers on one hand. Multiply the number of fingers showing on one player's hand by the number of fingers showing on the other player's hand. If the product is even, Player E wins. If the product is odd, Player O wins. Keep a tally for twenty rounds. **Which player wins the most rounds?**

You should have noticed that Player E won many more games than Player O. Will Player E still win if both players use a spinner instead of their fingers? Try it. Use a pencil to hold a paper clip at the center of the spinner. Flick the paper clip around the spinner. Keep a tally for twenty rounds. **Now, which player won the most games?**

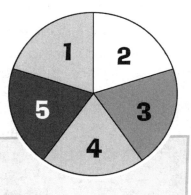

Space for Tallies

(see the following page for possible explanations)

Even and Odd—Explained

What's going on? Why does Player E keep winning? There are two possible explanations:

1. If Player E always shows either two or four fingers, the answer will **always** be even, regardless of the number of fingers Player O shows. Player E will win **every time.**

2. If Player E is totally honest and shows fingers randomly, then it is the same as using the spinner. Player E will win most of the time. To see why, **fill in this multiplication table** and circle all the even numbers. Wow!

×	1	2	3	4	5
1	1	2	3		
2	2	4			
3	3				
4					
5					

When you look at the results, it's easy to see which kind of number is more likely to win!

GET OUT OF HERE

Make your way from START to END by following a number path that goes even, odd, even, odd, etc.

How many different paths do you think you might start before you find the correct one?

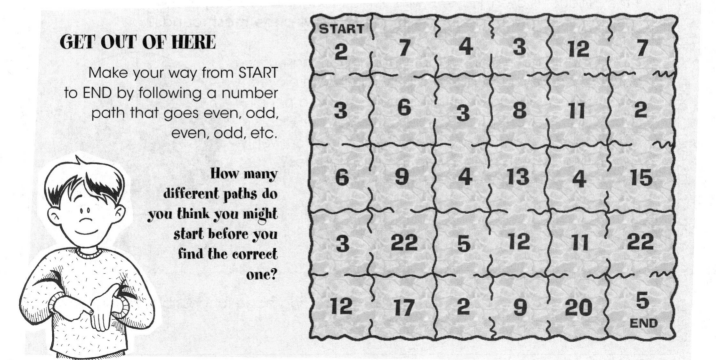

START					
2	7	4	3	12	7
3	6	3	8	11	2
6	9	4	13	4	15
3	22	5	12	11	22
12	17	2	9	20	5 END

An Average Day

What do you know about estimating averages? Each blank below represents an average value. Fill in the following story with your estimates:

I'm just an average ten-year-old who is ⬭ inches tall. I am in school for ⬭ hours per year. After school, I eat a snack. Usually it's popcorn. One popped kernel weighs about ⬭ grams and there are about ⬭ popped kernels in one cup. Today, we are out of popcorn, so I eat ice cream. My favorite flavor is ⬭ . I watch a half-hour TV show, but there is an average of ⬭ commercials every 30 minutes, so the show is really only ⬭ minutes long. Before I go to bed, I still check under the bed for monsters. After all, there is an average of ⬭ monsters per bed.

One of the averages above is a mode. Which one is it? _____

Q: What's an average pie?

A: Pie à la mode.

WORDS 2 KNOW

averages: There are three ways to calculate the average. The **mean** is what you get if you add up all the values and divide the total by the number of values. This is typically what people mean when they use the word **average**. The **median** of a set of values is the value in the middle of the set when the set is written in order. The **mode** of a set of values is the value that occurs most often. Mode is usually used as the average when the values are not numbers, like eye or hair color.

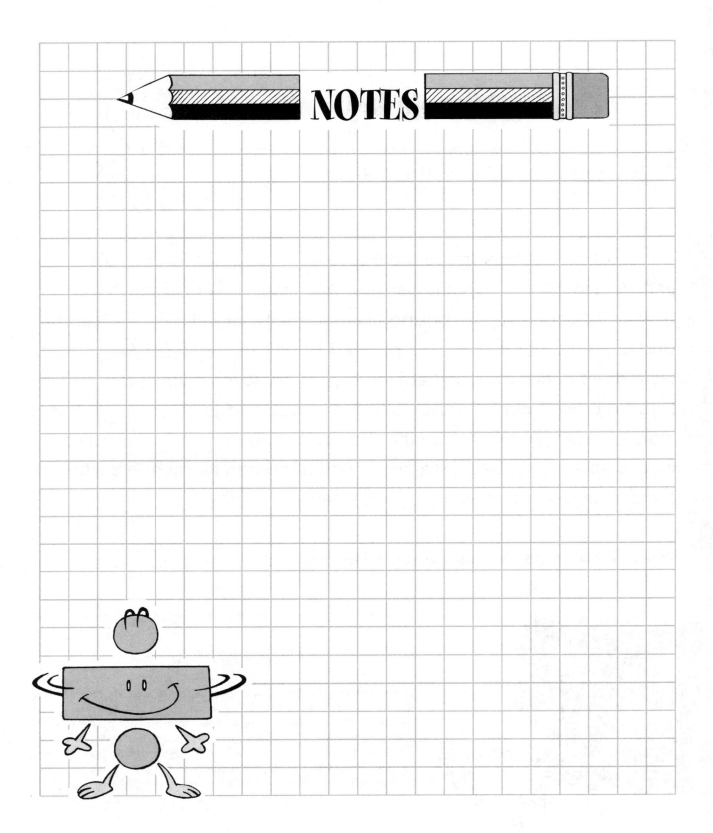

NOTES

Chapter 18

Random Remainders

Game Time

SO WHAT'S LEFT?

You may already know what a **remainder** is:-it's what's left over after a division problem. For example 35 ÷ 8 = 4 with a remainder of 3: 8 goes into 35 4 times, but since 4-x 8 = 32, there is still 3 left over.

The puzzles in this chapter are the remainder of the book—we've crammed it with fun activities that you didn't get a chance to see in any of the previous chapters.

Spellulator

Work out each problem with a calculator. When you are through figuring, turn the calculator upside down to read the answer to the clue in parentheses. **NOTE:** Some calculators automatically display a decimal point with two zeros—ignore those, because it may make your answer difficult to read!

9,645 / 3 = (small, medium, or large) ....

142 x 5 = (petroleum) ....

1,879 x 3 = (what you walk on) ....

10,000 – 4,662 = (honey makers) ....

50,029 – 15,023 = (barnyard animal) ....

206 + 206 + 206 = (the opposite of tiny) ....

188,308 + 188,308 = (laugh in a silly way) ....

10 + 13 = (not hard) ....

926 x 2 x 2 = (an empty space) ....

Calling Code

Sam is calling his friends to invite them to a party. Using the phone keypad as a decoder, figure out the names of the people invited. Each phone button has several letters on it, so be sure to look for the number after the slash. It tells you if the letter is in the second or third space. For example, 2/2 = B. A number with no slash after it means the letter is in the first space.

1. 4/3-6-2   6/2-8/2-8-8

2. 3/3-7/2-2-6/2-5/2

   6/2   7/3-8-3/2-4/3-6/2

3. 8-3/2-3   3/2   2/2-3/2-2-7/2

4. 8-2-3/3-3/3-3/9/3   7-8/2-5/3-5/3

5. 3-7/2-3/2-9   2   2/2-6/3-2-8

6. 7/3-8/2-6-6-3/2-7/2   8-4/3-6-3/2

7. 7/3-2-6/2-8-2   2/3-5/3-2-8/2-7/3

NETWORK PUZZLES

Network puzzles require you to make sense of a network that is presented to you. One of the most famous network puzzles is the **Seven Bridges of Königsberg** problem.

In Königsberg, Germany (now Kaliningrad, Russia), there was an island in the middle of a river that flowed through the city. After the river passed around the island, it separated into two branches. Seven bridges were built so that the people of the city could move around.

A map of the center of Königsberg looks like this:

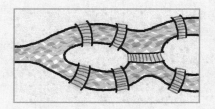

Can you walk around the city and only cross each bridge once?

Try it. Trace the map of the city on a sheet of paper and "walk" around the city with a pencil so that you trace over each bridge once and only once without lifting your pencil.

If the original problem seems hard, sometimes it helps to solve a simpler version:

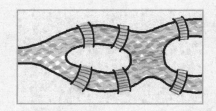

Suppose they built six bridges in Königsberg. Could you walk around the city and only cross each bridge once?

Why is this question easier? How is-it different from the first question?

**Q: What's the matter with the math book?
A: It has problems.**

An Approach That Makes Sense

Here's a method to help you with any number of bridge network problems—or any network problems, for that matter. First, turn the city map into a diagram, where each circle is a piece of land and each line is a bridge.

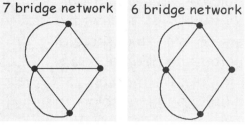

7 bridge network   6 bridge network

Each dot of land is called a node. You start and end at a node (not always ending at the place you started) and travel along the lines that connect them (the paths).

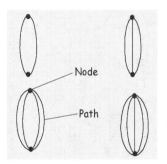

Node

Path

Here is the general rule for solving a network. You look at each node and count how many paths lead out of that node. An even node has an even number of paths leading out of it. An odd node has an odd number of paths. A network can be solved (traced without lifting a pencil and crossing each path exactly once) if the number of odd nodes is 0, 1, or 2.

Practice Solving Networks

For each of the following network puzzles, first figure out if it can be solved by counting the number of odd nodes. If it can be solved, then mark it with arrows to show how to trace around it and cross each path exactly once.

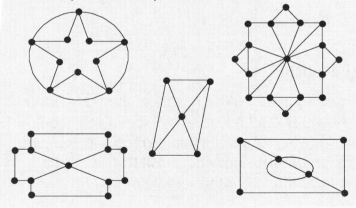

It's Perfect!

Have you ever heard of "perfect" numbers? They are whole numbers that are equal to the sum of their proper divisors. For example, 6 is a perfect number because 6 = 1 + 2 + 3. Other perfect numbers include 28, 496, 8128, 33550336, 8589869056, 137438691328, 2305843008139952128, and 26584559 9156983174465469261595 3842176. How do you think they calculated that one?

HEE HEE HEE

COLOR MY WORLD

In 1893, Francis Guthrie, a student, wondered whether any map could be colored with four colors or fewer—to illustrate the borders, countries that share a border must be different colors.

Try to color the map of Africa using only four colors. This may be harder than it sounds, but it isn't impossible! HINT: Choose one color and fill in as many countries as possible. Then move to the second color, the third, and—finally—the fourth. Countries that share a border cannot be the same color.

THE BURDEN OF PROOF

This seemingly simple question perplexed mathematicians for years. In 1976, two mathematicians, Appel and Haken, wrote a computer program to determine if any map could be colored with four colors. The program took over 1,200 hours to run, but finally verified that only four colors are needed to color any map.

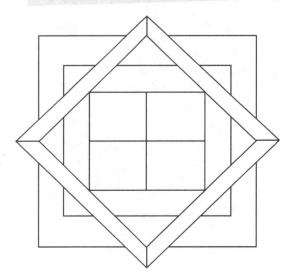

Crazy Quilting

This quilting figure isn't a map, but the same idea is true—you should be able to color all the sections using only four colors, so that no two sections that touch are the same color. **HINT:** This puzzle is easier if you start from the middle and work your way out.

AN UNSOLVED MYSTERY

T he puzzles in this book have answers, but there are some famous mathematical puzzles to which no one knows the answer yet. Maybe you will solve a famous unsolved puzzle.

One such puzzle is known as the **Goldbach's Conjecture.** The conjecture is as follows: **All even numbers greater than 2 can be written as the sum of two prime numbers.** (Remember, a prime number is one that can only be divided by 1-and itself.)

No one has proved that this is always true or disproved it by finding an example that doesn't work (a counter-example). Here are examples that illustrate Goldbach's Conjecture:

6 = 3 + 3
8 = 3 + 5
10 = 3 + 7 or 5 + 5 (there may be more than one answer)

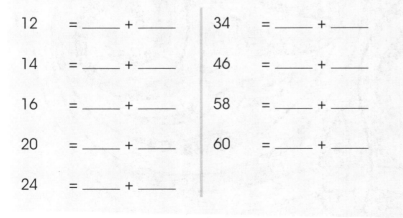

Can you find two prime numbers that add up to the following even numbers? (You may want to use the prime numbers you found in Chapter 3.)

12	= ___ + ___	34	= ___ + ___
14	= ___ + ___	46	= ___ + ___
16	= ___ + ___	58	= ___ + ___
20	= ___ + ___	60	= ___ + ___
24	= ___ + ___		

Young Math Geniuses

Solving famous puzzles is not only for mathematicians with a lot of education. In 1995, two ninth-graders found an original solution to this problem: Divide any line segment into a set number of equal parts using only a compass and straightedge. Variations of this problem date back to the time of Euclid (300 B.C.). Find out about their solution at *www.gfacademy.org/GLaD*.

Around, and Around, and Around We Go

This triple whirligig pattern, or "triskele," is a very old and powerful symbol. Since the ancient Celtic people of Ireland thought that the number 3 was both sacred and magical, they may have believed that this symbol brought good luck and protection from evil. Sometimes the artist would add tiny lines or dots to make the pattern look like an animal, a flower, or a human face.

As you wind your way through this mysterious triskele, find a bird in a nest, an elf in a pointy hat, a fish, two snakes looking at each other, and a bird with a big beak.

START

END

jumbo puzzle book

The Very Last Cross-Number Puzzle

Well, you've come to the end of the book.
But before you go on your way, here is one last cross-number puzzle you can enjoy!

Across

1. If "a cat has nine lives," then how many lives do nine cats have?
3. How many cards are in a full deck?
5. The number that is two numbers after 5, three times in a row!
7. How much is seven sevens?
8. How many days are in a year?
10. How many Dalmatians are in that classic movie?
11. How many hours are in a day?
12. What's between 5 and 9?
15. It takes eight rows of eight checkers to fill a checkerboard. How many checkers is that?
16. How many states are in the United States?

Down

1. A score is twenty years. How many years is "four score and seven"?
2. XVII in Arabic numbers.
3. How would you see "quarter to six" on a digital clock?
4. A month can have this many days, but not often.
6. What's an early bedtime?
9. This number is a palindrome.
10. A dozen dozens is called a "gross"! If you have a gross of pencils, how many pencils do you have?
11. Take an unlucky number and double it.
13. How many pennies equal three quarters?
14. What's left of a dollar if you spend a dime and two nickels?

201

NOTES

Introduction to Super Puzzles

Wacky for wordplay? Cuckoo for crisscrosses? This section is for you!

Not only did we cram as many kinds of puzzles into this section as possible, we also came up with all types of themes to interest you. You'll find everything from Pets to Pizza, Music to Monsters, Camping to Computers. And wherever there was room, we stuffed in fascinating facts and Fast n' Funny jokes.

To make things even more exciting, there are a couple of puzzles that run through the whole section. First, watch for Mervin the mouse. He's hidden somewhere on each and every spread (the two pages you have open at any one time). Sometimes he's easy to spot—but not always! You will also notice that there are random white letters mixed among the dark ones. These are not mistakes, but are clues to the White Out! puzzle found in the "What a Great Idea!" section.

So, flip ahead and dive right in. We wish you many happy puzzling hours ahead!

Puzzles

PILES OF PETS

Mouse Maze

Mervin is a very curious mouse, and he smells cheese! Can you get Mervin through the maze, left, to his favorite snack?

Pet Groupie

A groupie is a type of puzzle that has only one clue—the word provided. Your job is to figure out the other words that belong in the puzzle. Hint: Some of the animals pictured are clues!

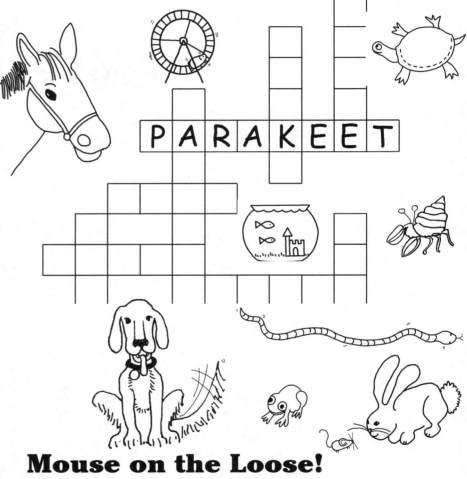

Mouse on the Loose!

Oh no! Mervin went right by the cheese and out of the maze! Look for him throughout the rest of this book. He'll show up at least once on every two pages, and sometimes twice! Look carefully—Mervin can be very good at hiding!

Kitty Compounds

Can you figure out the compound words in each of these pictures?

C A T _____ _____

YAKITTY
YAKITTY
YAKITTY

C A T _____
OUCH

Fast 'n' Funny
What does the vet keep outside his front door?

A welcome mutt!

C A T _____

Animal Antics

Try these tongue twisters!

Dirty dogs dig deep.

Seven slinky snakes sneak snacks.

Five fancy fish finish fixing fins.

Many mice make much music.

C A T _____ _____

C A T _____ _____

C A T _____ _____

CLOTHES CLOSET

Hat Hamper

To fill this hamper with hats, think of a name and a describing word that both start with the same first letter. Try your family's, friend's, or even your pet's names! A sample hat has been done for you.

Use this space to draw the hat that goes with your name!

ANNIE's hat is an _ARTSY_ hat.

Hamper Maze

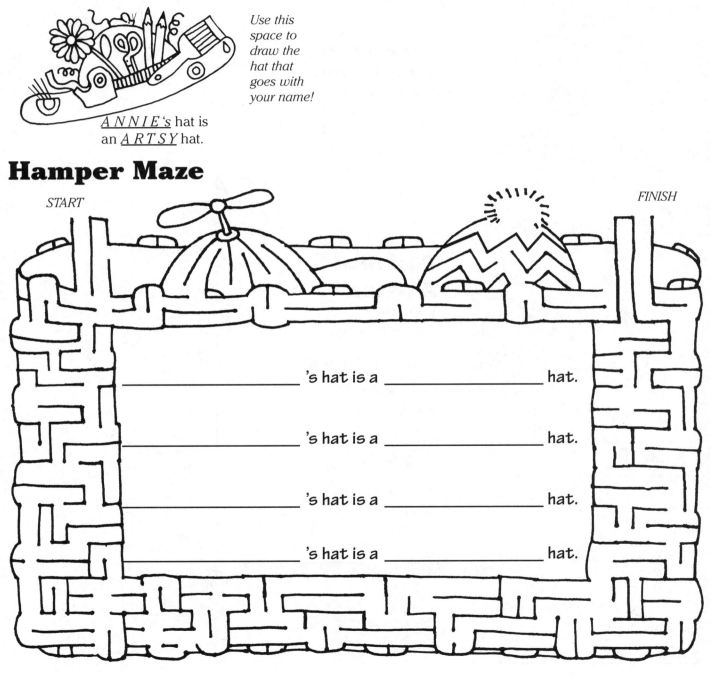

START   *FINISH*

_____ 's hat is a _____ hat.

_____ 's hat is a _____ hat.

_____ 's hat is a _____ hat.

_____ 's hat is a _____ hat.

PUZZLING PRESIDENTS

Capitol Maze

ENTER

EXIT

Hidden Presidents

Six presidents are hiding in the windows of the capitol building, below. Can you figure out which one is in each? Part of their first name is on the top line and part of their last name is on the bottom. A list of presidents is given, but not all of them are used!

Capitol Confusion

During the Civil War, the Capitol building was used for many different purposes. Read the list below and see if you can guess which are correct.

1. soldiers' barracks
2. hospital
3. bakery
4. stable
5. blacksmith shop

Fast 'n' Funny

Why was George Washington buried at Mount Vernon?

¡pɐǝp sɐʍ ǝɥ ǝsnɐɔǝꓭ

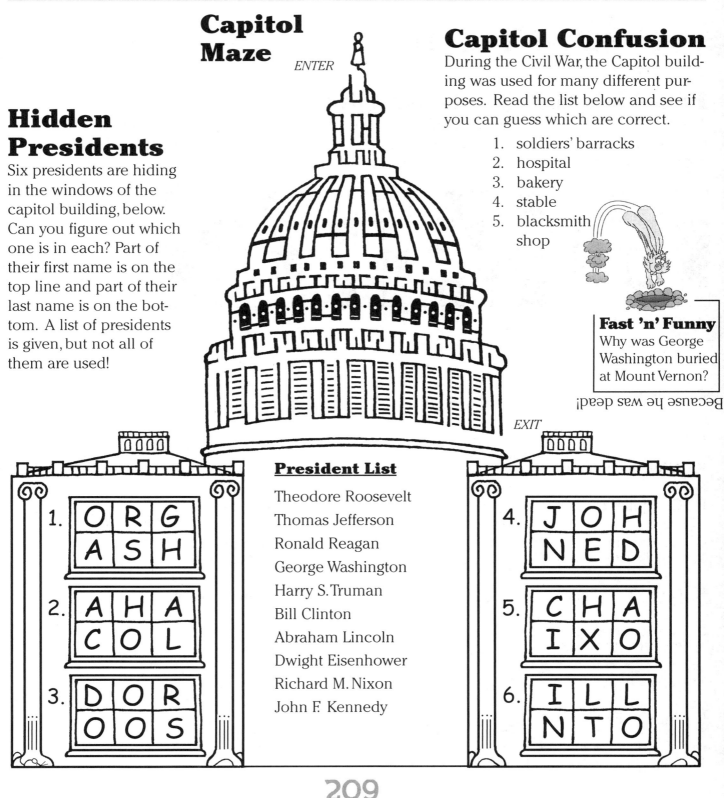

President List

Theodore Roosevelt
Thomas Jefferson
Ronald Reagan
George Washington
Harry S. Truman
Bill Clinton
Abraham Lincoln
Dwight Eisenhower
Richard M. Nixon
John F. Kennedy

1. | O | R | G |
   | A | S | H |

2. | A | H | A |
   | C | O | L |

3. | D | O | R |
   | O | O | S |

4. | J | O | H |
   | N | E | D |

5. | C | H | A |
   | I | X | O |

6. | I | L | L |
   | N | T | O |

Rebus for President!

Use this combination of pictures and letters to spell out the names of two well known presidents.

1. D + [WHITE paint can] [eye] + Z N + [hourglass]   2. G + [oar] + G [bush]

Presidential Quotable Quote

Answer as many clues as you can, and fill the letters you have into the grid. Work back and forth between the quotation box and clues until you can read this famous line once said by John F. Kennedy, the thirty-fifth President of the United States.

1	2	3		4	5		6	7		8	9	10	11	12	13		14	15	16	17	18	19	20	21	22
	23	24	25		26	27	28		29	30	31	32		33	34	35	36		37	38	39	40	41	42	43
	44	45	46		47	48		49	50	51		52	53	54		55	56	57		58	59	60	61		62
63	64		65	66	67		68	69		70	71	72		73	74	75	76		77	78	79	80	81	82	83

A. Person, place, or thing ‾67‾ ‾34‾ ‾54‾ ‾40‾

B. To fasten ‾10‾ ‾50‾ ‾65‾ ‾25‾

C. To hurry ‾72‾ ‾39‾ ‾24‾ ‾59‾

D. What a cow chews ‾19‾ ‾75‾ ‾68‾

E. Adult male human ‾15‾ ‾1‾ ‾21‾

F. Caterpillar case ‾44‾ ‾12‾ ‾37‾ ‾5‾ ‾71‾ ‾80‾

G. Building in which people live ‾30‾ ‾48‾ ‾79‾ ‾56‾ ‾9‾

H. Opposite of night ‾47‾ ‾14‾ ‾33‾

I. To move through the air with wings ‾49‾ ‾11‾ ‾43‾

J. A plaything ‾32‾ ‾69‾ ‾52‾

K. Pull suddenly ‾83‾ ‾20‾ ‾2‾ ‾57‾

L. A large number ‾6‾ ‾31‾ ‾46‾ ‾73‾

M. Sound a dog makes ‾13‾ ‾53‾ ‾38‾ ‾70‾

N. To attempt ‾81‾ ‾36‾ ‾62‾

O. Abrupt ‾77‾ ‾35‾ ‾17‾ ‾61‾

P. Unhappy ‾22‾ ‾66‾ ‾3‾

Q. In another direction ‾60‾ ‾29‾ ‾55‾ ‾7‾

R. Part of plant that grows underground ‾42‾ ‾78‾ ‾63‾ ‾28‾

S. Person trained to care for the sick ‾26‾ ‾64‾ ‾76‾ ‾4‾ ‾16‾

T. Twelve inches ‾8‾ ‾74‾ ‾27‾ ‾41‾

U. Mixture of gases surrounding Earth ‾45‾ ‾18‾ ‾82‾

V. Armed fighting between people ‾58‾ ‾23‾ ‾51‾

TUTTI-FRUTTI

Lost Lemons

No wonder Josh looks sour — Jess and his dog Rosie knocked over his lemonade stand! See if you can find the sixteen lemon slices splashed throughout the picture below.

Fruit Salad

Unscramble these words to find ingredients for a fruit salad.

1. RUEBELRIEBS
   _ _ _ _ _ _ _ _ _ _ _

2. LEMTERAWNO
   _ _ _ _ _ _ _ _ _ _

3. TALCNOPUAE
   _ _ _ _ _ _ _ _ _ _

4. PESPAL
   _ _ _ _ _ _

5. NASABAN
   _ _ _ _ _ _ _

6. PRGAES
   _ _ _ _ _ _

Serve 'em Up

Cross out all the odd numbers and capital letters. The remaining numbers and letters will remind you how many servings of fruit you should eat each day!

B 2 1 C 7 1
3 F † X 5 o
V 1 7 Y 4 K

Fast 'n' Funny

What do you call two bananas?

A pair of slippers!

Positively Peachy

Fill in the missing letters to find plenty of fruits that start with the letter P and one hard word that is found in the center of many fruits!

Tropical Maze

Find your way through this prickly pineapple.

START

FINISH

212

Mucho Dinero

START **Money Maze** Can you find the dollar sign in the maze? *FINISH*

Money Match

Draw a line from each denomination of money to the person whose portrait appears on it. Hint: Some names are used more than once.

penny	Ulysses S. Grant
nickel	Thomas Jefferson
dime	George Washington
quarter	Alexander Hamilton
$1.00	Abraham Lincoln
$2.00	George Washington
$5.00	Thomas Jefferson
$10.00	Abraham Lincoln
$20.00	Franklin D. Roosevelt
$50.00	Benjamin Franklin
$100.00	Andrew Jackson

Loose Change

Cross out every D-O-L-L-A-R in the grid below, and the remaining letters will tell you what is your nose's favorite money.

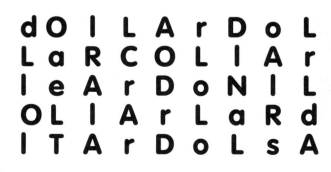

```
d O I L A r D o L
L a R C O L I A r
I e A r D o N I L
O L I A r L a R d
I T A r D o L s A
```

213

Can I Borrow a Drachma?

Money is called different things in different countries. See if you can fit all of these world currencies into the crisscross grid (use just the money name). We left some M-O-N-E-Y in the grid to get you started.

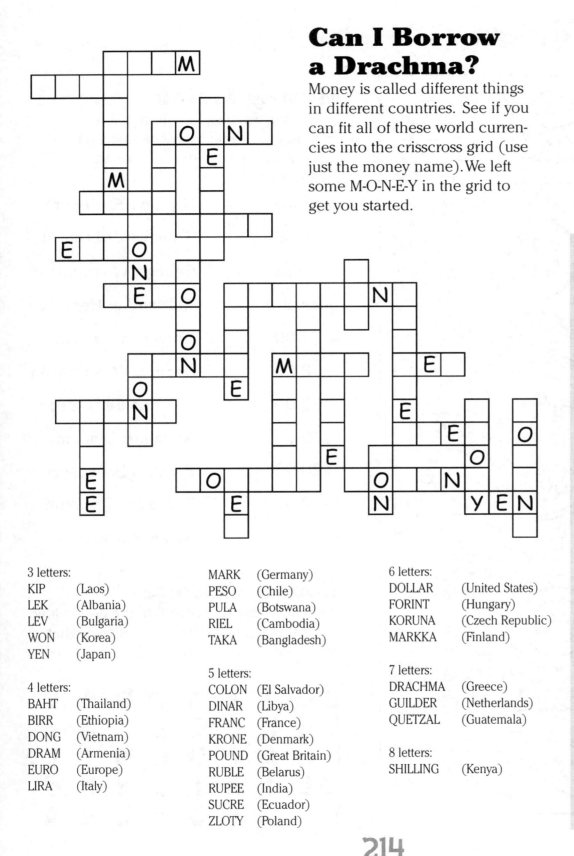

Fast 'n' Funny
Where does a polar bear keep his money?

In a snow bank!

F.Y.I.
Eleven European countries, including France, Germany, and Italy, began using the euro in January, 1999. On July 1, 2002, these countries will change over completely and money like the franc, mark, and lira will no longer be used.

● ● ● ● ● ● ● ●

Do you know who is the youngest multibillionaire?

Athina Onassis Roussel, granddaughter of Greek shipping magnate Aristotle Onassis. She inherited an estimated $5 billion in 1988.

3 letters:
KIP (Laos)
LEK (Albania)
LEV (Bulgaria)
WON (Korea)
YEN (Japan)

4 letters:
BAHT (Thailand)
BIRR (Ethiopia)
DONG (Vietnam)
DRAM (Armenia)
EURO (Europe)
LIRA (Italy)

MARK (Germany)
PESO (Chile)
PULA (Botswana)
RIEL (Cambodia)
TAKA (Bangladesh)

5 letters:
COLON (El Salvador)
DINAR (Libya)
FRANC (France)
KRONE (Denmark)
POUND (Great Britain)
RUBLE (Belarus)
RUPEE (India)
SUCRE (Ecuador)
ZLOTY (Poland)

6 letters:
DOLLAR (United States)
FORINT (Hungary)
KORUNA (Czech Republic)
MARKKA (Finland)

7 letters:
DRACHMA (Greece)
GUILDER (Netherlands)
QUETZAL (Guatemala)

8 letters:
SHILLING (Kenya)

Space Race

Space Maze
Follow each safety line to the correct astronaut.

Planet Groupie
Can you fit all the planets of our solar system into this grid?

Factoid
Oldest man to go into space: John Glenn at age 77.

NEPTUNE

Moon Phase Decoder

Use this decoder to find out how long it takes for the moon to go through all of its phases.

A B C D E

F G H I J

K L M N O

P Q R S T

U V W X Y

Z

One Small Step

Use this combination of astronauts to spell out the name of the first person to walk on the moon.

Factoid
John Glenn was also the first American to orbit the earth.

Fast 'n' Funny
Why couldn't the astronaut land on the moon?

Because the moon was full!

The most people in space at once was on March 18, 1995.
— 7 Americans (STS 67 Endeavor)
— 3 Cosmonauts (MIR Space Station)
— 2 Cosmonauts + 1 US Astronaut (Soyuz TM21)

It Takes Two: Tic-Tac-Toe

Classic Tic-Tac-Toe

Choose whether you want an X or an O to be your mark. Have a friend, sibling, or parent be the other mark. Taking turns, make your mark in one of the nine tic-tac-toe squares. The object is to get three of your marks in a row — horizontally, vertically, or diagonally. If you have done this, draw a line through all three marks and yell "Tic-Tac-Toe." You win!

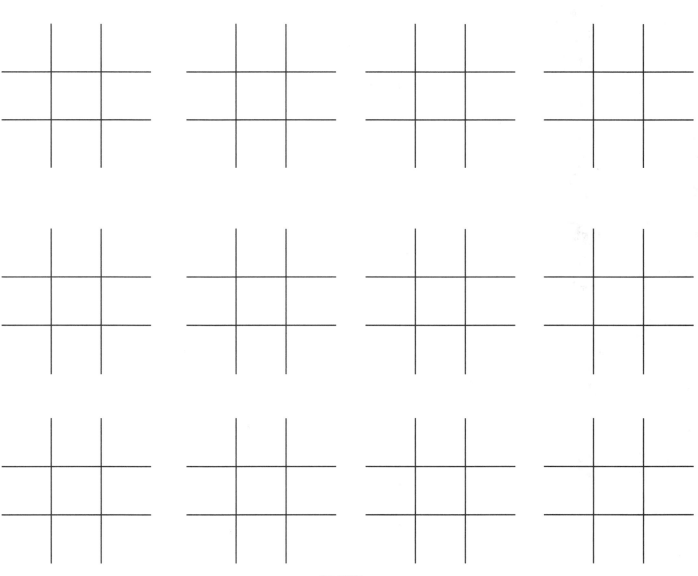

Super Duper Tic-Tac-Toe

In this larger game, each player tries to get three, four, or five marks in a row. You do not win with just one line — try to make as many as you can. Each X or O can be counted more than once if it is included in a different line.

When all the spaces are filled, each player adds up their score:

— 1 point for three marks in a row

— 3 points for four marks in a row

— 5 points for five marks in a row

High score wins!

If you want to play some more, make your own boards on the blank pages at the end of this book.

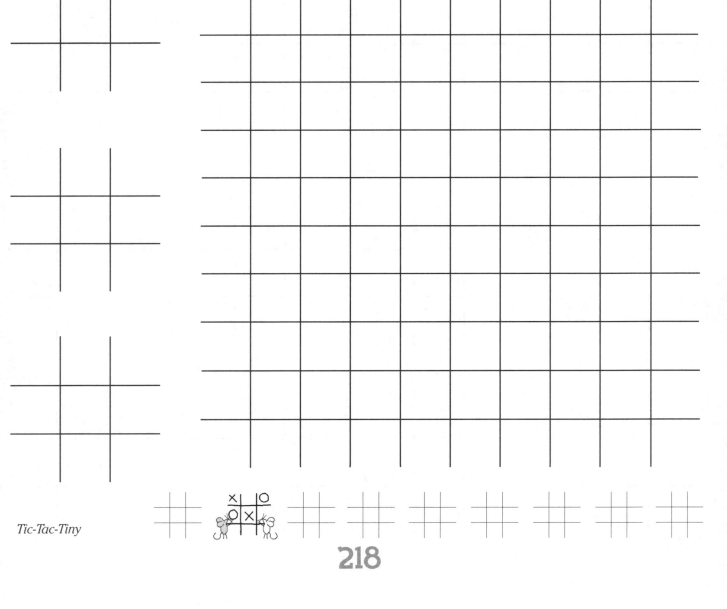

Tic-Tac-Tiny

It Takes Two: Hangman

Classic Hangman

This is a game of mystery words.

To play:

1. Find a partner to play with you. One of you will think up the word (the drawer) and the other will try to guess it (the guesser).

2. The drawer thinks up a word and tells the guesser how many letters it has.

3. The guesser guesses one letter at a time. If the letter is in the word, the drawer writes it in the proper space or spaces. If not, the drawer writes the used letter next to the hangman gallow and draws the head on the hangman.

4. Play continues and a new body part is added to the hangman each time a wrong letter is guessed (stick body, arms, legs, dots for eyes & nose, frown).

To win:

Either the guesser or the drawer can win. If the guesser figures out the word before the hangman is completely drawn, then he wins. But if he doesn't, then the drawer wins. The guesser can also try to solve the word at any time, but automatically loses the game if he or she is wrong.

Oops! The guesser in this game did not guess the word "stand" before the hangman was completed. The guesser loses.

Updating a Classic

Can you think of which current and popular game show is based on Hangman? Need a hint? Buy a vowel!

Wheel of Fortune

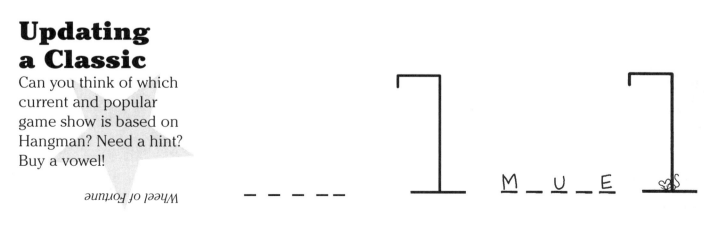

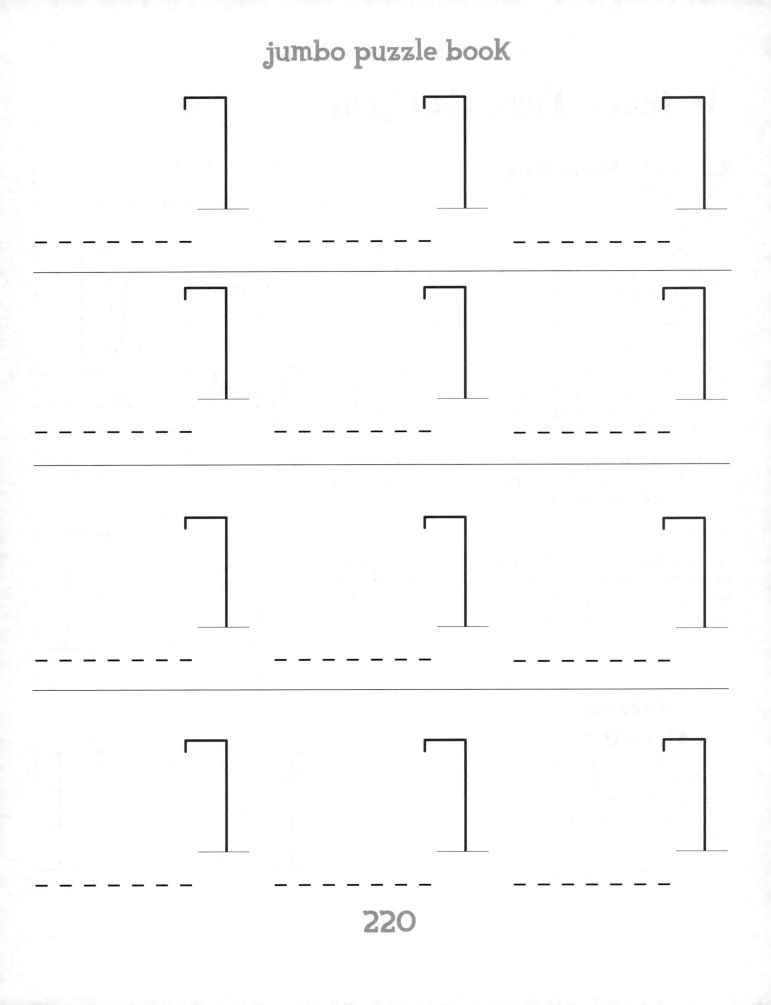

Artsy Smartsy

Color-a-Message

Color in all the F's, K's and M's and read the remaining letters to see what Johann Wolfgang von Goethe had to say about art.

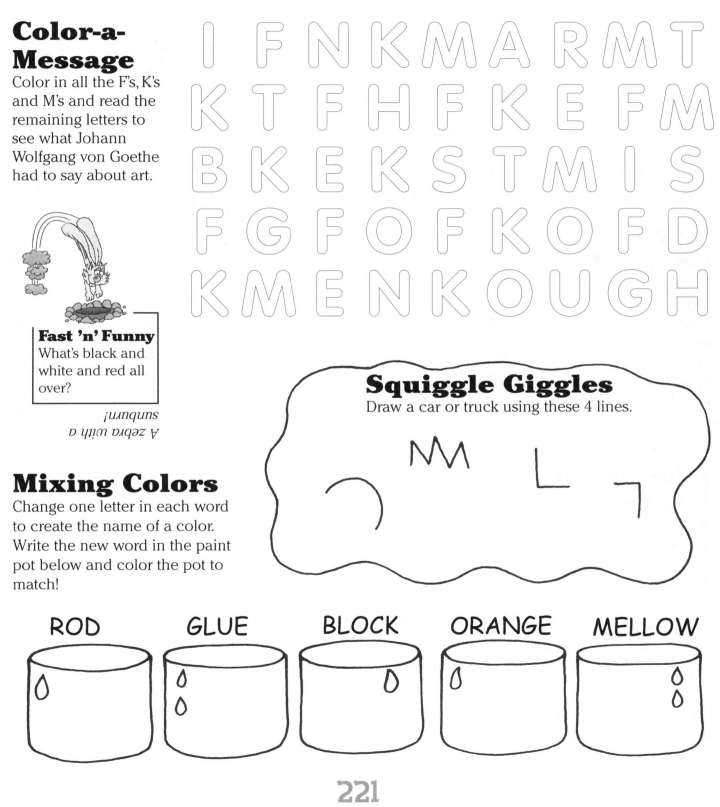

I F N K M A R M T
K T F H F K E F M
B K E K S T M I S
F G F O F K O F D
K M E N K O U G H

Fast 'n' Funny

What's black and white and red all over?

A zebra with a sunburn!

Mixing Colors

Change one letter in each word to create the name of a color. Write the new word in the paint pot below and color the pot to match!

Squiggle Giggles

Draw a car or truck using these 4 lines.

ROD   GLUE   BLOCK   ORANGE   MELLOW

221

Famous Artists

Six famous artists have signed the backs of their paintings, but they wrote too big! Part of their first name is on the top line, and part of their second name is on the bottom line. Can you figure them out?

Possible Artists:
Mary Cassatt
Winslow Homer
Leonardo da Vinci
Pablo Picasso
Paul Cezanne
Vincent van Gogh
Claude Monet
Georgia O'Keefe
Edgar Degas

Same Frames?

The artists are very different, but these frames sure look the same. Try to match the three pairs of frames that are exactly alike.

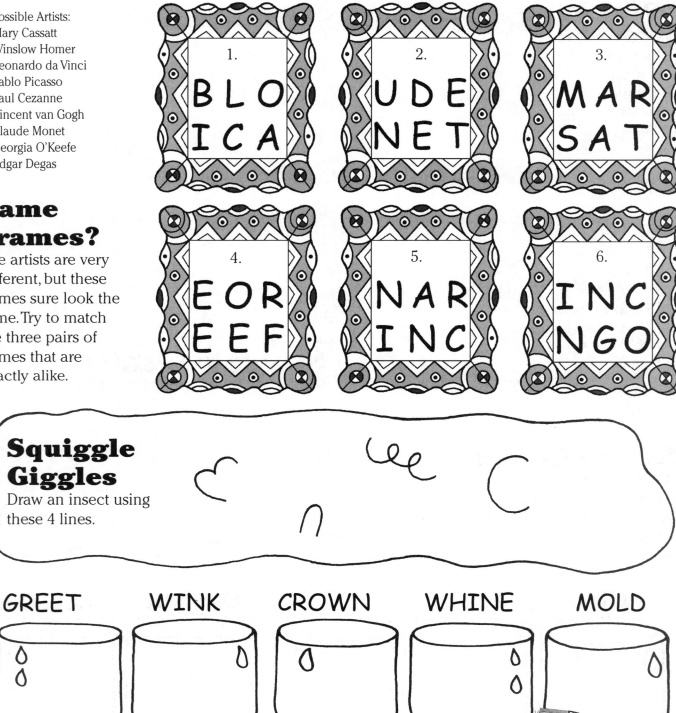

1. B L O / I C A
2. U D E / N E T
3. M A R / S A T
4. E O R / E E F
5. N A R / I N C
6. I N C / N G O

Squiggle Giggles

Draw an insect using these 4 lines.

GREET   WINK   CROWN   WHINE   MOLD

222

Listen To The Music

Strike Up the Band

How many band instruments can you identify and fit into the grid to the right? One of the instruments left you some O-O-M-P-A as a hint.

Off Key Riddle

Figure out where to put each of the scrambled letters. They all fit in spaces under their own column.

When you fill in the grid, you will have the answer to the following riddle:

What's the difference between a piano and a fish?

P	A	A			N		T		N	E		
C	I	N	T	C	B	U	T	N	Y	I	S	H
Y	O	U	N	O	A	U	N	A	U	F	O	U	A

Classical Composers

The names of six famous composers are hidden on the musical staff. Part of their first name is over part of their last name. Can you figure them out?

1. HAN RAH

2. ETE CHA

3. RAN AYD

4. GAN ART

5. OHA BAC

6. UDW EET

Composer List

Ludwig van Beethoven

Wolfgang Amadeus Mozart

Johann Sebastian Bach

Johannes Brahms

Franz Joseph Haydn

Franz Schubert

Peter Ilyich Tchaikovsky

Name That Tune

Each of the pictures below show the title of a well-known song. Can you guess what each one is?

1.

2.

Read the Music

Using the notes and musical symbols provided, decode this Italian proverb.

D	E	G	H	I	N

R S V W A Y

O SPACE

Fast 'n' Funny

Why did the busy musician spend so much time in bed?

Because he wrote sheet music.

Toothful Grin

Whose Teeth Are These?

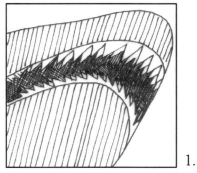

1.

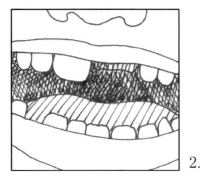

2.

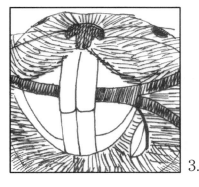

3.

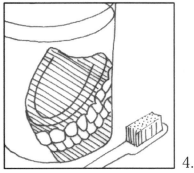

4.

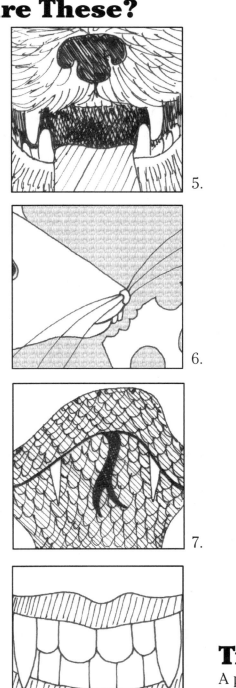

5.

6.

7.

8.

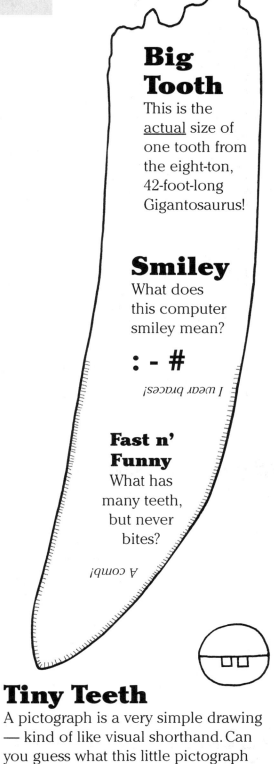

Big Tooth
This is the <u>actual</u> size of one tooth from the eight-ton, 42-foot-long Gigantosaurus!

Smiley
What does this computer smiley mean?

: - #

I wear braces!

Fast n' Funny
What has many teeth, but never bites?

A comb!

Tiny Teeth
A pictograph is a very simple drawing — kind of like visual shorthand. Can you guess what this little pictograph (above) shows?

Brace Yourself!   Find the path that uses the floss, toothbrush, and toothpaste!

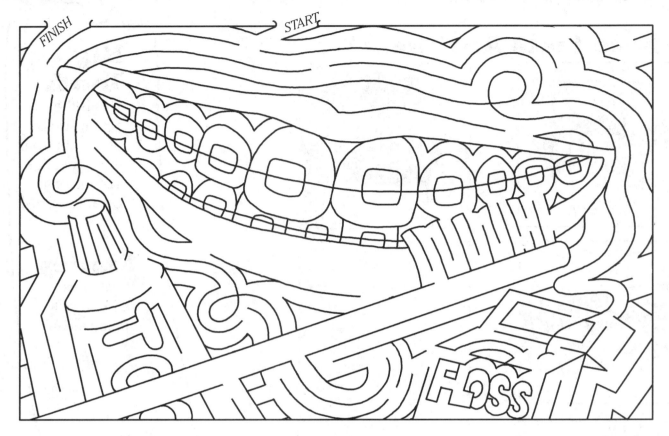

Mystery Words

Fill in the blanks in the following paragraph with words that have to do with the care of your teeth.

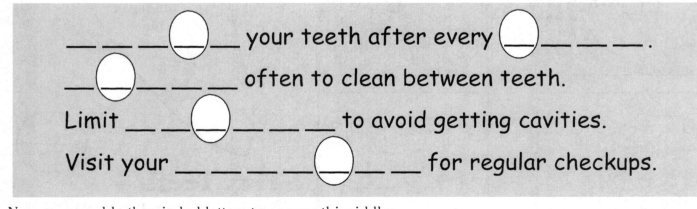

___ ___ ___ ___ your teeth after every ___ ___ ___ ___ .

___ ___ ___ ___ ___ often to clean between teeth.

Limit ___ ___ ___ ___ ___ to avoid getting cavities.

Visit your ___ ___ ___ ___ ___ ___ for regular checkups.

Now, unscramble the circled letters to answer this riddle:
**"I'm a road that stretches from left to right.
I'm often paved with pearly white. What am I?"**

226

Animal Hide And Seek

Follow vines over and under. Which one goes to the snake?

3.

1. 2.

Many Mammals

Find the fifty-six animals hidden in this grid. The sneaky gopher is in twice! Then, read the leftover letters from left to right and find the world's largest animal.

armadillo
ape
badger
bat
bear
beaver
bison
boar
bobcat
caribou
cat
chipmunk
cow
coyote
deer
dog
dolphin
elk
ferret
fox
goat
gopher
gopher
groundhog
horse
human
jaguar
kangaroo

lemming
lynx
lion
manatee
marmot
mole
moose
mouse
muskrat
ocelot
opossum
otter
pig
pika
porcupine
prairie dog
rabbit
raccoon
rat
seal
sheep
shrew
skunk
squirrel
vole
weasel
whale
wolf

```
S J A G U A R N G T H C A R I B O U
Q E F O X W M O O S E H T O L R T L
U D T P N T D O L P H I N A I S T W
I A L H Y A A C R G E P A S O T E E
R A N E L O V C O L E M M I N G R A
R T I R M A L A I W A U U S T E H S
E A E B P I G R L N S N H S E U E E
L C W F H G A L A K E K A D S E A L
A B L T O O O T R V N E W B R O L O
H O S P C D E A N U E E H A U N P K
W B H D E E T R K A R M A D I L L O
E E E D L I O S F H A E E G B T L O
R A E O O R Y N S R G P A E N A D R
A V P O T I O A M V E F E R R E T A
B E A R E A C O K G O H D N U O R G
B R R L T R T W O I H H O R S E A N
I U O N D P O R C U P I N E R E O A
T M D M O U S E T O N S N O S I B K
```

What Are These?

Each of these pictures is a close-up of a different mammal. Can you guess them all?

1. _____

2. _____

3. _____

4. _____

5. _____

6. _____

7. _____

8. _____

9. _____

10. _____

Practice Your Paw-menship

This mysterious note was found on the forest floor. Using the names belonging to the animal tracks provided, can you decipher the message?

robin

bobcat

bat

woodchuck

vole

fox

otter

chipmunk

deer

marten

gopher

muskrat

Can you play baseball later? ─lend you his ? We'll pizza, too. Tell your mom we be home by six.
Later,

Pizza Party

The Works

ANCHOVIES
MEATBALLS
MUSHROOMS
BROCCOLI
CHEESE
EGGPLANT
GARLIC
BACON
HAM
CLAM

PEPPERONI
SAUSAGE
TOMATO
ONIONS
PEPPERS
SALAMI
SPINACH
SHRIMP
OLIVES
PESTO

```
I L O C C O R B A C O N
M Y S R E P P E P H O U
E G G P L A N T S E S C
A A P E N D E F P E A S
T I M P E S T O I S L M
B N I P I T T V N E A O
A C R E E A O L A Y M O
L I H R M H N M C A I R
L L S O C A I K H E A H
S R T N L O O L I V E S
T A A I O F N D O U G U
E G A S U A S H C L A M
```

Pizza Maze

Dave is constantly delivering pizza to Mr. Gibson's store. How fast can you get the van across town? Find the route that has the least traffic lights. You can travel under the giant pizza slice.

P.S. How many triangular pizza pieces can you find on the way?

What do you like on your pizza? Find all twenty toppings in the grid of letters, above. Then, read the leftover letters from left to right to find out why someone might want to own a pizza shop.

CONSTANTLY PIZZA

229

Extra ZZZ's, Pleeze

Some people like pizza with extra cheese. Here's a bunch
of words with double Z's! How many can you figure out?

1. the sound a bee makes   _ _ **Z Z**

2. type of music   _ _ **Z Z**

3. to feel like you are spinning   _ _ **Z Z** _

4. a picture that's not clear   _ _ **Z Z** _

5. game with interlocking pieces   _ _ **Z Z** _ _

6. large bird with a bald head   _ _ **Z Z** _ _ _

7. big snow storm   _ _ _ **Z Z** _ _ _

8. several short tests   _ _ _ **Z Z** _ _

Fast 'n' Funny

Knock, Knock

Who's there?

Pizza

Pizza who?

Pizza boy
next door!
(Pete, the boy next
door!)

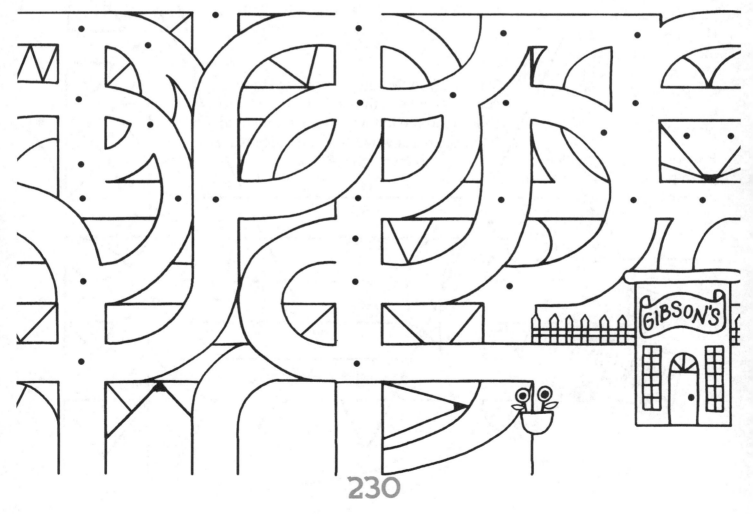

230

Bouncing Babies

Surprising Seven

Start with the B marked with the black dot. Move clockwise around the puzzle, picking up every third letter. Write the letters on the lines (we have given you the first two). When you are done, you will know who gave birth in 1997 to the first ever thriving set of septuplets.

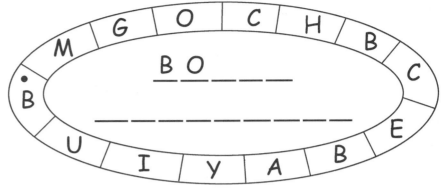

B O _ _ _ _ _

_ _ _ _ _ _ _ _ _ _

Where Are the Babies?

Drew was reading a story to all the children when Mom left the room. But when Mom returned, all she saw was Drew! Can you find the seven babies? Don't forget to look for their older sister, too.

What Do You Call a Baby?

Draw lines to match the pictures of animal mothers with the names of their babies.
Be careful — several different mamas have babies with the same name.
Other mamas have babies with more than one name!

CALF

KID

FOAL

CUB

LAMB

PIGLET

COLT

FAWN

KIT

PUPPY

DUCKLING

FILLY

Fast 'n' Funny
What did the
baby lightbulb
say to the mama
lightbulb?

I wuv you watts!

232

The Bookcase

Don't Forget About Mervin

Are you still looking for him? He's still hiding somewhere on every two pages.

Book-ish Words

How many of these "book" words do you know?

1. a support at the end of a row of books .... BOOK __ __ __

2. a small book or pamphlet .... BOOK __ __ __

3. a set of shelves to hold books .... BOOK __ __ __ __

4. something that holds your place in a book .... BOOK __ __ __ __

5. a person who loves to read .... BOOK __ __ __ __

6. owner's label in the front of a book .... BOOK __ __ __ __ __

7. a person who keeps the records of a business........................ BOOK __ __ __ __ __ __

8. a traveling library .... BOOK __ __ __ __ __ __

9. owner of a book store........................ BOOK __ __ __ __ __ __

Reading Rebuses

Need a good read? Solve these rebuses and you'll have an armload of great books to choose from!

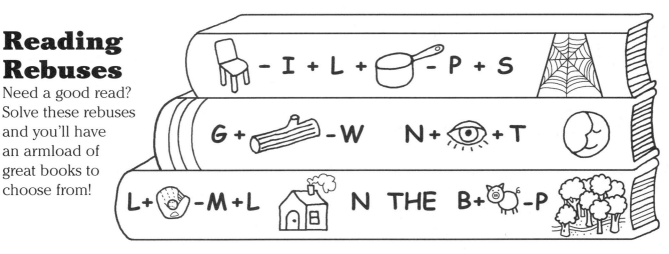

233

A Good Mystery

Using a simple reversed alphabet code (A = Z, B = Y, C = X, etc.), can you figure out this American proverb?

Z   Y L L P   R H   Z

—   — — — —   — —   —

U I R V M W

— — — — — —

The Book Nook

The answers to these riddles are two single syllable words that rhyme.

1. What do you call someone who steals volumes from the library?

   A _____

2. Where do you hang your wet books to dry?

   On a _____

3. What do you call a chef who boils a dictionary?

   A _____

Oops!

Mervin must be hungry after all his hiding. Use straight lines to finish the letters of the four word book title he just ate.

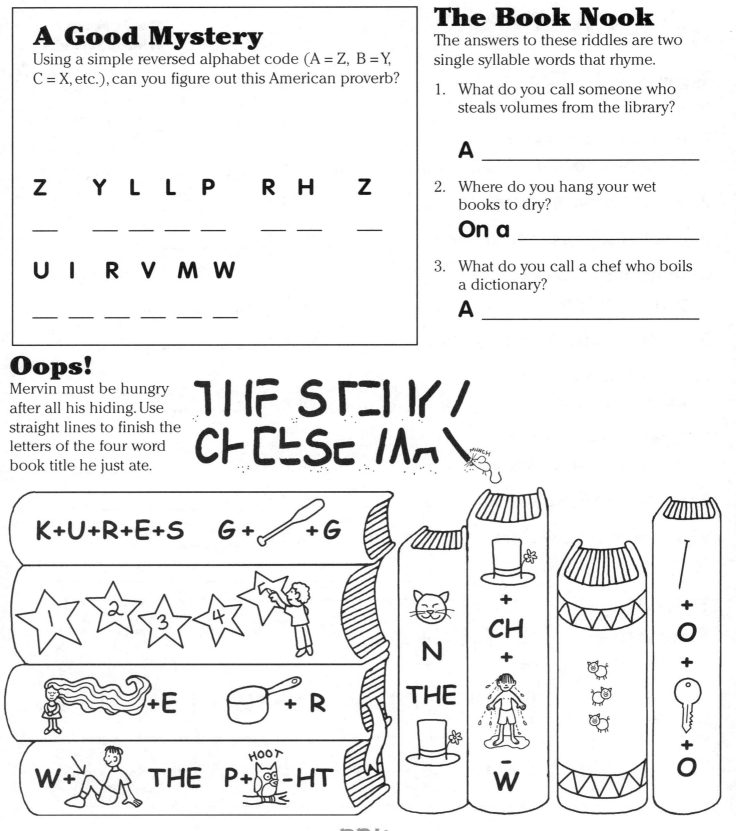

Travel USA

License Plate Lottery

Can you name the state from just the slogan on its
license plate? We left some U-S-A to help you out!

Across

2. Land of Enchantment
5. First in Flight
7. Famous for Potatoes

Down

1. Wild, Wonderful
2. Live Free or Die
3. 10,000 Lakes
4. Greatest Snow on Earth
6. The Last Frontier

State Scramble

Unscramble each state. After you have written them in the blanks, the shaded
letters will spell out the most popular time for travel in the United States.

1. A V E D N A   _ _ _ _ _ _

2. H A I O D   _ _ _ _ _

3. N C T U N T O E C I C   _ _ _ _ _ _ _ _ _ _ _

4. G A I V R I N I   _ _ _ _ _ _ _ _

5. H O U S T   T A D O A K   _ _ _ _ _   _ _ _ _ _ _

6. I S O U L A I A N   _ _ _ _ _ _ _ _ _

7. L I N I S O I L   _ _ _ _ _ _ _ _

8. W N E   C X I O E M   _ _ _   _ _ _ _ _ _

235

Fast 'n' Funny

What state is round
at both ends and
high in the middle?

Ohio

Cross-Country Trip

Sonja is driving with her family from your home in Maine back to her house in California. On the way, she stops in eighteen states. At each stop she mails you a postcard with the state abbreviation on it. But the postcards do not arrive in order! See if you can plot Sonja's trip on the map below.

Shade in each state as you put the postcards in order
from Maine to California.

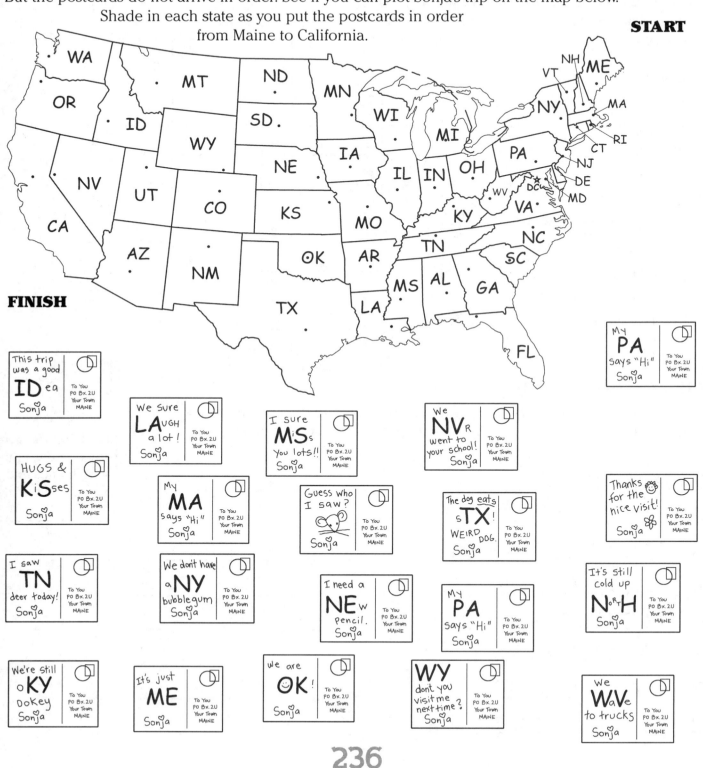

START

FINISH

This trip was a good **ID**ea Sonja
To You PO Bx.2U Your Town MAINE

We sure **LA**UGH a lot! Sonja
To You PO Bx.2U Your Town MAINE

I sure **MS**s you lots!! Sonja
To You PO Bx.2U Your Town MAINE

We **NV**r went to your school! Sonja
To You PO Bx.2U Your Town MAINE

My **PA** says "Hi" Sonja
To You PO Bx.2U Your Town MAINE

HUGS & **K:S**ses Sonja
To You PO Bx.2U Your Town MAINE

My **MA** says "Hi" Sonja
To You PO Bx.2U Your Town MAINE

Guess who I saw? Sonja
To You PO Bx.2U Your Town MAINE

The dog eats s**TX**! WEIRD DOG. Sonja
To You PO Bx.2U Your Town MAINE

Thanks for the nice visit! Sonja
To You PO Bx.2U Your Town MAINE

I saw **TN** deer today! Sonja
To You PO Bx.2U Your Town MAINE

We don't have a **NY** bubblegum Sonja
To You PO Bx.2U Your Town MAINE

I need a **NE**w pencil. Sonja
To You PO Bx.2U Your Town MAINE

My **PA** says "Hi" Sonja
To You PO Bx.2U Your Town MAINE

It's still cold up **N**o**RTH** Sonja
To You PO Bx.2U Your Town MAINE

We're still o**KY** Dokey Sonja
To You PO Bx.2U Your Town MAINE

It's just **ME** Sonja
To You PO Bx.2U Your Town MAINE

We are **OK**! Sonja
To You PO Bx.2U Your Town MAINE

WY dont you visit me next time? Sonja
To You PO Bx.2U Your Town MAINE

We **W**a**Ve** to trucks Sonja
To You PO Bx.2U Your Town MAINE

236

High Tide

A Day at the Beach

It's easy to get lost in a crowd. Can you spy where each of these small parts is located in the big picture? Hint: The small parts might be turned sideways or upside-down!

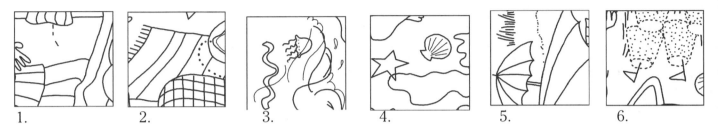

1.　　2.　　3.　　4.　　5.　　6.

Heading Home

Can you get from your vacation at the sea to your home in town? You must travel one space at a time making compound words as you go. You can move up and down, and side to side — but not diagonally!

START SEA	SHELL	FISH	HOOK
HORSE	BACK	HAND	BALL
FLY	YARD	OUT	GAME
PAPER	STICK	BREAK	DOWN
BACK	FIRE	FAST	TOWN FINISH

Building Project

Look carefully at the beach scene on the page to the left. Find eleven items that fit into the grid on this page. Each word should read from top to bottom. When you are finished, read across the shaded row of letters to find the name of popular beach houses.

238

Simply Sports

Race to the Finish

These athletes were in a rush to get home! Starting at number 1 and ending at 88, connect the dots to see what they have left on the stadium floor.

Who?

Can you figure out to which well-known athlete each piece of gear belongs? Part of their first name is over part of their last name. Here's a list of possibles:

Tiger Woods
Mark McGwire
Tara Lipinski
Wayne Gretzky
Andre Agassi
Mia Hamm

Michelle Kwan
Bobby Orr
Pete Sampras
Sammy Sousa
Michael Jordan
John Elway

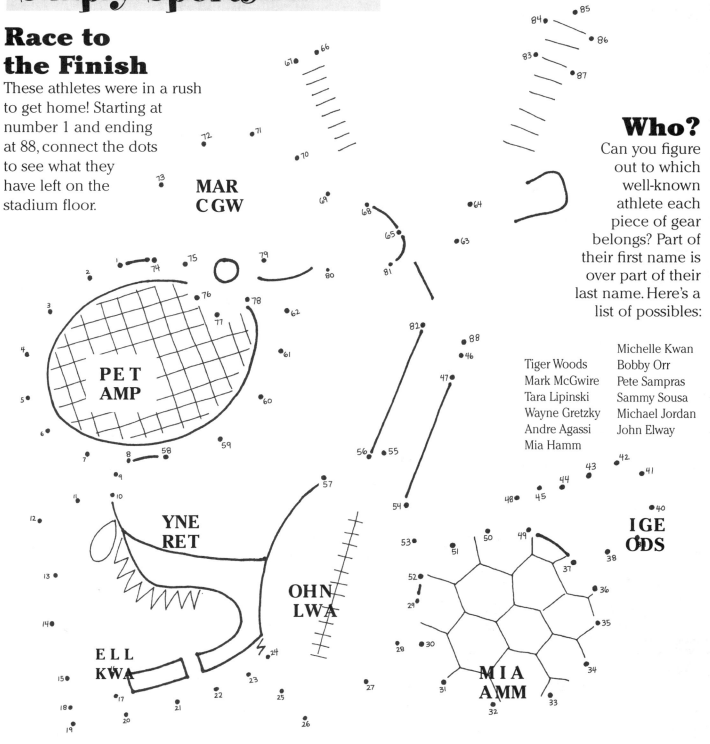

MAR
C GW

PE T
AMP

YNE
RET

OHN
LWA

E L L
KWA

I GE
ODS

M I A
AMM

Take Me Out to the Ball Game

See if you can name eleven popular sports that use balls and fit the names into the crisscross grid. We left you some B-O-U-N-C-E and R-O-L-L as hints.

1. _____
2. _____
3. _____
4. _____
5. _____
6. _____
7. _____
8. _____
9. _____
10. _____
11. _____

You Win Some, You Lose Some

Figure out where to put each of the scrambled letters. They all fit in spaces under their own column. When you have filled in the grid, you will be able to read this classic saying about winning and losing.

Fast 'n' Funny
What should a boxer drink before a fight?

Punch!

Hot Hobbies

Cool Collections

Fill in as many collectibles as you can. We left you some D-U-S-T
as a hint, since that's what a lot of collections collect!

Across

2. A kind of magazine full of colorful action drawings
4. Soft toys that children cuddle
6. Pieces of metal used as money
8. Hard outer covering of certain animals found at the beach
9. Big paper signs that often have pictures

Down

1. A person's signature, usually someone well known
3. Small circular objects used to fasten clothing
5. Small pieces of paper stuck on letters to show a mailing fee has been paid
7. Toys that look like babies, children, or grown-ups

Similar Stamps

Bill loves to collect stamps. But he doesn't want two of the same kind! Can you find the two stamps that are exactly alike and cross out one of them?

241

Build a Model

To construct the model airplane, write the correct part number for each piece on the lines provided. The number shows where each piece belongs in the puzzle grid. We've given you a small picture of the completed airplane to guide you. Caution: Some of the pieces may be upside down!

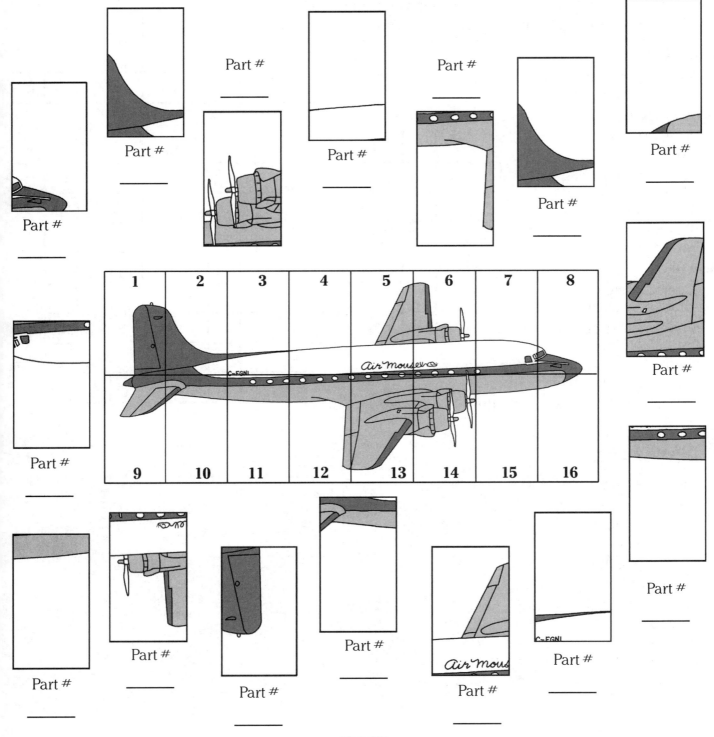

Part #

Part #

Part #

Part #

Part #

Part #

Part #

Part #

Part #

Part #

Part #

Part #

Part #

Part #

Part #

Part #

Part #

Part #

242

Name That Number

Roman Numerals

People didn't always count 1, 2, 3. They used to count I, II, III, IV!

These are the basic numbers used in the Roman system. The Romans used these seven numbers to make up all their numbers.

I	= **1**
V	= **5**
X	= **10**
L	= **50**
C	= **100**
D	= **500**
M	= **1000**

Here's how the system works:

If one Roman numeral is followed by a larger one, then the first number is subtracted from the second number.

For example: **IX = 10 - 1**

But if one Roman numeral is followed by a number that is the same or smaller, you add the numbers together.

For example: **VII = 5 + 1 + 1**

See if you can write the following in Roman Numerals.

1. Your age: _____

2. The number of minutes in an hour: _____

3. The number of hours in a day: _____

4. The number of days in a year: _____

What's a Googol?

A googol is a REALLY big number. If a ten has one zero (10), how many zeros do you think a googol has? Using a simple number substitution (A=1, B=2, C=3, etc.), see if you can break this number code.

1   7·15·15·7·15·12   8·1·19

— — — — — — —   — — —

15·14·5   8·21·14·4·18·5·4

— — —   — — — — — — —

26·5·18·15·19

— — — — —

Hidden Numbers

There is at least one number hidden in each of these sentences. Circle the ones you can find!

1. I love my computer — when it works!

2. Beth reeked of smoke after sitting by the campfire.

3. My mother likes to weigh tomatoes on every scale in the store.

4. Annie was even early for school last week!

5. We can stuff our dirty clothes in your bag.

Quick

Can you turn this number into a mouse?

2

Four Squares

Begin at the white number 4 that is in the dark box. Move up, down, or sideways four spaces in any direction. Add the numbers as you go and reach all four corners, but only one time each. What path must you take to have the sum of all the numbers you land on add up to 46? Hint: The pattern forms the outline of a letter of the alphabet.

```
4 2 4 3 1 3 4 2 4
2 1 2 4 3 4 2 1 2
1 2 4 3 2 3 4 2 3
3 4 3 2 1 2 3 4 1
4 3 2 1 4 1 2 1 2
3 4 3 2 1 2 3 4 1
1 2 4 3 2 3 4 2 3
2 1 2 4 1 4 2 1 2
4 2 4 1 3 1 4 2 4
```

Cross Sums

You must figure out what combination of numbers to use so that each column or row adds up to the totals shown in the white numbers. The white arrows show you in which direction you will be adding, and we have left you some numbers as hints. Better sharpen your pencil!

Here are a few simple rules:

— You are only adding the numbers in any set of white boxes that are touching each other.

— Use only the numbers 1 through 9. Each number can only be used <u>once</u> in each set.

Remember, you need to think ahead a little bit. Each number has to be correct both across <u>and</u> down!

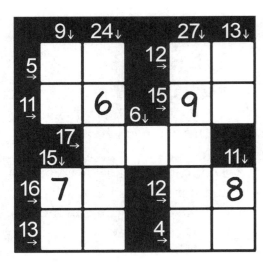

What A Great Idea!

Travel Back in Time

Can you place the following inventions on the time line in the correct order in which they were invented?

Bicycle

X-Ray

Paper

Telephone

Sewing Machine

Windshield Wipers

Microwave Oven

Helicopter

Zipper

Parachute

White Out!

Bette Nesmith Graham invented a very functional fluid! It is something which makes life much easier for people who need to correct mistakes. Turn to each page listed below and find the "white" letter. Fill these letters into their proper square. When you are finished, you will have the name of her invention.

Page **4**

Page **6**

Page **9**

Page **11**

Page **21**

Page **37**

Page **45**

Page **54**

Page **79**

Page **97**

Page **114**

Fast 'n' Funny

What did the inventor get when he crossed a turkey with an octopus?

Enough drumsticks for everyone at dinner!

AD105   1785   1846   1876   1885

Why Didn't I Think of That?

Can you guess each of these famous inventions? Write your guess in each box.

1.
I'm an invention that your mom, dad, or other adult probably reminds you to use every night before you go to bed. What am I?

2.
I come in fun flavors and am perfect to lick on a hot day. What am I?

3.
I'm such a talented invention that I can sleep, walk the dog, and shoot the moon! What am I?

4.
I'm a good writer, but not an author. I leave blue or black lines on white sheets, but not in a bed. I have a ball in my point, but don't bounce! What am I?

Fast 'n' Famous

Thomas Alva Edison, inventor of the lightbulb, phonograph, movie projector, and over 1,000 other patented inventions, said "To invent, you need a good imagination and a pile of junk."

5.
I'm a mixed-up invention — in a car accident, I explode to keep you safe! What am I?

6.
I'm an invention that gets right to the heart of the matter. I love listening to a good beat. What am I?

7.
I can get rid of your headache or bring down your fever, but I'm not a doctor. What am I?

8.
I have more memory than an elephant, but you can lift me with one hand. What am I?

9.
I was invented by someone who was impressed by the way certain prickly plants stick to your clothes. What am I?

1891   1895   1903   1939   1947

Signs & Symbols

Shape-ly Squares

Use the following six shapes to fill in the holes in the grid: circle, star, diamond, square, hexagon, triangle. The object is to have each shape appear only ONCE in each row or column.

Fast Signs

Can you guess what these symbols stand for?

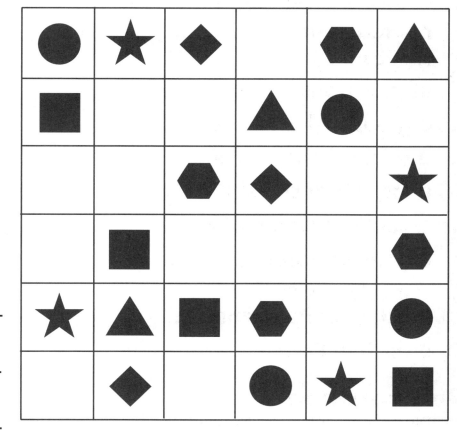

It's Symbolic!

Crack this code to find a tongue twister about symbols. Some of the letters have been provided to help you get started. Write your answers on the lines under the code.

A = !   > = V
S = $ (= I
L = #   B = +

$! # # ‹ $! &
— — — — —   — — —

$ = > = @ ! # $ (# # ‹
— — — — — — —   — — — — —

$ ‹) + % # $ ε:›
— — — — — — —   — — — — — —

Hink Pinks

The answers to Hink Pinks are two rhyming words of one syllable each. We did the first one for you!

1. happy boy .... <u>G</u> L <u>A</u> D   <u>L A</u> <u>D</u>
2. not real reptile .... _ _ _ _   _ _ _ _ _
3. splendid group
   of musicians .... _ _ _ _ _   _ _ _ _
4. a group yell .... _ _ _ _   _ _ _ _ _
5. a skinny female ruler .... _ _ _ _   _ _ _ _ _
6. a large branch .... _ _ _   _ _ _ _
7. a cold swimming place .... _ _ _ _   _ _ _ _
8. a drink at noon .... _ _ _ _ _   _ _ _ _
9. a made smaller
   black & white animal .... _ _ _ _ _ _   _ _ _ _ _
10. a ditch in Paris .... _ _ _ _ _ _   _ _ _ _ _ _

Teeny Weeny Hink Pink
What is Mervin dreaming about?

Onomatopoeia

Onomatopoeia simply means a word that sounds like its meaning, for example <u>click</u> or <u>hum</u>. Look at the pictures below and see if you can find their sounds in the letter grid.

```
S D H O N K U V P
J L R G W R E L Z
H S U I U J U Z R
B I P R P G U E E
L K S L P B P V V
A Y Q S A S P G M
Z K U O I S C O Z
I H O H Z I H B P
P M W I F M E O W
```

248

Simply Synonyms

Synonyms are words that have the same, or almost the same, meaning.
We have chosen four synonyms for each word listed below. How quickly
can you find them in the word list and write them where they belong?

LITTLE = _____ _____ _____ _____

WALK = _____ _____ _____ _____

FUNNY = _____ _____ _____ _____

POKE = _____ _____ _____ _____

GROUP = _____ _____ _____ _____

STAY = _____ _____ _____ _____

BEND = _____ _____ _____ _____

WORD LIST

JAB	WEIRD	SMALL	BATCH	TWIST	STROLL	CURIOUS
STEP	WAIT	PROD	TURN	LINGER	CLUSTER	HIKE
STOP	TINY	CROWD	REMAIN	PLOD	SKIMPY	BUNCH
ODD	STAB	WIND	SLIGHT	STICK	CURVE	STRANGE

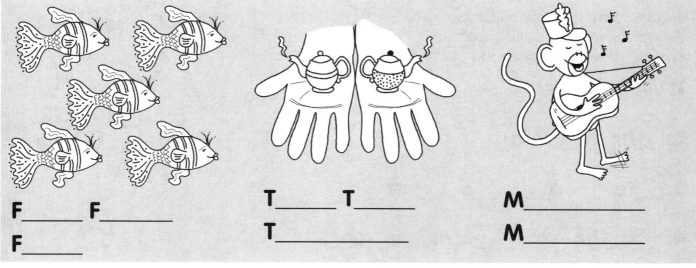

F_____ F_____
F_____

T_____ T_____
T_____

M_____
M_____

Wackiest Word Play Ever!

Blended Words

Many words are a combinaton of two words.
Can you unscramble the following blended words?

1. breakfast + lunch = NUBHRC

2. flutter + hurry = RYULFR

3. motor + hotel = LEMOT

4. smack + mash = SHAMS

5. smoke + fog = OGMS

6. squirm + wiggle = QUEGIGSL

7. twist + whirl = WLRIT

8. chuckle + snort = HELTROC

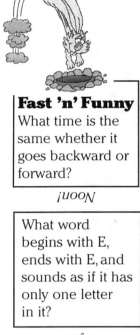

Fast 'n' Funny
What time is the same whether it goes backward or forward?

Noon!

What word begins with E, ends with E, and sounds as if it has only one letter in it?

Eye!

Perfect Palindromes

A palindrome is a word or sentence that reads the same both forward and backward. Can you figure out the missing letters in each of these palindromes?

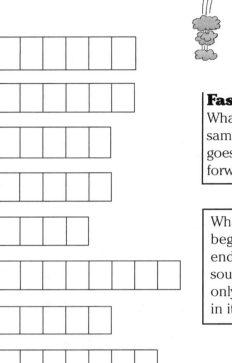

W__ __ it __
r__t
l __ __w?

1. W__ s__w

2. __ur__e__ ru__

3. __te__ o__ __o __et__

4. __e__er o__ __ or e__e__

250

Short n' Sweet

Acronyms are abbreviations formed from the first letters or other parts of a group of words. See if you can guess what each acronym stands for by looking at the pictures. Write your answer on the lines.

Use It Again, Sam

Recycled Words

See if you can turn the first word into the last word by changing ONE letter at a time to make the next new word in line.

1. PIG - _____ - _____ - LEG

2. FOOD - _____ - _____ - COOK

3. HAND - _____ - _____ - SEED

4. CAN - _____ - _____ - _____ - BET

5. JUNK - _____ - _____ - _____ - BANK

Fast 'n' Funny
What has four wheels and flies?

A garbage truck!

Don't Throw It Out!

Hey, there's lots of good junk in this pile! Can you find five things that don't have to go to the dump, but could be recycled or reused?

1. _____
2. _____
3. _____
4. _____
5. _____

Can you also find three things that could be hazardous and should definitely <u>not</u> be just dumped?

1. _____

2. _____

3. _____

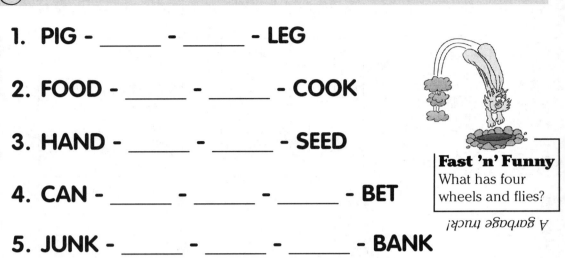

252

New Life for an Old Joke

To solve this puzzle, figure out where to put each of the scrambled letters. They all fit in spaces under their own column. When you have correctly filled in the grid, you will have the answer to this riddle:

Why are garbage collectors sometimes sad?

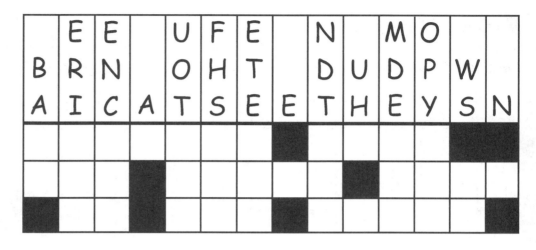

Back to Nature

Figure out the mystery words from the clues. Then read the circled letters to discover what you get when you mix all of these things together in a pile out in the yard. We left you some W-O-R-M-S as a hint, because they <u>love</u> this stuff (and they're good for it, too)!

1. Left over after a dark brown breakfast drink is brewed.

   ( )o _ _ _ _   _ _ ro _ _ _ s

2. What is left after you burn logs in the fireplace.

   w ( )o _   _ s _ _ _ _

3. Waste matter from farm animals.

   (m) _ _ _ r _

4. The vegetable skins that are removed before cooking.

   ( ) _ _ _ s

5. These creatures are good for the soil.

   w (o) r m s

6. These fall off trees in the fall.

   _ _ _ _ _ ( )

7. Apples, bananas, cherries, etc.

   _ r _ _ ( )

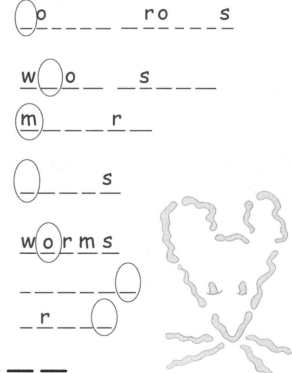

Mystery Word _ _ _ _ _ _ _ _

Let's Play!

Kriss Kross
Don't be bored — see if you can get all ten of
these board games into their proper place!

PARCHEESI   CLUE
MONOPOLY   CHESS
LIFE   SCRABBLE
BACKGAMMON   RISK
CHECKERS   CANDYLAND

Disappearing Dots
Dylan has Dominoes with disappearing dots!
Can you replace the correct number of dots
(one through six) on each disturbed domino?

Hopscotch Addition
Bet you've never played hopscotch this
way! Use the numbered hopscotch board
below and for each "turn" add up the
numbers in the spaces on which you hop.

For example, on your first
turn you would "hop"
over number one, so
don't count it. As
you keep hopping
up the board, add
2+3+4+5+6+7
+8+9+10. Turn
around and hop
back down the
board adding
9+8+7+6+5+4+3+2
for a total
of 98 points.

On your second
turn you would
hop on 1, hop over
2 (so don't count
it), and keep on going.

QUESTION: How many
turns would it take to
get 380 points?

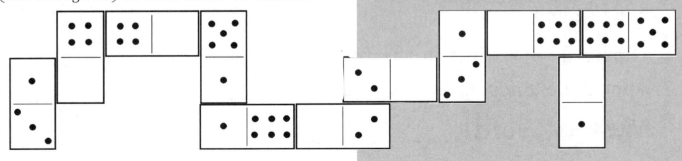

254

How Many Marbles?

Sandy, Peter, and Flo are playing marbles. To find out how many marbles each child has, add the numbers that make a straight line through the circle from where each player shoots.

Jumble of Jacks

Find your way from the first jack to the ball.

START

FINISH

Two of a Kind

You are holding a handful of Kings, and two of them are exactly the same. Which two are they?

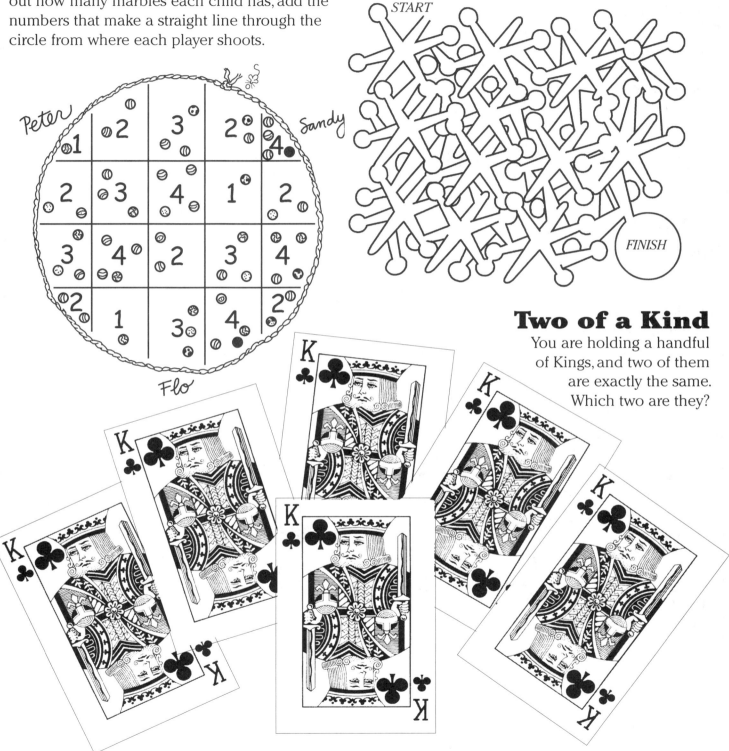

A Camping We Will Go

In the Wild

Ryan's family packed in a hurry for their camping trip. Take a good look at the picture of their campsite, right. Can you see what fourteen items they brought by mistake?

Triangle Teaser

Color in each three-sided shape to find out where your dog sleeps when he goes camping with you.

256

Midnight Morse Message

Late at night Ryan sends his brother Danny this secret message using his flashlight. But you know Morse code, too, so you can tell what the two of them are planning to do. Hint: The slash mark (/) in the message is the space between letters.

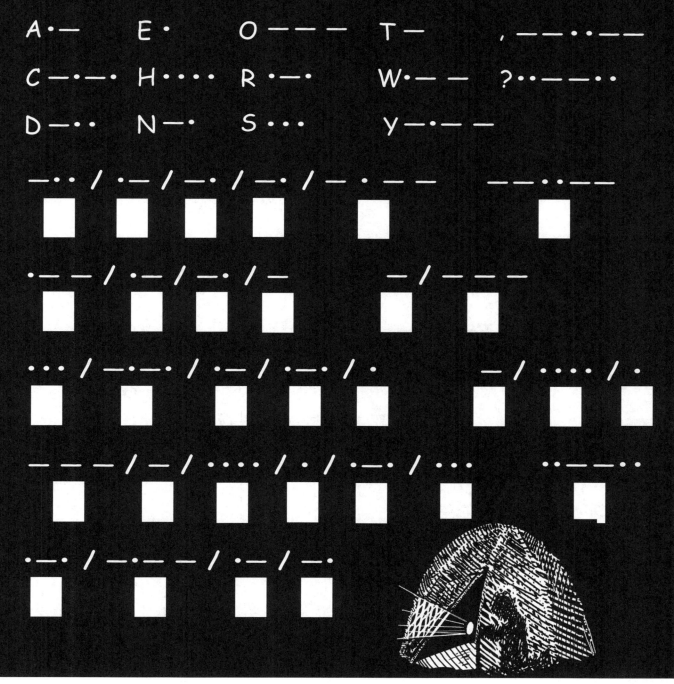

A —   E ·   O — — —   T —   , — — · · — —

C — · — ·   H · · · ·   R · — ·   W · — —   ? · · — — · ·

D — · ·   N — ·   S · · ·   Y — · — —

— · · / · — / — · / — · / · — · — / — — · · — —

· — — · / — · / — · / · — · / — · / — — —

· · · / — · — · / · — / · — / · — / · / — · / · · · · / ·

— — — / — / · · · · / · / · — · / · · · / · · — · ·

· — · / — · — · / · — / — ·

Quotable Quote

Answer as many clues as you can, and fill the letters you have into the grid. Work back and forth between the quotation box and clues until you can read what former First Lady Eleanor Roosevelt had to say about feelings. To make it more challenging we've left one letter out for you to guess.

1	2		3	4	5		6	7	8		9	10	11	12		13	14	15
	16	17	18	19		20	21	22	23	24	25	26	27		28	29	30	31
32	33	34		35	36	37	38		39	40	41	42	43	44	45			

A. Sing without words = $\overline{31}\ \overline{33}\ \overline{9}$

B. Seven days = $\overline{28}\ \overline{5}\ \overline{18}\ \overline{11}$

C. To touch = $\overline{16}\ \overline{23}\ \overline{12}\ \overline{19}$

D. Not me = $\overline{35}\ \overline{3}\ \overline{37}$

E. In a little while = $\overline{42}\ \overline{14}\ \overline{36}\ \overline{1}$

F. Midday = $\overline{4}\ \overline{40}\ \overline{32}\ \overline{44}$

G. Not skinny = $\overline{22}\ \overline{7}\ \overline{30}$

H. Larger than a town = $\overline{39}\ \overline{25}\ \overline{34}\ \overline{13}$

I. Faster than a walk = $\overline{24}\ \overline{15}\ \overline{21}$

J. More pleasant = $\overline{41}\ \overline{20}\ \overline{6}\ \overline{43}\ \overline{38}$

K. Not far = $\overline{41}\ \overline{17}\ \overline{10}\ \overline{27}$

L. Toward the inside = $\overline{29}\ \overline{8}\ \overline{45}\ \overline{26}$

How Do You Feel?

Look at the picture below. Try and guess the phrase that means you are VERY happy.

" _ _ _ _ _ _ _ _ _ _ _ "

Love to Laugh

Laugh out loud or quietly to yourself — can you fill in five different kinds of laughs? We gave you a couple of L-A-U-G-Hs to get you started.

258

Family Reunion

The Newlywed Name

Some people combine their last names when they get married. See if you can make some familiar compound words by matching up these couples. Write their new married name on the lines below.

Katie

Franny

Paula

Julie

Rita

Tammy

Nathan

Frank

Brian

Peter

Steven

Chris

1. Mrs. Katie _____
2. Mrs. Franny _____
3. Mrs. Paula _____
4. Mrs. Julie _____
5. Mrs. Rita _____
6. Mrs. Tammy _____

Oh, Brother!

Jennifer comes from a large family. How many brothers and sisters do you think she has? Find out by crossing out the following names from the grid, below.

1. Cross out all the names that start with the letter S.
2. Cross out all the names that end with the letter N.
3. Cross out all the names that start and end with the same letter.

Sara	Allan	Bob	Billy
David	Sylvia	Kathy	Elise
Ryan	Simon	Anna	Kevin
Sonja	Philip	Sandy	Georg
Tom	Therese	John	Ian
Otto	Sharon	Mervin	Fran
Brian	Seth	Mary	Lynn
Sam	Nan	Robin	Erin
Susan	Karen	Steven	Jim

Jennifer has _____ brothers and _____ sisters.

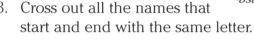

Fast 'n' Funny

What happens when a mouse marries a baker?

They have cheese-cake at the reception!

Fast 'n' Funny

What happens when a snake marries an undertaker?

For presents they get towels marked "Hiss" and "Hearse"!

259

A Flurry of Families

A family is a group, but not all groups are called families.
Unscramble the letters to find which kind of animal lives
in what kind of group.

1. IHSF_____ live in a SCHOOL

2. SNILO _____ live in a PRIDE

3. XEON_____ live in a YOKE

4. ESBE_____ live in a SWARM

5. EHPSE _____ live in a FLOCK

6. SANT _____ live in a COLONY

7. EEESG _____ live in a GAGGLE

8. DKSCU _____ live in a BRACE

9. SODG _____ live in a PACK

10. IHSKCC _____ live in a CLUTCH

11. VESDO_____ live in a COVEY

12. EMOSKNY_____ live in a TROOP

13. SAMCL_____ live in a BED

14. TBAIBRS _____ live in a DOWN

15. ANSWS _____ live in a BEVY

16. SEHALW _____ live in a POD

Just Like Your Mom!

Parents and children may not look exactly alike, but often people can pick family members out of a group. Study the following faces and see if you can do it, too. Draw a line matching each pair of relatives.

Best Friends

Quotable Quote

Answer as many clues as you can, and fill the letters you have into the grid. Work back and forth between the quotation box and clues until you can read what writer and poet Ralph Waldo Emerson had to say about being a friend.

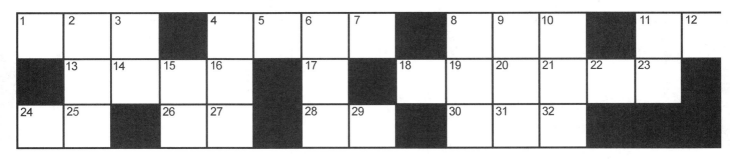

1	2	3		4	5	6	7		8	9	10		11	12
	13	14	15	16		17		18	19	20	21	22	23	
24	25		26	27		28	29		30	31	32			

A. One more than four

$\overline{18}\ \overline{24}\ \overline{15}\ \overline{3}$

B. Person between the
    ages of 13 - 19

$\overline{1}\ \overline{29}\ \overline{21}\ \overline{31}$

C. Noise an owl makes

$\overline{13}\ \overline{27}\ \overline{30}\ \overline{11}$

D. To show the way

$\overline{6}\ \overline{32}\ \overline{9}\ \overline{23}$

E. To melt

$\overline{26}\ \overline{2}\ \overline{17}\ \overline{8}$

F. Not a girl

$\overline{28}\ \overline{12}\ \overline{7}$

G. Cats like to play
    with a ball of this

$\overline{10}\ \overline{14}\ \overline{19}\ \overline{5}$

H. A loud sound

$\overline{22}\ \overline{4}\ \overline{20}\ \overline{25}\ \overline{16}$

One Scoop — Or Two?

Joey, Mark, and Aaron want to buy ice cream. They empty their pockets to see how much money they have.

Joey	=	$1.15
Mark	=	$1.78
Aaron	=	$1.42

A single-scoop cone costs $1.25 and a double-scoop cone costs $1.50. If the boys pool all their money, do they have enough to each get double scoops?

Share & Share Alike

Andrew, Jay, and Josh are friends who share everything. Today they went apple picking and came home with thirteen apples. Some of the apples are really big, and some are pretty tiny. How can the three boys divide the apples evenly if they don't have a scale with which to weigh them?

Stephanie's Sleepover

Stephanie had a gigantic sleepover party — there were 15 kids all together! The girls were being silly and arranged their sleeping bags to look like the following impossible math equation:

However, four of the guests had to go home early. After they left, Stephanie noticed that the math equation now worked! Can you figure out which four bags were taken away? Color in the remaining bags to see the numbers clearly.

• • • • • • • • • • • • • • • • • • • •

Nice Neighbors

Nina, Lauren, Blair, and Dylan all live in the same neighborhood. Using the clues, can you decide in which house each child lives?

* Nina lives on Pine Street.

* Dylan lives diagonally across the street from Blair.

* Lauren lives down the street from Nina, but on the opposite side.

* Blair lives across the street from Nina.

* Lauren and Dylan live in the same block, but not on the same street.

* Blair does not live on Pine Street.

* Nina must cross Pine Street to visit Blair or Dylan.

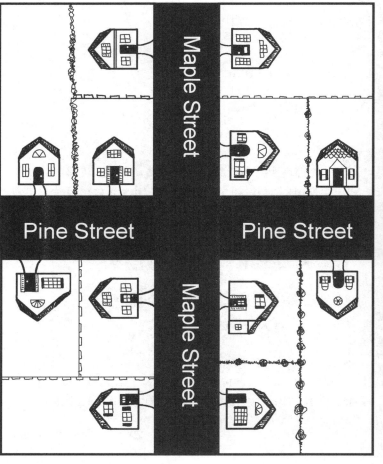

262

Home Sweet Home

Household Words

There are lots of compound words that begin with the word "house." How many can you figure out?

1. A grayish winged bug that eats garbage .... **H O U S E** _ _ _

2. A floating vessel that people live on .... **H O U S E** _ _ _ _

3. All the people who live in a home .... **H O U S E** _ _ _ _

4. Cleaning, cooking, etc. .... **H O U S E** _ _ _ _

5. It is green and is grown indoors .... **H O U S E** _ _ _ _

6. A person who is paid to take care of a large household .... **H O U S E** _ _ _ _ _ _

At Home Wherever They Go

Unscramble the names of these four creatures that carry their homes with them on their backs.

1. **LAINS** _____

2. **MERITH BRAC** _____

3. **LETRUT** _____

4. **KPARABCKCE** _____

A House for Me

Draw a line to match each character with their home.

263

Habitat Is Where It's At

There are many different places where animals live. Each has its own climate and types of plants. Think of six different habitats that can be found around the world and fit them into the grid, below. The numbered clues are a big hint — they show you one animal from each of the regions!

ACROSS

2. "There is a lot of tall, skinny stuff all over the ground in my habitat."

4. "My habitat can get VERY cold and dark for six months of the year."

6. "If you come to my habitat, you'd better bring an umbrella!"

DOWN

1. "Most people would need ropes and special boots to climb all the way up to my habitat."

3. "My habitat is full of sand. Better bring some water to drink!"

5. "It's a long swim to land from my habitat."

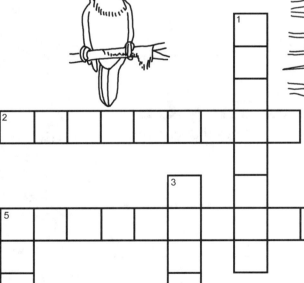

Fast 'n' Funny
Why did the old house go to the doctor?

It was having window pains (windowpanes)!

Fast 'n' Funny
What kind of house is like a book?

A tall house, because it has many stories!

Completely Computers

Can You Speak the Language?

Using a computer requires its own sort of language. Do a search for all twenty-four of the computer terms listed below in the grid.

```
Y L D E L E T E B K P Y
F D Y I C O N S U X R P
I C A N K S I D G O O O
L M B T H O S D M I G C
E O N E A F R E D S R D
S N E R R T M N A E A R
R I S N D W G V T R M A
N T U E W A E Y Q A C H
B O O T A R B S A M D H
I R M O R E T N I R P S
T C L K E Y B O A R D U
```

BIT
BOOT
BUG
BYTE
DATA   MEMORY
DELETE   MONITOR
DISK   MOUSE
EMAIL   PRINTER
FILES   PROGRAM
HARDCOPY   RAM
HARDWARE   ROM
ICONS   SAVE
INTERNET   SEARCH
KEYBOARD   SOFTWARE

Fast 'n' Funny
What's a sign of old age in a computer?

Loss of memory!

Keyboard Code

An English mathematician named Charles Babbage was the first person to figure out how a machine could perform calculations and store the results. Crack this keyboard code to find out his nickname.

5Y3

RQ5Y34

9R

D9J07534W

Dumb Deletions

Doug e-mailed Dave some of his favorite tongue twisters, but he accidentally kept hitting the delete key. Can you figure out what each phrase was supposed to say?

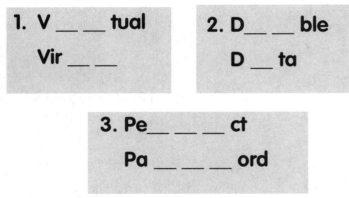

1. V __ __ tual

   Vir __ __

2. D__ __ ble

   D __ ta

3. Pe__ __ __ ct

   Pa __ __ __ ord

Micro Maze

Can you get Tanya's e-mail through the Internet to her Aunt Mia? Follow the black line from computer to computer. Don't stop for any on-line shopping!

Smiley E-Mail

Smilies are little pictures you can type on your computer using punctuation marks, numbers, and letters. Tilt your head to the left to correctly see the smilies. For example, the original smiley looks like this :-) . Can you see the smiling face? Now, finish the following e-mail letter using only five of the smilies provided.

Possible Smilies

> :)	: - D
: - *	: - o
: - c	; -)
: - ı ı	: X<

_____! My _____ ate
Uh oh!   cat

something _____
            sour

and is very _____.
              unhappy

What a little _____
                devil

he is!

266

School Daze

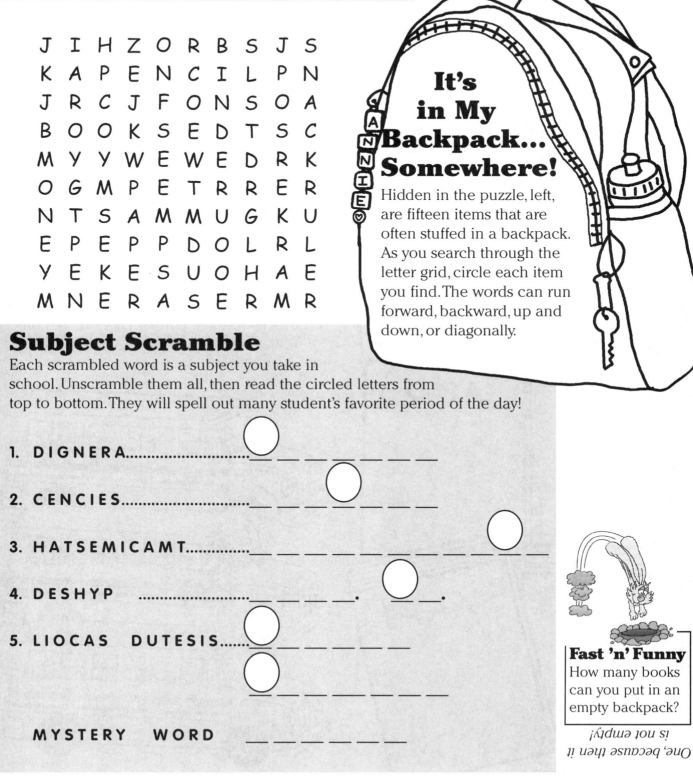

```
J  I  H  Z  O  R  B  S  J  S
K  A  P  E  N  C  I  L  P  N
J  R  C  J  F  O  N  S  O  A
B  O  O  K  S  E  D  T  S  C
M  Y  Y  W  E  W  E  D  R  K
O  G  M  P  E  T  R  R  E  R
N  T  S  A  M  M  U  G  K  U
E  P  P  P  D  O  L  R  L
Y  E  K  E  S  U  O  H  A  E
M  N  E  R  A  S  E  R  M  R
```

It's in My Backpack... Somewhere!

Hidden in the puzzle, left, are fifteen items that are often stuffed in a backpack. As you search through the letter grid, circle each item you find. The words can run forward, backward, up and down, or diagonally.

Subject Scramble

Each scrambled word is a subject you take in school. Unscramble them all, then read the circled letters from top to bottom. They will spell out many student's favorite period of the day!

1. DIGNERA.............................◯ __ __ __ __ __ __

2. CENCIES................................__ __ ◯ __ __ __ __

3. HATSEMICAMT...............__ __ __ __ __ __ __ __ __ ◯ __

4. DESHYP ....__ __ __ . ◯ __ .

5. LIOCAS   DUTESIS......◯ __ __ __ __ __ __

   ◯ __ __ __ __ __ __

MYSTERY   WORD   __ __ __ __ __ __ __

267

Whose Is Whose?

Laura is looking for her Math book. Unfortunately, the whole class has the same book and parts of each kid's name have rubbed off. Can you figure out which book is Laura's? See if you can figure out the names of her classmates, too.

Hot Lunch

Ryan's mom gave him $2.00 for lunch. If he buys an apple and a cookie, what hot lunch item and drink will he have to get?

MENU
Pizza $1.00
Hot Dog $1.25
Cheeseburger $1.50

Milk $.50	Cookie $.50
Juice $.75	Chips $.50
Water Free	Fruit $.50

Bus Stop

John can't remember the number of his school bus, but he does remember that his bus is different from all the others. Can you tell which bus John should take?

268

Around The World

Stars & Stripes

These three flags are very similar to each other. But each country uses a different symbol in the upper left-hand corner. Can you break the code that tells you which symbol goes on which flag? When you have, complete each flag by drawing in the proper symbol.

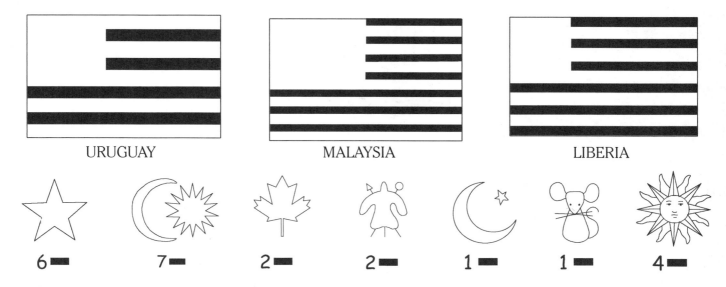

URUGUAY   MALAYSIA   LIBERIA

6 ■━   7 ■━   2 ■━   2 ■━   1 ■━   1 ■━   4 ■━

Hello Friend

You have just gotten a letter from your new pen pal, but he wrote it in Portuguese! Use the dictionary below to read his letter.

Dictionary

amigo	friend	meu	my
anos	years	moro	live
contar	to sing	na	in
dez	ten	nome	name
e	and	novo	new
é	is	Oi!	Hi!
escrever	to write	por favor	please
você escreve	you write	que	what
fazer	to do	seu	your
gostar	to like	ter	to have
eu gosto	I like	eu tenho	I have
você gosto	you like	tocar	to play music
logo	soon	violão	guitar
morar	to live	você	you

Oi!

Meu nome é Rodolfo. Eu tenho dez anos e moro na Brazil. Eu gosto de contar e tocar violão. E você, o que gosta de fazer? Por favor me escreve logo!

seu novo amigo, Rodolfo

269

Under The Sea

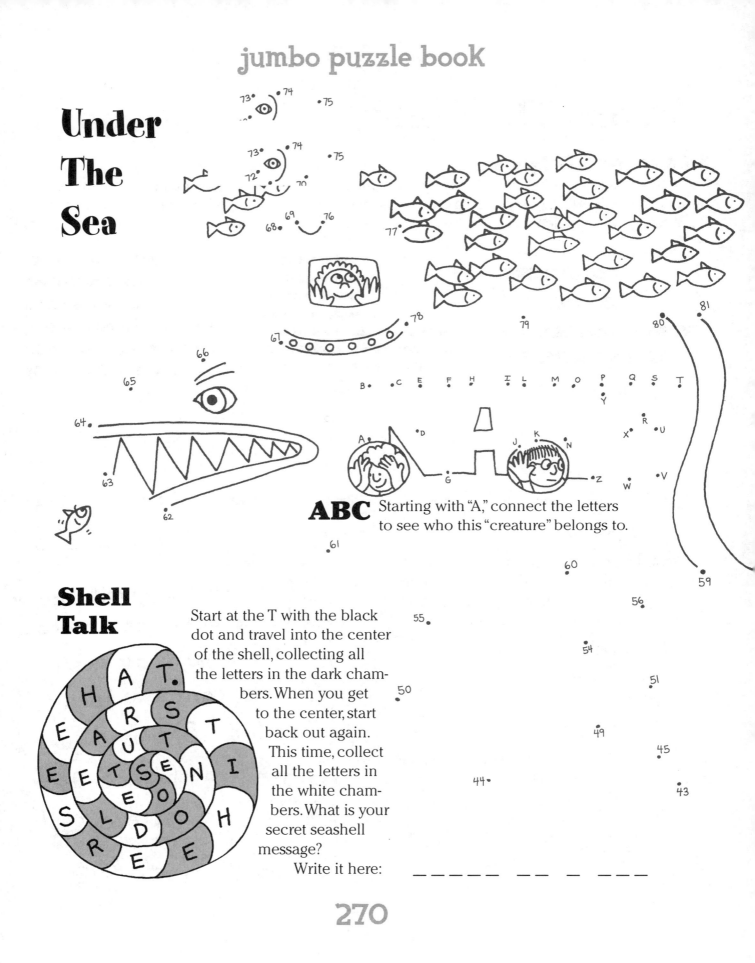

ABC Starting with "A," connect the letters to see who this "creature" belongs to.

Shell Talk

Start at the T with the black dot and travel into the center of the shell, collecting all the letters in the dark chambers. When you get to the center, start back out again. This time, collect all the letters in the white chambers. What is your secret seashell message?

Write it here: _ _ _ _ _ _   _ _   _   _ _ _

School of Fish

Fish traveling in groups called schools move so fast that they are hard to count! First, guess how many fish are in this school. Then, circle them in groups of five. Catching them this way makes counting easier.

Your Guess | *Exact Number*

What's Dot?

Starting with 1 and ending with 82, connect the dots to discover two kinds of things that travel under the sea.

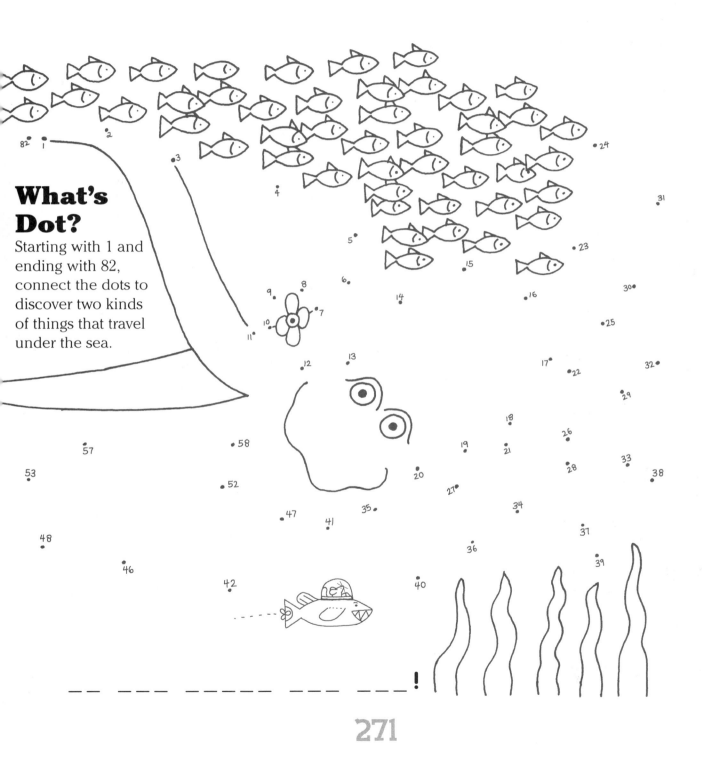

All Knight Long

Missing Parts

Part of each of these words has magically disappeared. Can you find the missing section of each word in the column of word parts on the right?

1. W I Z _ _ _

2. _ _ _ G H T

3. U N I _ _ _ N

4. T _ _ _ L

5. F A I _ _ _ S

6. _ _ _ M E

7. D R _ _ _ N

8. _ _ _ N C E S S

Missing Parts
AGO
COR
GNO
RIE
ROL
PRI
KNI
ARD

A Corner Castle

Can you count how many squares and rectangles it takes to make this castle?

Elf Talk

Use the decoder at right to read the message below. When you're finished, you will have the answer to this riddle:

Why can only two elves sit under a toadstool?

Help!

Connect the dots quickly to find out the helpful answer to this riddle:

What time is it when a princess gets captured by a dragon?

Fast 'n' Funny
Why shouldn't you pollute the ocean?

Because you make the sea sick!

273

Someone's In The Kitchen

Cookies

Jimmy had great fun decorating these gingerbread men. Can you tell which two are EXACTLY alike? Be sure to look on both pages.

Serve It Up!

Can you find all twenty-six cooking terms in the grid?

```
T S Q H E A T Q T G
P L T A S T E U S H
P I K C A R C H O P
R C R O L L H O P R
E E T L E M I S O J
H M S B O I L P U K
E Q E H A X L R R S
A A R A U K S I F T
T Q V U S N E N W U
S A E T I U F K A F
Q S I M M E R L S F
K R W H I P Y E H I
```

BAKE
BEAT
BOIL
CHILL
CHOP
COOK
CRACK
CUT
FRY
HEAT
MEASURE
MELT
MIX
POUR
PREHEAT
ROLL
SERVE
SIFT
SIMMER
SLICE
SPRINKLE
STIR
STUFF
TASTE
WASH
WHIP

Totally Tablespoons

Margarita is baking a cake. The recipe calls for:

* 2 cups of flour

* 1 1/2 cups of sugar

* 1/4 cup of cocoa

Unfortunately, Margarita only has a tablespoon with which to measure. Do you know how many tablespoons (Tbsp.) she will need for each ingredient?

Hint: 1 cup = 16 Tbsp.

Flour = _____ Tbsp.

Sugar = _____ Tbsp.

Cocoa = _____ Tbsp.

Mystery Meals

Someone forgot to tell us what they are cooking! Can you tell what each recipe will make from reading the list of ingredients? Write the name of the finished food at the top of each card.

Here's What's Cookin': _____

1/2 cup butter

1 cup brown sugar

2 eggs

1 1/2 tsp. vanilla

2 1/2 cups flour

1 tsp. baking soda

1/2 tsp. salt

6 oz. semi-sweet chocolate pieces

Here's What's Cookin': _____

_____

1 head lettuce

cherry tomatoes

1 cucumber

2 carrots

1 green pepper

4 radishes

onion

Italian Dressing

Here's What's Cookin': _____

8 cups water

1 3/4 cups uncooked macaroni

8 oz. cheddar cheese

1/4 cup flour

2 cups milk

dash of pepper

Fast 'n' Funny
What stays hot even if you put it in the refrigerator?

Pepper!

Fast 'n' Funny
What tastes better before it is cooked?

Burnt toast!

Here's What's Cookin': _____

8 slices bread

2 eggs

butter

1/2 cup milk

1 Tbsp. sugar

1/4 tsp. cinnamon

maple syrup

Zooey Zoo

Seeing Double

The animals with double letters in their names have gotten all mixed up. Can you straighten them out? Move the double letters from one animal to another until all the animals make sense again!

1. **OORDVARK** = _ _ RDVARK

2. **KANGAREE** = KANGAR _ _

3. **MONGAASE** = MONG _ _ SE

4. **RASSIT** = RA _ _ IT

5. **OPOPPUM** = OPO_ _ UM

6. **GIRABBE** = GIRA _ _ E

7. **GIRRON** = GI _ _ ON

8. **HIFFO** = HI _ _ O

9. **PABBOT** = PA _ _ OT

Fast 'n' Funny
What do you call two bananas?

A pair of slippers!

Fast 'n' Funny
What two flowers can be found at the zoo?

Dandelion and Tiger Lily!

Color-a-Message

Color in every letter that is <u>not</u> a Z to find a special message from the zookeeper.

```
Z  Z  P  Z  L
E  Z  Z  Z  A
Z  S  Z  Z  E
D  Z  Z  O  Z
N  Z  Z  Z  Z
Z  O  T  Z  F
Z  Z  E  Z  Z
E  Z  Z  D  Z
T  H  Z  Z  Z
Z  E  A  Z  N
Z  I  M  Z  Z
A  Z  Z  L  S
```

Zack's Favorite

Fill in all the triangles to show the
path to Zack's favorite animal.
When you're done, finish each of
the signs with Zack's favorite
letter. Can you guess
what it is?

Fast 'n' Funny
Which animal at
the zoo eats with
its tail?

*They all do—they
can't take them off!*

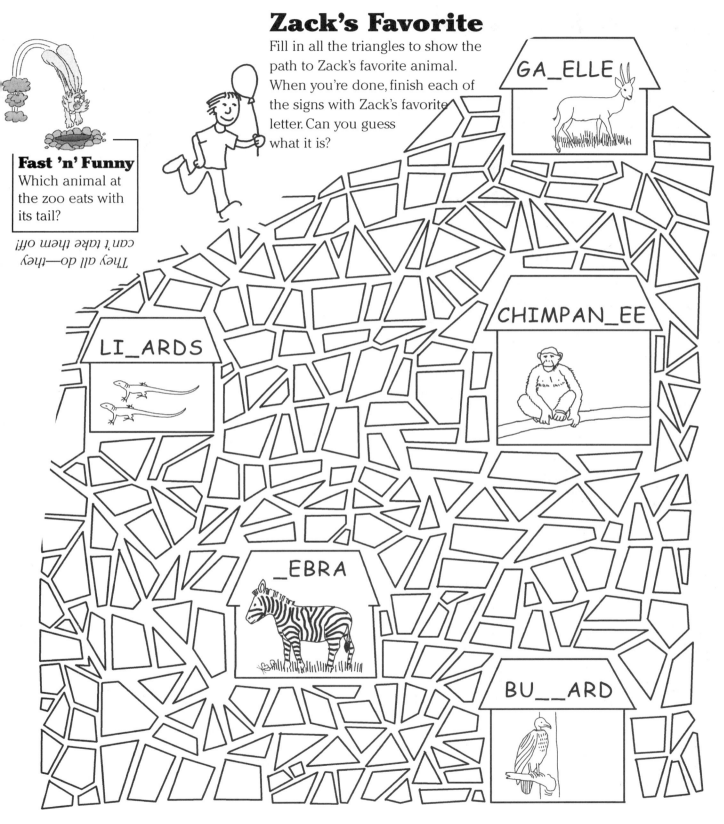

GA_ELLE

CHIMPAN_EE

LI_ARDS

_EBRA

BU__ARD

277

Creepy Crawlies

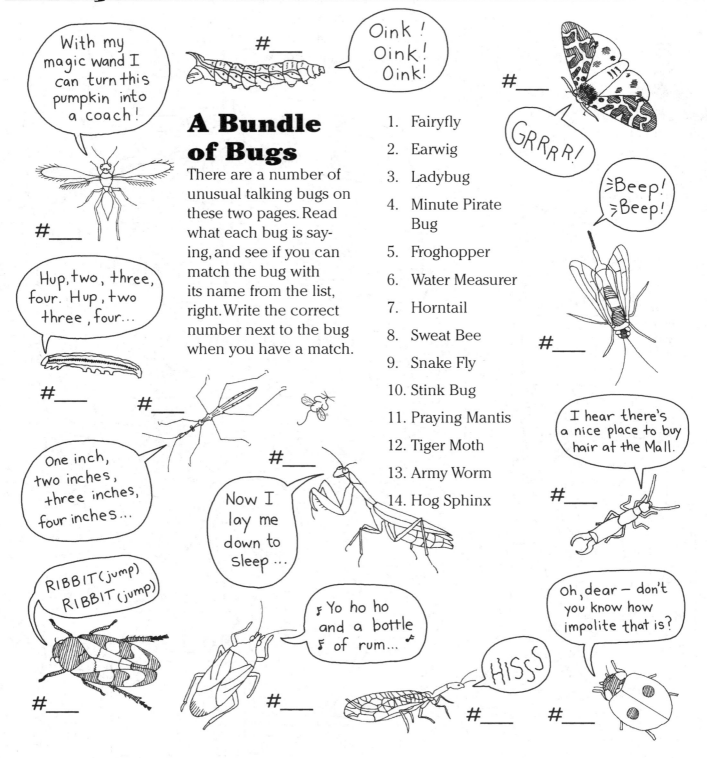

A Bundle of Bugs

There are a number of unusual talking bugs on these two pages. Read what each bug is saying, and see if you can match the bug with its name from the list, right. Write the correct number next to the bug when you have a match.

1. Fairyfly
2. Earwig
3. Ladybug
4. Minute Pirate Bug
5. Froghopper
6. Water Measurer
7. Horntail
8. Sweat Bee
9. Snake Fly
10. Stink Bug
11. Praying Mantis
12. Tiger Moth
13. Army Worm
14. Hog Sphinx

Mixed-Up Metamorphosis

Everybody knows that caterpillars change into butterflies. But did you know that a butterfly can become a firefly? You can do it in four steps if you make the right compound words.

BUTTERFLY to

FLY_____ to

_____ to

_____ to

FIREFLY

Itsy Bitsy

A pictograph is a very simple drawing — kind of like visual shorthand. Can you guess what this little pictograph shows?

Charlotte's Riddle

Start at the T marked with the spiders. Read the letters in a spiral toward the center to find the answer to this riddle: What day is it when two spiders get married?

Boy, am I HOT!

#__

Hiding in a Honeycomb

There are six bugs hiding in this honeycomb. Can you find them? Start at any letter and move one space at a time in any direction. Once you've found all the bugs, see what other words you can make.

I don't know why I'm way over here. I don't smell *that* bad!

#__

279

In The Garden

Tools of the Trade

Can you find eight things that don't belong in this garden?

Pick a Bouquet

Iris wants to pick flowers for her friends. Use two straight lines to divide this flower bed into four equal bunches. Each bouquet should have the same amount of tulips, roses, and daisies.

Bee to Flower

How can you get the bee to land on the flower?

Mixed-Up Garden

Unscramble each of the words in this garden. Write your answers in the rows provided. When you are finished, read the letters under the garden hoops from top to bottom. You will see that all these plants have something in common.

They are all

_____ .

DINVEE

CREUUBCM

NTELPGGA

EANB

OAPTOT

ARROCT

LOCIBCOR

LUTETCE

PPERPE

PNHCASI

Fast 'n' Funny
What do you call a tired gardener?

Bushed!

Herbal Seed Packets

Using straight lines only, finish the letters on these seed packets to form the names of some familiar herbs.

Fast 'n' Funny
How did the gardener fix the broken tomato plants?

With tomato paste!

Head To Toe

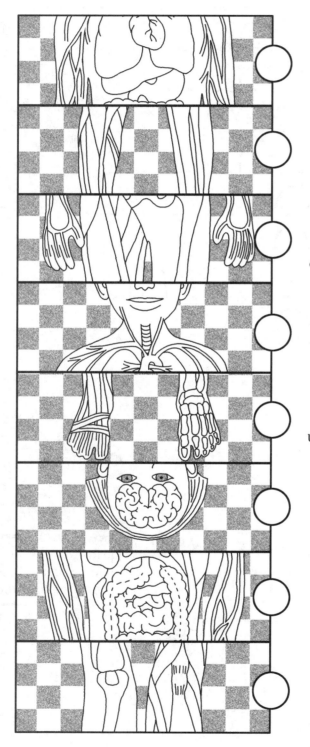

The Inner You

Whoa—the body on the left is all mixed-up! See if you can number the body parts in the correct order to match the picture on the right. The head is number one. Be careful—some of the pieces are upside down!

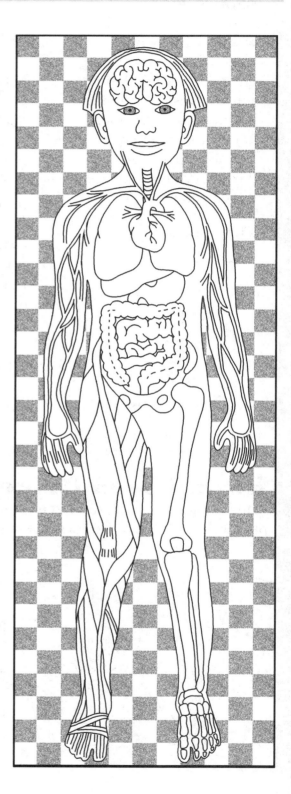

It All Makes Sense

Use your brain to figure out these small picture clues.
The shaded row tells you what they are called as a
group. We left you some E's for your Excellent Effort!

Fast 'n' Funny
What did one ear
say to the other ear?

*Something between
us really smells!*

Why did the bones
chase the skull?

*They wanted to get
a-head!*

Say What?

Do you know where the three
smallest bones in your body
are found? Here's a hint — clap
your hands loudly or whisper
softly and you'll be using these
bones!

Body Scramble

Unscramble the names of each part of the body, then put them in order from head to toes.

OTES _____ #__

DAEH _____ #__

SWAIT _____ #__

STECH _____ #__

GLES _____ #__

SHIP _____ #__

CKNE _____ #__

EFET _____ #__

DOSHULRES _____ #__

283

Community

New Neighbors

Each member of the Thomas family has a sign. Follow the directions below to find out the message they have for their new neighbors.

1. Fill in all the blocks on the left side of each person's sign.

2. Fill in all the top blocks on Gramma, Jesse, Dad, and Sally's signs.

3. Fill in all the blocks on the right side of Rachel, Mom, and Dad's signs.

4. Fill in the center block on Mom, Gramma, Rachel, and Sally's signs.

5. Fill in the bottom block in columns 2 & 4 of Mom's sign. Also fill in the block just below the center in Mom's sign.

6. Fill in the second block from the top in columns 2 & 4 on Rachel's sign.

7. Fill in all the bottom blocks on Gramma, Chrissy, Jesse, and Sally's signs.

8. Fill in the remaining square on the bottom row of Dad's sign.

All Over Town

Here is a list of errands your mother asked you to do today. Mom reminds you to do the grocery shopping last so the milk won't spoil. If you start at your house, in what order should you do the errands to get them finished as quickly as possible? When you have figured out the fastest route, number the errands on the list correctly from first to last.

Hint: Count the spaces from one place to the next to see which way is the shortest. The "driveway" for each parking lot counts as one square.

— Drop books at library.
— Pick up pie at bakery.
— Get mail at post office.
— Pick up paper at computer store.
— Buy flea soap at pet store.
— Get milk at grocery store.
Thanks!
♡♡♡ Mom
Do this ↑ last!

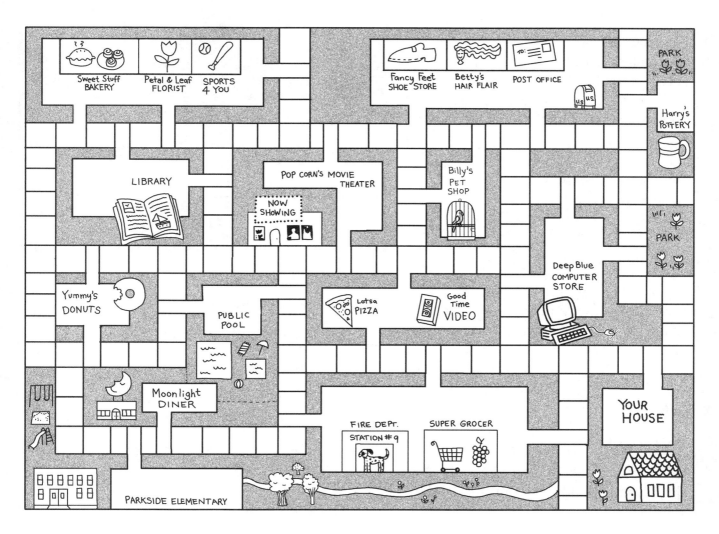

Only Opposites

Opposites Crossword

Figure out the answers to the questions below and fill them into the numbered crossword grid. All the answers will be the opposite of the clues. Bad Curse! (Oops, that should be "Good Luck!")

ACROSS

1. Opposite of friend

3. Opposite of bottom

6. Opposite of frown

7. Opposite of dry

9. Opposite of E.A.T.
   (Estimated Arrival Time)
   HINT: If the question is an acronym or abbreviation, the answer will be an acronym or abbreviation, too.

10. Opposite of happy

12. Opposite of disarm
    (take away weapons)

14. Opposite of unusual

15. Opposite of getting up is going to _ _ _

16. Opposite of followed
    HINT: Remember, if the clue is in the past tense, the answer must be in the past tense, too.

DOWN

1. Opposite of many

2. Suffix that means the opposite of the least.
   HINT: If something is the opposite of the least tall, it is the tall _ _ _

3. Opposite of untie

4. Opposite of younger

5. Opposite of an animal that is wild

8. Opposite of write down

10. A prefix that is the opposite of over
    HINT: A "_ _ _ marine" goes under the water.

11. Opposite of a thing that works correctly

12. Opposite of none

13. Opposite of not angry

What's Wrong?

Circle the twenty things that seem
odd or out of place in this room.

Party Party

Calling Code

Susan is calling her friends to invite them to a party. Using the phone keypad as a decoder, figure out the names of the people invited. Each phone button has several letters on it, so be sure to look for the number after the slash. It tells you if the letter is in the second or third space. For example, 2/2 = B. A number with no slash after it means the letter is in the first space.

1. 4/3-6-2   6/2-8/2-8-8

   _____

2. 3/3-7/2-2-6/2-5/2

   _____

   6/2   7/3-8-3/2-4/3-6/2

   _____

3. 8-3/2-3   3/2   2/2-3/2-2-7/2

   _____

4. 8-2-3/3-3/3-9/3   7-8/2-5/3-5/3

   _____

5. 3-7/2-3/2-9   2   2/2-6/3-2-8

   _____

6. 7/3-8/2-6-6-3/2-7/2   8-4/3-6-3/2

   _____

7. 7/3-2-6/2-8-2   2/3-5/3-2-8/2-7/3

   _____

Cut the Cake

How would you cut a round cake into nine pieces with only four cuts of a knife?

I Can't Believe My Eyes!

Optical illusions are a kind of puzzle designed to fool your eyes. See if you can tell the difference between illusion and reality in the following popular optical illusions.

1. Do you see a <u>13</u> or a <u>B</u> in the center of the figures above?

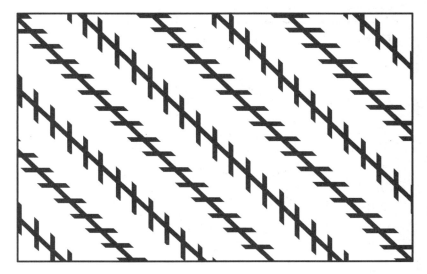

2. Are the long black lines parallel (even) with each other, or are they crooked?

3. Do you see two faces — or a vase?

4. Which of these girls is the tallest?

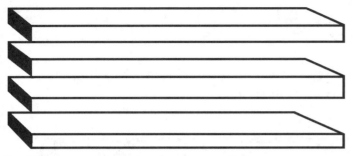

5. How many planks do you see?

6. What is strange about these bunnies?

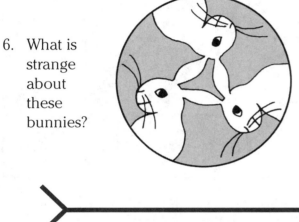

7. Which line is longer?

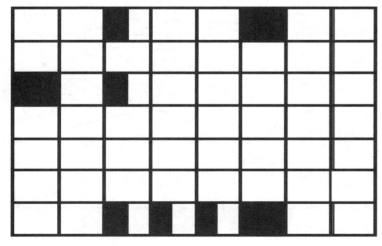

8. Can you read the secret message?

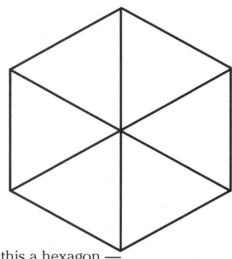

9. Is this a hexagon — or can you see something else?

10. What do you see where the white lines cross?

11. Can you see the white triangle?

Plundering Pirates

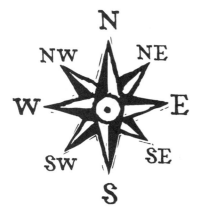

X Marks the Spot

Treasure could be buried at any of the X spots on this map. Using the compass and following the directions below, you should be able to find the right one.

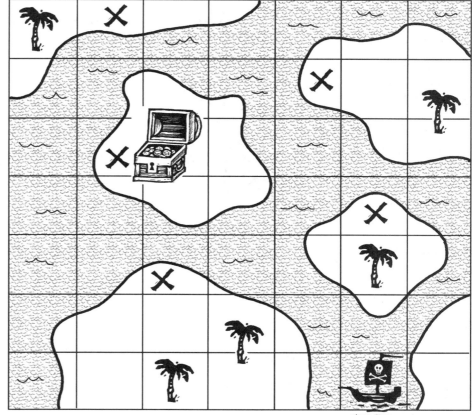

START

N one block
NW one block
N two blocks
NW two blocks
SW two blocks
E one block

291

Dividing the Booty

Captain Jack and his crew are dividing up their treasure. Using the information given below, can you figure out how many gold coins each pirate will get?

✠ One-Eyed Pete and Peg-Leg Larry get the same amount of gold coins.

✠ Captain Jack gets half of the total treasure.

✠ Each pirate's share can be divided by the number five.

✠ The total treasure is 50 gold coins.

Captain Jack gets ____ coins

One-Eyed Pete gets ____ coins

Barnacle Bill gets ____ coins

Peg-Leg Larry gets ____ coins

Walk the Plank

Can you fill in the blanks for these words that also end in the letters A-N-K?

1. A pirate would probably not deposit his money in a

_ _ _ _ .

2. Stealing a pirate's wooden leg and replacing it with an umbrella might be considered a silly

_ _ _ _ _ .

3. Pirates probably _ _ _ _ _ because they couldn't bathe very often.

4. On board a pirate ship they might use a _ _ _ _ _ to turn a wheel.

5. If pirates _ _ _ _ _ sea water, they would get really sick.

6. Many pirate ships _ _ _ _ _ during a bad storm or after a battle.

All Through The Week

Places of Worship

Throughout the week, people of all religions gather to worship. Can you fit the names of seven places of worship into the grid? We left you some beautiful M-U-S-I-C as a hint.

Fast 'n' Funny
How many days are there in a year?

Only seven — Sunday, Monday, Tuesday, Wednesday, Thursday, Friday and Saturday!

Household Chores

Find an action word in the list to fit with each of these items. Write it on the line in front of the item and you will have a long list of common household chores. How many of them do you do at home?

1. _____ **floor**

2. _____ **dishes**

3. _____ **table**

4. _____ **rugs**

5. _____ **furniture**

6. _____ **newspapers**

7. _____ **trash cans**

8. _____ **laundry**

9. _____ **sink**

10. _____ **plants**

11. _____ **meals**

12. _____ **pets**

Word List

wash	recycle	sweep
feed	empty	fold
vacuum	water	cook
scrub	dust	set

After-School Activities

James is very busy after school. Using the clues below, figure out on which day of the week he has each activity planned. Fill in the calendar at the bottom of this page for James.

✐   He plans to go to the library three days before his piano lesson.

✐   He has a swimming lesson two days after his baseball game.

✐   He is going to the movies with Tim at the end of the week.

✐   His piano lesson is scheduled on Thursday.

✐   His scout meeting is the day before his swimming lesson.

✐   He will go to the library and the baseball game on the same day.

Weekly Maze

Can you start at the word "Monday" on the calendar below and work your way through the WEEK until you reach Friday?

Monday	Tuesday	Wednesday	Thursday	Friday

Monster Mash

An Ugly Crowd

Can you use two straight lines to divide this group of monsters into four equal groups? Each group should have eight monster <u>heads</u>. Your line can go over the tips of tails or feet, but <u>not</u> through any bodies or necks!

Scared?

Did you know there's a word that means "fear of monsters"? Use the decoder to read the monster's eyes and see what this scary word is.

A B E H I O P R T

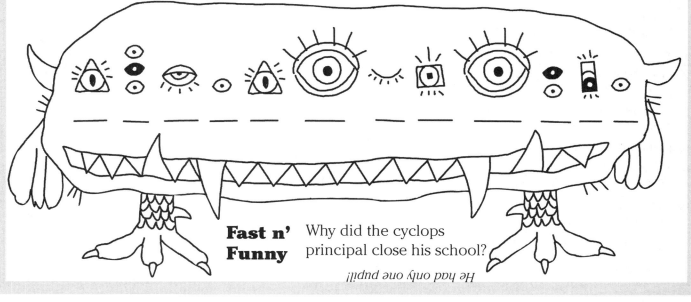

Fast n' Funny   Why did the cyclops principal close his school?

He had only one pupil!

Late at Night

How much do you know about those creepy creatures in late night movies and TV shows?

Way to Grow

This monster is growing eyes — and other parts, too! Figure out the pattern, then draw the correct number of eyes on the last head!

ACROSS

2. What do you call a crazy vampire?

4. The sound of a lightning bolt

6. "The _____" is a monster with no particular shape, but a big appetite

9. This is the name of a doctor who brought a famous monster to life

11. A famous Egyptian monster

12. "The Creature from the Black _____"

13. You might confuse this big green monster with a dinosaur

16. Dr. Jekyll's evil monster twin

18. "7 Down" climbed to the ____ of the Empire State Building

20. Vampires must be home by this time of day

21. This gentle blue monster lives on Sesame Street and loves crunchy, sweet treats

DOWN

1. A monster who should be dead but is still walking around

3. If this monster was smaller, you would swat it!

5. "The _____ of the Opera" is now a popular musical monster

6. A mad scientist's laboratory is always being hit by _____ of lightning

7. A super-giant-gorilla-monster

8. The most famous movie vampire

10. This monster needs to shave when the moon is full

14. Many TV stations show monster movies _____ at night

15. This type of scientist is always making monsters

17. What you yell when you run into a monster

19. Wolfman leaves ____ prints when he walks

Going On A Picnic

Having Fun

There are many ways to amuse yourself on a picnic. In each of the following, the words making up an activity have been squished together. Can you figure them all out?

1. FLKIYTE   _ _ _   _ _ _ _
2. EAFOOTD   _ _ _   _ _ _ _
3. REBADOOK   _ _ _ _   _ _ _ _
4. TANAKEP   _ _ _ _   _ _ _
5. WADOLKG   _ _ _ _   _ _ _
6. CLITREMEB   _ _ _ _ _ _   _ _ _ _
7. THBROWALL   _ _ _ _ _   _ _ _ _
8. PLACAYRDS   _ _ _ _   _ _ _ _ _

Ready to Go

Look carefully at the picnic scene, below. Figure out what object is by each number and write that word in the spaces provided. Then, take the circled letters and unscramble them. They will spell the answer to this riddle:

You bring me to the picnic, and I bring the picnic with me. What am I?

1. ⃝ _ _ _ ⃝ _ _
2. _ _ ⃝ _ _ ⃝ _ _ _ _
3. ⃝ ⃝ ⃝ _ _
4. _ _ ⃝ _ ⃝ _ _ _
5. _ ⃝ _ _ _ ⃝ _ _
6. _ _ _ _ ⃝

Answer: _ _ _ _ _ _

_ _ _ _ _ _

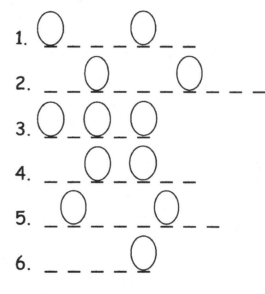

297

Ants

Help the ants find their way across the blanket to the picnic. Stop at all the sweet treats, but go past the silverware.

Start

Vanity Plates

Some license plates tell a lot about their owners. Can you match the following people with their license plate? Write the correct owner under each plate.

Mom
Newlyweds
Clown
Computer Wiz
Pretty Girl

Santa Claus
Tennis Player
Star Trek Fan
Math Teacher
Artist

ICR8

HOHOHO

2PLS2Z4

HRDDRV

TNSNY1

IMFUNE

5KDZ

IDOLUVU

QTPIE

BMMEUP

Skid Marks

These tire tracks tell a lot about what the owner of each vehicle does. Draw a line to match each vehicle with its tracks.

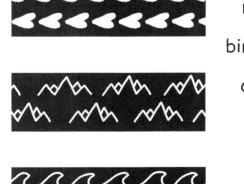

climbs mountains

bird watcher

curls hair

delivers flowers

surfs

fishes

It's Tree-Mendous!

Tallest Tree

You will be reading the growth rings on this tree stump in a clockwise direction. Start at the letter in the center ring marked with a black dot. Read around the ring until you reach the black dot again. Then, jump out to the next ring and continue reading in a clockwise direction. When you are finished you will know the answer to the question:

What is the tallest tree?

Properly Pronounced

Each type of tree here is listed by its dictionary pronunciation.
Watch your spelling as you write each one correctly in the space provided.

1. mā′pəl _____

2. bēch _____

3. ōk _____

4. sprüs _____

5. bûrch _____

6. päm _____

7. wil′ō _____

8. fûr _____

9. jü′nə pər _____

10. mə hog′ə nē _____

11. pop′lər _____

12. sē′dər _____

13. bôl′səm _____

14. hik′ə rē _____

300

Good Things Grow on Trees

Circle those things that grow on trees.

Cross out the things that
DO NOT grow on trees.

Shade in those items that
are made from trees!

Fast 'n' Funny
What is a tree's favorite game?

Follow the cedar!

Fast 'n' Funny
What does a tree yell at sporting events?

I'm rooting for you!

Snow Day

Bundle Up!

Snow What?

Staring at 1, connect the dots to see what Beth made in her yard.

ACROSS

Unscramble these winter clothing words and write them in the crossword grid.

2. TOBOS
3. SVELOG
4. STAPOWNNS
5. RAKAP
6. WERTEAS
7. ATH
8. CRAFS

DOWN

1. When you have filled in all the other words, see if you can guess this last important item of warm winter clothing!

Hot Chocolate

Keith, Jon, and Adam have just come in from sledding. Using the following clues, can you figure out how many marshmallows each boy likes in his cocoa?

- Jon has three less marshmallows than Adam.

- There are nine marshmallows.

- Keith has twice as many marshmallows as Adam.

Jon ___ Keith ___ Adam ___

Snowy Words

Do you know all of these words that begin with "snow"?

1. A packed sphere of snow......................**SNOW** _ _ _ _

2. One of these small ice crystals.............**SNOW** _ _ _ _ _

3. A person made out of snow ....**SNOW** _ _ _

4. A vehicle for traveling on snow............**SNOW** _ _ _ _ _ _

5. Flat webbed frames attached
   to boots for walking on snow...............**SNOW** _ _ _ _ _

6. A heavy, curved metal blade
   used to push snow off the road............**SNOW** _ _ _ _

7. Strong winds and heavy snow..............**SNOW** _ _ _ _ _

Fast 'n' Funny
Why does it snow
in the winter?

*Because snow would
melt in the summer!*

Similar Snowflakes

No two snowflakes are supposed to be exactly alike. But two of these are. Can you spot them?

Playing At The Movies

Popcorn Maze

Help Mervin get through this handful of popcorn.

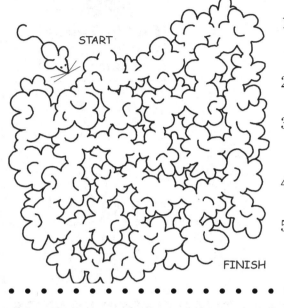

START

FINISH

Merry Poppin'

Popcorn isn't the only word with "pop" in it. How many of these words do you know that start with P-O-P?

1. Cartoon character who
   eats spinach to get strong .... **POP** _ _ _

2. Tall tree with wide leaves........ **POP** _ _ _

3. Garden plant with
   round red flowers.................... **POP** _ _

4. Liked by many people............. **POP** _ _ _ _

5. Tradename for a frozen
   ice treat on two flat sticks .... **POP** _ _ _ _ _

Mystery Menu

You can get a really good deal at the refreshment counter if you can find the secret message hidden in the menu.

refreshmenTs:

Fast 'n' Funny
What is a reptile's
favorite movie?

The Lizard of Oz

Water candy
Orange SODA nachoS
cofFee popcORn
hoT dog HamburgEr
Peanuts RICE cakes
cOla french Fries lemONadE

Secret Message: _____

Now Showing

Fill in the triangles on the screen to see what
movie is being shown at the matinee today.

Happy Endings

The Last Word

This crazy crossword is all squashed together. Not only that, but you can spell some of the answers around corners, and even bottom to top! When you have filled in every square, read the letters from left to right. You will find a funny final message!

The Tail End

These animals are too shy to say goodbye, so they are hiding. But somehow their tails got mixed up with their noses! Draw a line between each happy tail and its proper nose. Can you name the animals, too?

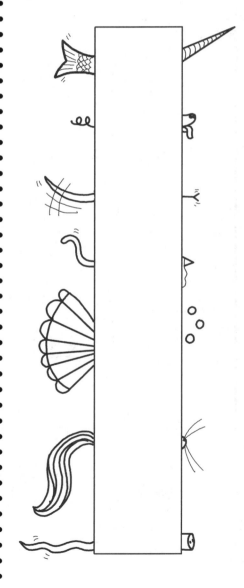

ACROSS

1. The begining of a famous USA song: "Oh say can you _____ ..."
4. The past tense of eat
6. The opposite of none
11. A casual way to say "no"
16. ROCK minus RK
20. The answer to a simple question can be either yes ___ ___ (two words)

DOWN

3. Shirts come in the following sizes: SM, MD and ___
5. A two letter abbreviation for railroad
8. To help
12. Santa usually says three of these in a row
14. Long distance truckers talk to each other on this kind of radio

UP

21. If you are going out with two friends, you would say "___ are leaving now."

AROUND THE CORNER

9. You have a big one on your foot
15. A popular sandwich is ham on _____

SINGLES

2. Q is always found with it
7. The ninth letter of the alphabet
10. The letter after H
13. "Hello" has two of these. Put one of them here
17. The letter before J
18. See 13 — put the other one here
19. The start of "finish"

Tasty Endings

A bit of dessert is a great end to a meal. Can you circle six favorites in the grid below? Then, read the leftover letters to find an end-of-day message!

```
D O C N S O I
T F O O U R C
B R O W N I E
G E K T D K N
T O I B A R R
U S E C E H E
T I H O S E A
P T E E T H M
```

Fast 'n' Funny

How does a bee say goodbye?

Gotta buzz!

How about a marathon racer?

Gotta run!

A gardener?

Seed you later!

A baseball player?

Catch you later!

A salesman?

Buy, buy!

A cheesemaker?

Gouda bye!

Bye, Mervin!

Mervin has finally reached the last page. Look what's waiting for him at the end of the maze! Help Mervin find his way to his new home as quickly as possible. He can follow the roads over and under. Do you think Mervin will be traveling again soon?

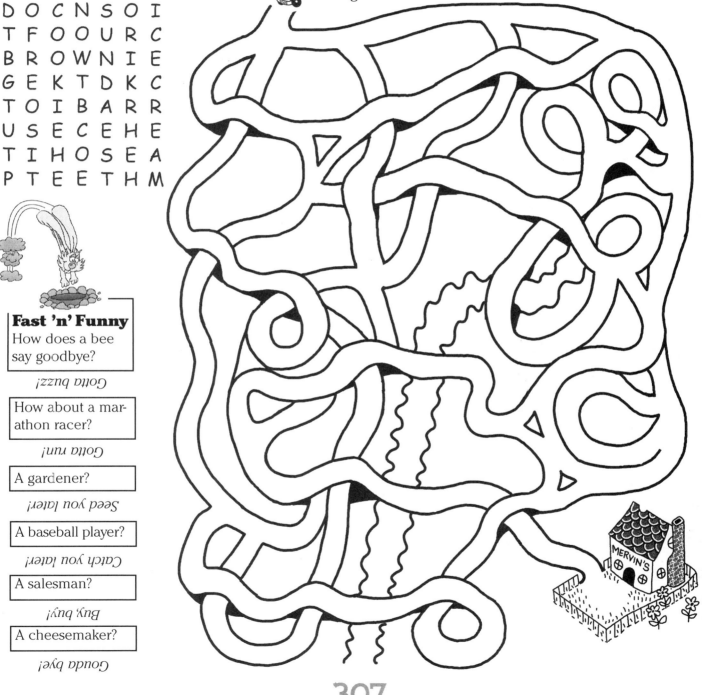

puzzle answers

page 2 • Funny Faces

YOUR NAME!

page 4 • Houses in Houses

I live in a frame. ___PICTURE___
I live in a piggybank. ___MONEY___
I live in a vase. ___FLOWER___
I live in a carton. ___MILK___
I live in a tube. ___TOOTHPASTE___
I live in a deck. ___CARD___
I live in a trashcan. ___GARBAGE___
I live in a book. ___BOOKMARK___
I live in a tank. ___FISH___

I live in a jar. ___COOKIE___
I live in a lamp. ___LIGHTBULB___
I live in a box. ___TISSUE___
I live in a hamper. ___LAUNDRY___
I live in a clock. ___CUCKOO___

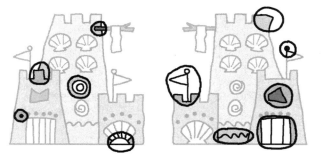

page 5 • Knock, Knock!

1. Anita minute to think it over.

2. Canoe come out and play?

3. Harry up, it's cold out here!

4. Ketchup with me and I'll tell you.

5. Don't you know your own name?

page 6 • No Way!

BECAUSE HE
CAN'T BE A
BROTHER AND
A SISTER,
TOO.

page 7 • Silly Sand

page 7 • Muddy Madness

slithery snake tracks
turtle tracks (tail drags between feet)
web-footed goose tracks
BIG elephant tracks

You can tell that the top track is made by the snake because it is shaped like a snake slithering along. The elephant leaves big, round tracks with his big, round feet. The duck leaves triangular-shaped footprints with his webbed feet. The turtle leaves footprints with a wiggly line running down the middle. That's his tail dragging along behind him! You might have thought these were mouse tracks, but look how big they are compared to the other tracks on the floor. A mouse would leave a MUCH smaller bunch of footprints!

puzzle answers

page 8 • Name Game

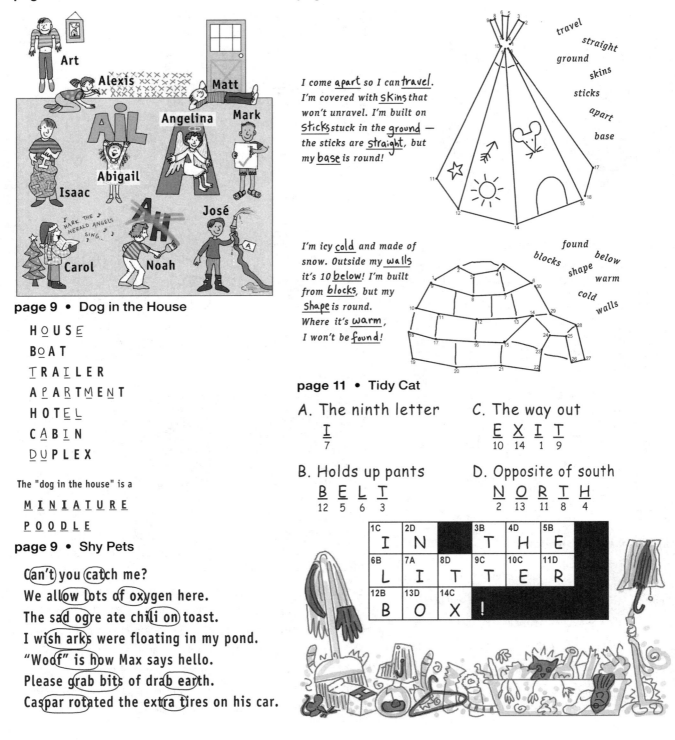

Art, Alexis, Matt, Angelina, Mark, Abigail, Isaac, Carol, Noah, José

page 9 • Dog in the House

H O U S E
B O A T
T R A I L E R
A P A R T M E N T
H O T E L
C A B I N
D U P L E X

The "dog in the house" is a

M I N I A T U R E
P O O D L E

page 9 • Shy Pets

Can't you catch me?
We allow lots of oxygen here.
The sad ogre ate chili on toast.
I wish arks were floating in my pond.
"Woof" is how Max says hello.
Please grab bits of drab earth.
Caspar rotated the extra tires on his car.

page 10 • That's Different!

I come apart so I can travel.
I'm covered with skins that
won't unravel. I'm built on
sticks stuck in the ground —
the sticks are straight, but
my base is round!

travel, straight, ground, skins, sticks, apart, base

I'm icy cold and made of
snow. Outside my walls
it's 10 below! I'm built
from blocks, but my
shape is round.
Where it's warm,
I won't be found!

found, blocks, below, shape, warm, cold, walls

page 11 • Tidy Cat

A. The ninth letter
I
7

B. Holds up pants
B E L T
12 5 6 3

C. The way out
E X I T
10 14 1 9

D. Opposite of south
N O R T H
2 13 11 8 4

1C	2D		3B	4D	5B
I	N		T	H	E
6B	7A	8D	9C	10C	11D
L	I	T	T	E	R
12B	13D	14C			
B	O	X	!		

puzzle answers

page 12 • Who Lives Where?

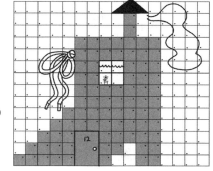

1. LIGHT HOUSE
2. BIRD HOUSE
3. CARD HOUSE
4. HAUNTED HOUSE
5. GINGERBREAD HOUSE

page 13 • What's Weird?

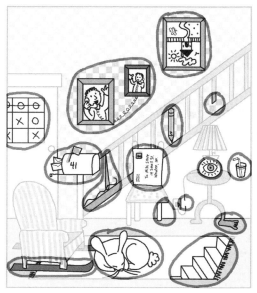

page 14 • The Ha-Ha House

1F, 2E, 3C, 4D, 5A, 6B

page 16 • Autograph Fun

page 17 • Loony Language

Hello, Nadia.
What are you up to?

> Hello, Aidan. I
> just got out of school.

Did you have a good day?

> No! I had
> a lot of tests.

That's too bad. Tomorrow
will be different.

> I hope so!

Well, I have to go. Goodbye!

> Goodbye!

311

puzzle answers

page 17 • Friendly Hink Pinks

A girl friend
<u>G</u> <u>A</u> <u>L</u>
<u>P</u> <u>A</u> <u>L</u>

A dirty friend
<u>M</u> <u>U</u> <u>D</u> <u>D</u> <u>Y</u>
<u>B</u> <u>U</u> <u>D</u> <u>D</u> <u>Y</u>

A wonderful friend
<u>G</u> <u>R</u> <u>E</u> <u>A</u> <u>T</u>
<u>M</u> <u>A</u> <u>T</u> <u>E</u>

A sad friend
<u>G</u> <u>L</u> <u>U</u> <u>M</u>
<u>C</u> <u>H</u> <u>U</u> <u>M</u>

page 18 • Almost Twins

color of daisy
curly stem
brim of hat
neck of T-shirt
pocket on overalls
edge of sleeves
belt
length of shorts
stripes on socks
shoes

page 18 • Looks the Same, But...

bass (kind of fish/deep voice); bow (weapon for shooting arrows/to bend forward); lead (heavy, soft metal/to show the way); sewer (one who sews/pipe to carry away waste); wind (air moving across Earth/wrap something around something else); tear (water from the eye/a rip in fabric)

page 19 • Bead Buddies

YOU
ARE
THE
BEST

page 19 • Just Friends

Boys	Girls
11	10

page 20 • Pucker Up!

Josie and Arlo will make the same amount of money ($3.50) if they sell all their lemonade!

page 20 • Crazy Keyboard

To decipher each letter, number, or symbol in the message, look down one row, and to the right one key.

Y 9 2   E 9   6 9 7   J 9 F 3
HOW   DO   YOU   MOVE

Q   D 9 2 !   7 W 3   Q
A   COW?   USE   A

J 9 9 F 8 H T   F Q H P
MOOVING   VAN!

312

puzzle answers

page 21 • Tough for Two

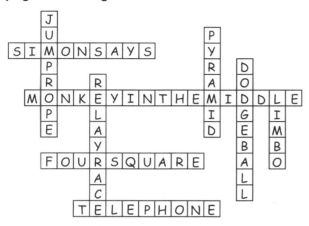

page 22 • Silly Sleepover

The bathtub is a very silly place for a sleepover!

page 23 • Pass It On

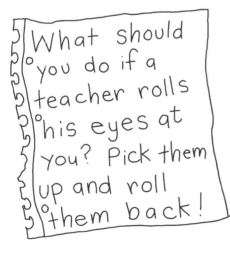

What should you do if a teacher rolls his eyes at you? Pick them up and roll them back!

page 24 • Ready, Set, Go!

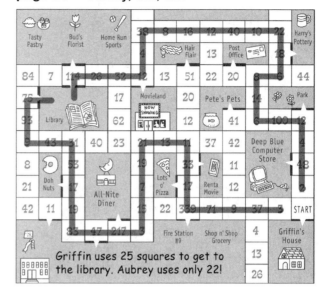

Griffin uses 25 squares to get to the library. Aubrey uses only 22!

page 25 • In the Shadows

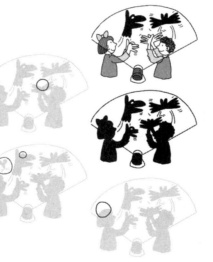

page 28 • Birthday Bowling

Total of pins left standing (86) minus total of pins knocked down (74) is 12. Nayib is 12 years old.

page 26 • Friends to the End

<u>F R I E N D</u> = a person you like who likes you

<u>L E N D</u> = to let a person borrow something

<u>B L E N D</u> = to mix together completely

<u>S P E N D</u> = to pay money

<u>L A V E N D E R</u> = pale purple

<u>M E N D</u> = to fix or repair

<u>T E N D E R</u> = kind or loving

<u>A G E N D A</u> = a list of things to be done

<u>D E F E N D</u> = to protect against danger

<u>E X T E N D</u> = to make longer

<u>L E G E N D</u> = story told for many years

<u>O F F E N D</u> = to cause to be angry

<u>E N D L E S S</u> = never stopping

<u>S L E N D E R</u> = long and thin

<u>A P P E N D I X</u> = info at the end of a book

<u>C A L E N D A R</u> = place to write special dates

<u>S P L E N D I D</u> = really awesome

<u>F E N D E R</u> = metal piece over a bike's wheel

puzzle answers

page 29 • Happy Half

page 29 • Peculiari-tea

MILK SHAKE

SODA (Code: A=1, B=2, C=3, etc.)

JUICE (Code: Substitute the letter before each letter of the message.)

ICED TEA

page 30 • Hink Pinks

A quick present = S W I F T   G I F T

A not real dessert = F A K E   C A K E

A dumb party activity = L A M E   G A M E

page 30 • Kooky Carnival

page 31 • Cake-o-licious

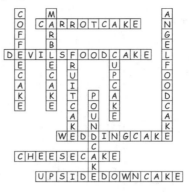

page 32 • Why Do Candles . . .

B	E	C	A	U	S	E		Y	O	U
	C	A	N	'	T		P	U	T	
T	H	E	M		O	N		T	H	E
	B	O	T	T	O	M		O	F	
T	H	E		C	A	K	E	!		

page 32 • What Should You . . .

SPIT OUT THE CANDLES!

page 33 • You're Invited!

Please come to my party!
Date: Saturday, April 1
Time: 5–7 p.m.
Place: 3223 Eva Ave.
Acaloola, CA
Breakfast will be served.
Wear your clothes
backward!
Hannah Anna

To read the invitation, hold it up to a mirror—it is printed backward! Hannah wanted to have this kind of party because she has two names that are the same spelled backward or forward. Parts of her address can be read either way, too.

puzzle answers

page 33 • Goofy Guests

- IMA TROUT
- OLIVE OYL
- STAR E. NITE
- BILL DING
- BEN DOVER
- AL B. RIGHTBACK
- CANDY KANE

page 34 • Crazy Costume

Chloe decided to go as a mermaid!

page 35 • Silly Song

HAPPY BIRTHDAY TO YOU!

HAPPY BIRTHDAY TO YOU!

YOU LOOK LIKE A MONKEY,

AND SMELL LIKE ONE, TOO!

page 36 • Balls of String

T mtutsicatl cthatirts
H bhlhihnd mhahn's hbhlufhf
E esiemoen esaeyes
Y byinygyo
W cwhawrawdes
E feolleow thee eleeaeder
R rrerd lrigrht rgreren rlrigrht
E eleeaepferog
T thot ptotattot
I iduick diuicki goiosie
E heidee eande eseeke
D dstatdudes

page 36 • Find Your Way

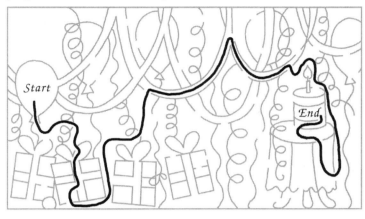

Start — End

page 37 • Looking for Loot

page 38 • Tons of Fun

S R U A S O N I D H I P P I E L G N U J
W M M A C A R N I V A L X P A J A M A S
I Y A B H C E O X A E S E H T R E D N U
M S E C R E T A G E N T S P I Z Z A O S
M T R P I B S S D B E G N I T A K S T T
I E C R S A R T S A N D C R A F T S R H
G Y C N M B T O I T I S T W S D L V I
G N I C A E N P V E N P E E H Y L L E N
N E D E S C I S O R E P X S X O O Y L K
I E W S D U W S M I L Y A D H T R I B D
V W C S B E A G H N A C I G A M A S E N
I O O R O L A F A A V D A N C I N G E A
G L O E S R D W W S H A N U K K A H C S
S L K T S O E C A P S R E T U O S I A N
K A I S O C O M I C B O O K S L R X M O
N H E A D X W W I L D W E S T C L D P G
A T S E I F E D A L S X L B U G S W I A
H S L L O D M O N S T E R S U O S X N R
T S E O R E H R E P U S F I S H I N G D

page 40 • Soup's On!

CLAM CHOWDER *Kind of Soup*

- onions
- clams
- flour
- ~~bathing suit~~
- ~~plastic shovel~~
- potatoes
- ~~clam shells~~
- salt
- ~~dry sand~~
- pepper
- milk
- ~~pebbles~~
- ~~sunscreen~~
- butter

CHICKEN *Kind of Soup*

- water
- chicken
- ~~chicken wire~~
- pepper
- celery
- ~~straw~~
- egg carton
- onion
- ~~chicken feed~~
- carrots
- ~~grit~~
- noodles
- salt
- ~~feathers~~

VEGETABLE *Kind of Soup*

- onion
- celery
- carrots
- zucchini
- potatoes
- ~~glove~~
- tomatoes
- green beans
- water
- ~~watering can~~
- salt
- pepper
- ~~fertilizer~~
- basil
- ~~dirt~~

RED, HOW, WHO, WED, DEW, HER, ROW, OWE, HOE, WOE

puzzle answers

page 41 • What a Mouthful

ap´ əl sôs	*applesauce*
kū´ kum bər	*cucumber*
sī´ dər	*cider*
bə nan´ ə	*banana*
kô´ lə flou´ ər	*cauliflower*
brok´ ə lē	*broccoli*
cher´ ē	*cherry*
säl´ sə	*salsa*
sə lä´ mē	*salami*
av´ ə kä´ dō	*avocado*
bā´ ken	*bacon*

page 43 • Splash!

page 41 • Berry Good

<u>S T R A W</u> BERRY

<u>B L U E</u> BERRY

<u>B L A C K</u> BERRY

<u>C R A N</u> BERRY

<u>R A S P</u> BERRY

<u>G O O S E</u> BERRY

page 42 • Where should you go . . .

K	N	E	A	D	L	E
A	S	F	R	Y	T	E
B	A	K	E	S	A	N
S	I	M	S	T	I	R
D	I	S	T	E	W	C
A	R	O	A	S	T	S
C	E	C	U	T	E	N
O	N	B	R	O	I	L
U	T	O	A	S	T	Y
B	L	E	N	D	I	X
M	E	L	T	A	R	D

page 42 • Dizzy Donuts

Chocolate   Coconut

Powdered

Glazed   Sprinkled

Dad ate 4 donuts, Mom ate 2, Austin ate 3, Caleb ate 3, and Brooke ate only 1 donut!

316

page 44 • Second Helpings

page 46 • S-L-L-L-L-U-U-U-R-R-R-P!

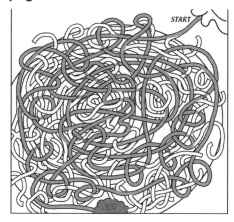

page 47 • How Do You Make . . .

hoT dog   YOgurt   chiPs

Ice cream   hambURger   grilLed cheese

miLk   sAlad

Tuna fish   Taco

french friEs

Answer: Tilt your plate!

page 47 • Fill 'er Up!

page 48 • Scrambled Eggs

WOOFLES   BACON AND LEGS   SCREAM OF WHEAT

puzzle answers

page 48 • Leftovers

CUP <u>CAKE</u>
STRAW <u>BERRY</u>
POTATO <u>SALAD</u>
PEANUT <u>BUTTER</u>
POP <u>CORN</u>
CORN <u>CHIPS</u>
COLE <u>SLAW</u>
HOT <u>DOG</u>
HAM <u>BURGER</u>
FRENCH <u>FRIES</u>
TUNA <u>MELT</u>
APPLE <u>SAUCE</u>
EGG <u>ROLL</u>

page 50 • Daffy Descriptions

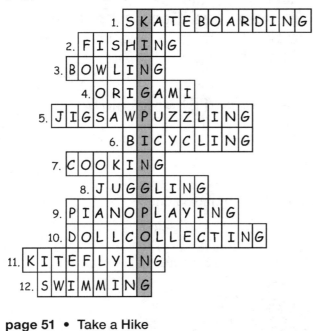

1. SKATEBOARDING
2. FISHING
3. BOWLING
4. ORIGAMI
5. JIGSAWPUZZLING
6. BICYCLING
7. COOKING
8. JUGGLING
9. PIANOPLAYING
10. DOLLCOLLECTING
11. KITEFLYING
12. SWIMMING

page 51 • Take a Hike

WHY		IS	MOUNTAIN		CLIMBING		AN
EASY		HOBBY		TO	START		IF	YOU
ARE	OLD?		BECAUSE		YOU		ARE
ALREADY	OVER		THE		HILL!

page 52 • Tacky Ties

page 53 • Too Much Fun

being a clown, riding a unicycle, juggling, reading about cats, photography, listening to music, playing the trumpet, cards, collecting butterflies, collecting stamps

page 53 • Cool Collections

```
S T A M P S H O V E G
F O O S H B I N G P O
F L O C O I N S C A L
X J E L L Y F I S H O
T Y P E S H E L L S H
O K R O W E M O H T A
M A R B L E S M I L E
B A N A T I S S U E S
F O H A T S D U S K Y
S L L O D L P E A S N
O P A L G R E E N Q U
L I G H T B U L B S P
R U N T R R O C K S I
Q S T A P L E S A N D
N O T S E L D O O N O
O V E R D U C A R D S
C O T T O N C A N D Y
S K O O B W O R M S T
```

Might Collect: stamps, coins, shells, rocks, marbles, books, cards, dolls, hats. Would Never Collect: worms, jellyfish, homework, peas, tissues, light bulbs, noodles, staples, cotton candy

puzzle answers

page 54 • Absurd Authors

page 54 • Camera Chaos

page 55 • Movie Night

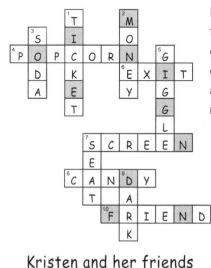

Kristen and her friends like doing crossword puzzles, doing scrambles, and going to the movies!

Kristen and her friends saw *Finding Nemo.*

page 56 • Whittle Away

page 56 • Totally Tiles

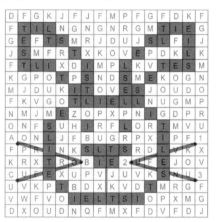

page 57 • Milo's Magic

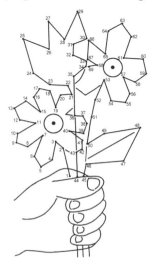

puzzle answers

page 57 • Go Fly a Kite

Kaity's kite was red and _white_ .
To her _delight_ , it flew to a
great _height_ . She hung on
tight with all her _might_ ,
but the kite veered sharply to
the _right_ . Snap went the
string! "Oh, no!" Kaity cried with
fright , as her _bright_
new _kite_ flew out of
sight .

page 58 • Loony Tunes

page 59 • Sticky Stamps

1. There are five bird stamps and only four patriotic
stamps. 2. Birds are on the most number of stamps.
3. Teddy bears are on the four almost-identical
stamps. 4. The stamp with the fox on it has the
most postage (.48 cents).

page 60 • What do you ask . . .

TENT-ACLES
80 32 56 80 - 8 24 48 32 72

page 60 • Dot's Dominoes

```
-3  +7  +7  -2  -2  +8  -3  -2  +5  -3  -3
-3                                      +5
+7                                      +5
+5                                      -3
-3  +5  -4  +7   8   START    -4  +6  +6  -1
```

45. Here's a helpful hint—First make a list of the number of dots on each of the dominoes from START to
END. Then go back and add the plus and minus signs
according to the rules!

page 62 • Loopy Hoops

Dark Shirts: 212 points
Light Shirts: 201 points

Light shirts win!

320

puzzle answers

page 63 • Happy Camper

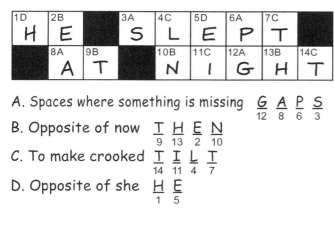

1D	2B		3A	4C	5D	6A	7C	
H	E		S	L	E	P	T	
	8A	9B		10B	11C	12A	13B	14C
	A	T		N	I	G	H	T

A. Spaces where something is missing G A P S
$\quad$ 12 8 6 3

B. Opposite of now T H E N
$\quad$ 9 13 2 10

C. To make crooked T I L T
$\quad$ 14 11 4 7

D. Opposite of she H E
$\quad$ 1 5

page 63 • What Should You Put . . .

What should you put on
before you get dressed
to be in a relay race?

RUN-DERWEAR!

page 64 • Why does everyone . . .

THEY ARE GREAT
AT CATCHING FLIES!

page 65 • Which ghost . . .

1. Player wears this on his head = METHEL H E L M E T
2. Score! = CHDOTOUWN T O U C H D O W N
3. To handle clumsily = LEBMUF F U M B L E
4. To bring a player to the ground = CAKTEL T A C K L E
5. Shirt with a number on it = SERJYE J E R S E Y
6. To receive the ball = CHATC C A T C H
7. Midway through the game = METIHAFL H A L F T I M E
8. Important January game = PRUES LOWB S U P E R B O W L
9. Throw ball to another player = SAPS P A S S
10. Catch ball meant for other team = CEPTERINT I N T E R C E P T
11. Three feet = DAYR Y A R D
12. The game is played on this = LEDIF F I E L D
13. He leads the team = TRAQUEBRACK Q U A R T E R B A C K

page 66 • What is the hardest . . .

page 67 • Go Team!

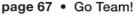

puzzle answers

page 68 • Why do soccer . . .

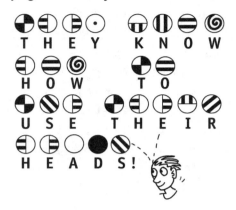

THEY KNOW
HOW TO
USE THEIR
HEADS!

page 69 • Archery Addition

Archibald
$$30 + 40 = 70$$
$$70 - 10 = 60$$

Annibelle
$$50 + 30 = 80$$
$$80 - 20 = 60$$

Ace
$$30 + 20 + 10 = 60$$
$$60 + 5 \text{ (bonus)} = 65$$

page 70 • X-treme Sports

BUNGEE JUMPING

ROCK CLIMBING

SKY DIVING

MOTORCYCLE RACING

page 70 • On Your Mark!

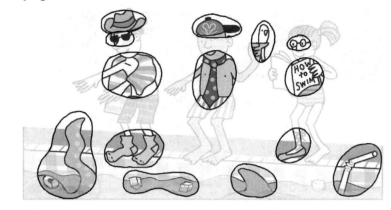

page 71 • Goofy Golf

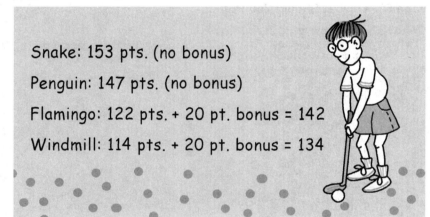

Snake: 153 pts. (no bonus)

Penguin: 147 pts. (no bonus)

Flamingo: 122 pts. + 20 pt. bonus = 142

Windmill: 114 pts. + 20 pt. bonus = 134

page 72 • Crazy Coach

D **Bassocketcerball**
Basketball and Soccer

C **Gymtennasnistics**
Gymnastics and Tennis

A **Icefootskatballing**
Ice Skating and Football

E **Tracycckling**
Track and Cycling

B **Golarcherfy**
Golf and Archery

puzzle answers

page 72 • Shadow Race

page 74 • To the Top!

page 74 • What is a tornado's favorite party game?

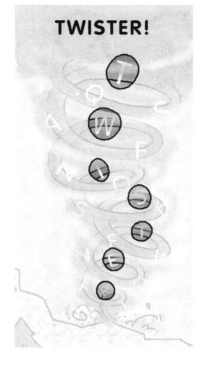

page 75 • Not Hot!

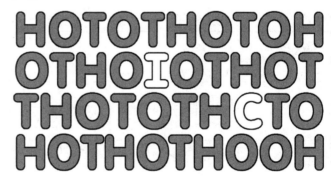

page 75 • The Silly Answer Is "Sunlight"!

323

puzzle answers

page 76 • Whoooosh!

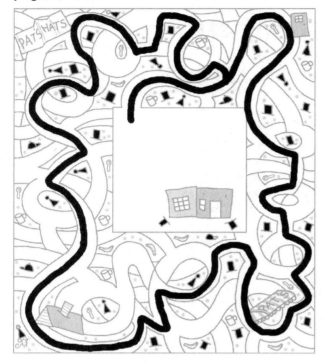

page 78 • What Is a Tree's Favorite Drink?

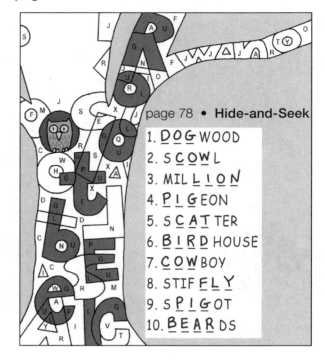

page 78 • Hide-and-Seek

1. D<u>O</u><u>G</u>WOOD
2. S<u>C</u>OWL
3. MIL<u>LI</u>ON
4. P<u>I</u><u>G</u>EON
5. S<u>CAT</u>TER
6. <u>BIRD</u>HOUSE
7. <u>COW</u>BOY
8. STIF<u>FLY</u>
9. S<u>PI</u><u>G</u>OT
10. <u>BEAR</u>DS

page 77 • Wacky Weather

March

Sun.	Mon.	Tues.	Wed.	Thurs.	Fri.	Sat.
		1	2	3	4	5
6	7	8	9	10	11	12
13	14	15	16	17	18	19
20	21	22	23	24	25	26
27	28	29	30	31	Notes: A very nice month!	

page 79 • Animal Addition

word for soil	GROUND
+ word for pig	HOG
= a woodchuck	GROUNDHOG
breathe quickly	PANT
+ opposite of him	HER
= dark leopard	PANTHER
pet you ride	HORSE
+ foot covering	SHOE
+ cranky person	CRAB
= seashore animal	HORSESHOE CRAB
role in a play	PART
+ chain of hills	RIDGE
= game bird	PARTRIDGE
pull slowly	DRAG
+ atop =	ON
+ move through the air	FLY
= long, thin insect	DRAGONFLY
a small boy	TAD
+ long, thin piece of wood	POLE
= baby frog	TADPOLE

puzzle answers

page 80 • The Silly Answer Is "You"!

W	H	A	T		L	O	O	K	S		L	I	K	E
A		M	O	N	K	E	Y	,		C	A	N		B	E
	F	O	U	N	D		I	N		Z	O	O	S	,
A	N	D		I	S		A	S		L	A	R	G	E
A	S		A		H	U	M	A	N		C	H	I	L	D	?

page 80 • Where's the Weather?

How **ind**ependent Kevin **is now**!

I certainly hope the river **runs und**er our house.

Kami stole the cobra **in** Concord.

The twins were **both under** the bed.

Two gruff ogres **hum id**entical tunes.

The Earth **ails** when recycling fails.

Winston **scolds** Eric loudly.

The **aisle Ethan** walked down was skinny.

page 81 • Rain Man, Sun Man

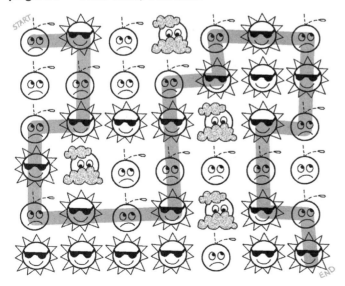

page 81 • What nickname do . . .

SUNNY!

page 82 • Secret Garden

1. gets cut in summer	7.	TREE
2. smells nice	2.	FLOWER
3. falls in Fall	11.	WORM
4. freezes in Winter	4.	WATER
5. makes walls	10.	BUTTERFLY
6. grows from seeds	5.	STONE
7. blooms in Spring	6.	PLANTS
8. grows in pods	8.	PEAS
9. running water	1.	GRASS
10. sips flowers	9.	STREAM
11. eats dirt	3.	LEAF

page 83 • The Silly Answer Is "Water"!

CARE	WAS	WIN
ONCE	RUN	**WHAT**
OCEAN	**RUNS**	SUN
MAN	WEAR	BEAR
AIR	ONLY	STARE
POND	**BUT**	FUN
NEVER	BUN	LAKE
CAR	OKAY	**WALKS**

puzzle answers

page 83 • Zany Rainy

page 84 • Dark Shadows

page 86 • What Do You Call It . . .

meat = **S T E A K**   phony = **F A K E**   damage = **B R E A K**

pain = **A C H E**   reptile = **S N A K E**   dessert = **C A K E**

cook = **B A K E**   male duck = **D R A K E**   error = **M I S T A K E**

snow = **F L A K E**   alert = **A W A K E**

tool = **R A K E**

page 87 • Go! Go! Go!

Not silver = G O L D

Long dress = G O W N

Turkey noise = G O B B L E

Large ape = G O R I L L A

Not hello = G O O D B Y E

A cart = W A G O N

Fairytale lizard = D R A G O N

Didn't remember = F O R G O T

Western state = O R E G O N

Spanish friend = A M I G O

Deep blue = I N D I G O

City in Illinois = C H I C A G O

puzzle answers

page 88 • Peculiar Passport

New Zealand
England
Mexico
United States
Thailand
North Korea
Norway
China
Yugoslavia
Australia

In 2003, the country of Yugoslavia was renamed Serbia and Montenegro. This happened after Yugoslavia's 10-year civil war.

page 89 • Potholes

<u>road</u> hog   <u>car</u> go

<u>road</u> map   <u>car</u> pet

<u>road</u> way   <u>car</u> fare

<u>road</u> runner   <u>car</u> pool

<u>road</u> side   <u>car</u> sick

page 89 • Amazing Liberty

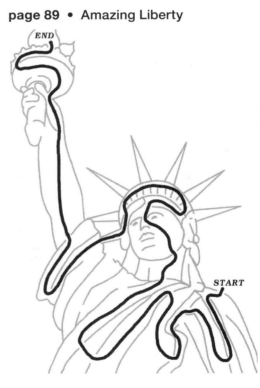

page 89 • USA, ABC

National Monuments

FORT SUM<u>T</u>ER

<u>M</u>OU<u>N</u>T RUSHM<u>O</u>RE

<u>ST</u>AT<u>U</u>E OF LIBERTY

<u>C</u>ASA GRAN<u>D</u>E

National Parks

G<u>R</u>EAT <u>S</u>MOKEY MOUN<u>T</u>AINS

VALL<u>E</u>Y F<u>O</u>R<u>G</u>E

C<u>A</u>RLS<u>B</u>AD <u>C</u>AVERNS

PET<u>R</u>IFIED FORE<u>ST</u>

page 90 • Totally Travel

<u>P</u>eter's <u>P</u>lane <u>P</u>owered <u>P</u>ast <u>P</u>aper <u>P</u>yramids.

<u>T</u>om <u>T</u>ook <u>T</u>en <u>T</u>iny <u>T</u>rains <u>T</u>o <u>T</u>oronto.

<u>C</u>arla's <u>C</u>amera <u>C</u>aught <u>C</u>amping <u>C</u>amels.

<u>S</u>teven <u>S</u>ilently <u>S</u>ailed <u>S</u>ideways.

<u>B</u>ob's <u>B</u>us <u>B</u>ounced <u>B</u>riskly <u>B</u>ackwards.

<u>M</u>itch <u>M</u>errily <u>M</u>aneuvered <u>M</u>ama's <u>M</u>otorcycle.

puzzle answers

page 90 • Hi-Ho Hink Pinks

Undecorated track-rider = <u>P L A I N</u>   <u>T R A I N</u>

Celebrity vehicle = <u>S T A R</u>   <u>C A R</u>

Commotion on public transport = <u>B U S</u>   <u>F U S S</u>

Not-crazy flying vehicle = <u>S A N E</u>   <u>P L A N E</u>

Long trip on two-wheeler = <u>B I K E</u>   <u>H I K E</u>

Jacket for floating vehicle = <u>B O A T</u>   <u>C O A T</u>

Big vehicle for chickens = <u>C L U C K</u>   <u>T R U C K</u>

Huge car for hire = <u>M A X I</u>   <u>T A X I</u>

An intelligent, small wagon = <u>S M A R T</u>   <u>C A R T</u>

page 91 • What 10-letter word . . .

The fifth letter	E
Right after K	L
Between H and J	I
Right before C	B
Right before P	O
Right after L	M
Between N and P	O
Right after S	T
One before V	U
The first letter	A

page 91 • Why is traveling by boat . . .

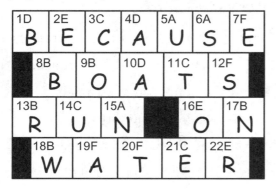

1D	2E	3C	4D	5A	6A	7F
B	E	C	A	U	S	E

	8B	9B	10D	11C	12F	
	B	O	A	T	S	

13B	14C	15A		16E	17B
R	U	N		O	N

	18B	19F	20F	21C	22E	
	W	A	T	E	R	

page 91 • Why is traveling by boat . . . (continued)

A. Shines in the sky

<u>S</u> <u>U</u> <u>N</u>
6 5 15

D. Sheep sound

<u>B</u> <u>A</u> <u>A</u>
1 4 10

B. Color of mud

<u>B</u> <u>R</u> <u>O</u> <u>W</u> <u>N</u>
8 13 9 18 17

E. Rock, mineral

<u>O</u> <u>R</u> <u>E</u>
16 22 2

C. Pretty, charming

<u>C</u> <u>U</u> <u>T</u> <u>E</u>
3 14 11 21

F. You sit on this

<u>S</u> <u>E</u> <u>A</u> <u>T</u>
12 7 19 20

page 92 • Out the Window

page 92 • What has eight wheels and flies?

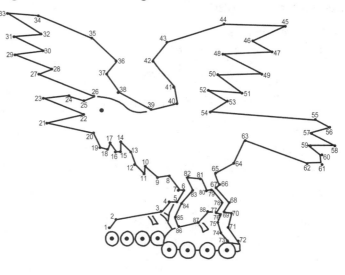

puzzle answers

page 93 • Hidden Jungle

page 94 • Time to Get Up!

The correct time for the Avion family to get up is 5:45 A.M.

page 94 • Time to Leave!

The correct time to leave for the airport is 6:30 A.M.

page 95 • The Great Race

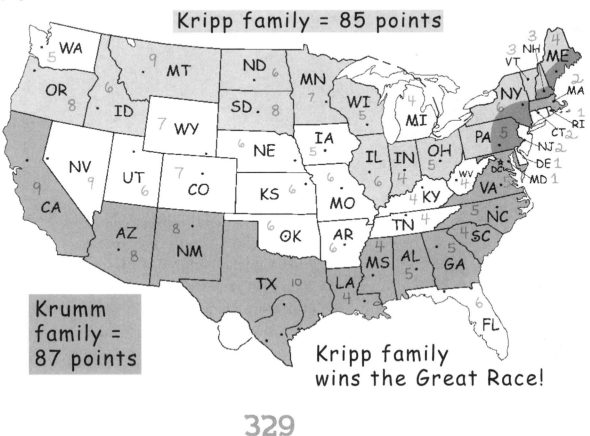

Kripp family = 85 points

Krumm family = 87 points

Kripp family wins the Great Race!

puzzle answers

page 96 • See You Later

```
        C I A O
    S E S H A L O M G E
    Y O U L E T O F A O A T
    E R Z A L E L H I T O S G A
    T K W A H E R I A O U D A A R I
    N A W I H I I L E C S B Y N R O
    C O D I J E A O S E E C Y O T Y O U
    A U F W I E D E R S E H E N I B L A
    T E R S A A I L L H I G A A O L T O
    W T T F N R O I N E A F A R V E L W
    H I L E C S R O J C O D A I S L
    T O T Z I E N S H E S E E Y S O
    U L A R R I V E D E R C I A
    T E R A L L J I F A T O
    R A U R E V O I R I
        N A W H
```

page 98 • Wanda Wonders

page 99 • Wish Upon a Star

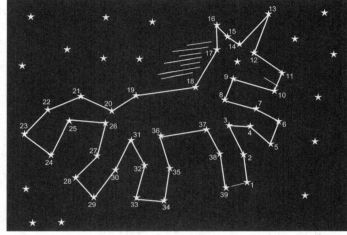

page 100 • Gnop Gnip

Hold the book up to a mirror, and tilt the top edge of the book slightly toward you. You will see that the message reads" "A ping pong ball bouncing backward!"

page 100 • Gobbledygook

1. What are you doing?
2. Where is the party?
3. I can't see you anywhere!
4. What is your favorite color?
5. Who is your best friend?

puzzle answers

page 101 • Imagine That!

pocketbook into medical person
PURSE to NURSE

baked dessert into garden tool
CAKE to RAKE

what you read into curved metal hanger
BOOK to HOOK

middle of your face into a flower
NOSE to ROSE

finger jewelry into male royalty
RING to KING

bird's home into a sleeveless sweater
NEST to VEST

penny into portable shelter
CENT to TENT

baby bear into bathtime place
CUB to TUB

long, soft seat into a drawstring bag
COUCH to POUCH

feline pet into baseball stick
CAT to BAT

dotted cubes into small rodents
DICE to MICE

street into cousin of a frog
ROAD to TOAD

teddy into fruit
BEAR to PEAR

page 102 • Hand in Glove

paper and pencil, comb and brush, stamp and envelope, hammer and nail, table and chair, sock and shoe, pot and pan, key and lock, spoon and fork, needle and thread, hide and seek, now and then

page 103 • Noble Knight

H	A	U	O	R
T	E	N	R	K
H	O	L	T	T
V	P	A	N	H
S	R	U	O	R

1. HONOR
2. TRUTH
3. HEART
4. VALOR
5. SPUNK

page 103 • Creative Cook

SOUP

SOAP — makes bubbles

SOAR — to fly up high

OARS — used to row boats

OATS — cereal grains

RATS — big rodents

RUTS — grooves in the ground

NUTS

page 104 • Hopping Harry

8	22	40	**25**	**9**	**43**	66	**START 19**
90	**39**	**7**	**53**	32	**81**	14	**51**
46	**3**	18	64	6	**77**	**95**	**3**
12	**49**	**27**	**17**	**35**	58	12	34
2	10	82	70	**19**	4	86	27
7	**23**	**41**	96	**1**	18	54	9
11	16	**9**	44	**65**	33	17	45
5	38	**55**	**13**	**3**	76	8	20
7 END	22	12	8	6	13	10	3

331

puzzle answers

page 105 • **Lotsa Lists**

1. Holidays: New Year's, Valentine's, Easter, Fourth of July, Halloween, Thanksgiving, Hanukkah, Christmas
2. Weather: Sunny, cloudy, rainy, foggy, windy, snowy
3. Pets: Cat, dog, bird, fish, gerbil or guinea pig, horse or hamster, snake
4. Colors: Red, yellow, blue, green, orange, purple, black, white
5. Vehicles: Car, bus, train, bike, plane, motorcycle, boat

page 105 • **Quick Catalog**

cot, cat, log, tag, got, lot, lag, oat, ago, cog, gal. Did you happen to find a coat and a goat and a goal hiding in the catalog, too?

page 106 • **Triple Triangles**

page 106 • **Double Trouble**

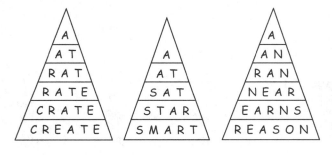

page 107 • **Crossed Creatures**

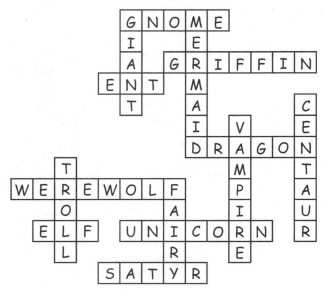

page 108 • **Black or White?**

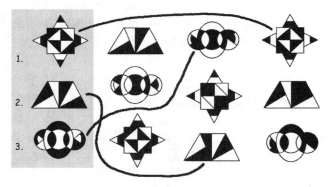

page 108 • **Who's Crazy Now?**

WHAT DO YOU CALL A CRAZY BAKER?

A DOUGH NUT!

332

puzzle answers

page 112 • Roman Numerals

Answer: CLOCK

+

Answer: WATCH

page 114 • When in Rome

149	14	2660	922	1606	14	61
N	A	T	U	R	A	L

149	922	411	29	8	1606	751
N	U	M	B	E	R	S

page 115 • Hidden Numbers

1. I love my computer — when it works!
2. Beth reeked of smoke after sitting by the campfire.
3. My mother likes to weigh tomatoes on every scale in the store.
4. Annie was even early for school last week!
5. We can stuff our dirty backpacks in your tent.
6. We like the mirrored maze room at the fun park.

page 116 • Practice Your Digits

START 3	3	4	2	3
4	1	1	2	2
2	4	3	1	4
2	3	1	4	3
4	2	1	2	END E

START 4	2	1	2	3	4
3	3	4	2	3	4
4	2	4	2	4	3
3	2	1	3	2	4
2	2	4	2	3	4
4	1	4	1	2	END E

page 117 • On or Off?
T-O-O-T-H   T-H-I-R-T-Y

333

puzzle answers

pages 118–119 • Making Sense of the Irrational

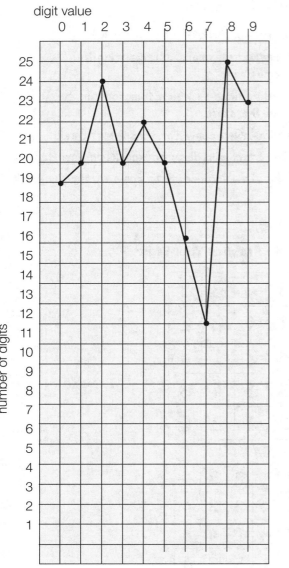

page 121 • See What I Mean?

page 124 • Clock Math

10 + 12 = **T**
3 + 4 = **O**
10 + 9 = **O**
1 − 3 = **T**
5 − 2 = **H**

11 + 4 = **H**
8 + 3 = **U**
11 − 3 = **R**
11 − 1 = **T**
12 + 12 = **Y**

page 126 • Magic Squares

There is more than one way to complete the magic squares, but the solutions will be similar. Here is one way of solving each magic square.

Magic Square 5

8	3	4
1	5	9
6	7	2

Magic Square 10

16	6	8
2	10	18
12	14	4

Magic Square 9

15	5	7
1	9	17
11	13	3

Magic Square 0

3	-2	-1
-4	0	4
1	2	-3

Magic Square 1

4	-1	0
-3	1	5
2	3	-2

Magic Square 4X4

16	2	3	13
5	11	10	8
9	7	6	12
4	14	15	1

page 120 • Let's Get Packing

1. Call Kelly Short for directions to State park.
2. Buy sun block and bug spray.
3. Check the flashlight batteries.
4. Fill water bottles, make snacks, and get chocolate!
5. Pack ponchos and extra socks.
6. Find binoculars and bird books.

334

puzzle answers

pages 129–132 •
Solve a Cross-
Number Puzzle

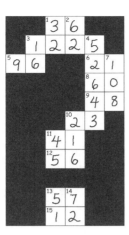

page 133 • Cross Sums

page 134 • It's My Favorite!

I LOVE TO ADD

page 138 • Multiplication Boxes

-4	5	-20
-9	6	-54
36	30	1080

7	10	70
11	-1	-11
77	-10	-770

7	3	21
-5	-2	10
-35	-6	210

-3	6	-18
7	-8	-56
-21	-48	1008

page 139 • Musical Math

$5\overline{)95} = 19$ $4\overline{)72} = 18$ $3\overline{)87} = 29$ $6\overline{)84} = 14$

$7\overline{)175} = 25$ $3\overline{)141} = 47$

$8\overline{)168} = 21$ $6\overline{)264} = 44$

$8\overline{)264} = 33$ $6\overline{)186} = 31$

Y	A	U	O	R	N	Y	M
31	45	47	16	19	12	21	29
R	E	B	R	M	G	A	W
44	13	15	33	25	18	22	14

What comes before a tuba?
Answer: A one-ba!

puzzle answers

page 141 • The Sieve of Eratosthenes

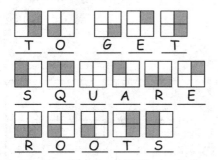

Prime Numbers: 2, 3, 5, 7, 11, 13, 17, 19, 23, 29, 31, 37, 41, 43, 47, 53, 59, 61, 67, 71, 73, 79, 83, 89, 97

page 145 • Squares and Radicals

$5^2 = 25$; $6^2 = 36$; $7^2 = 49$; $8^2 = 64$; $9^2 = 81$; $10^2 = 100$; $11^2 = 121$; $12^2 = 144$; $13^2 = 169$; $14^2 = 196$; $15^2 = 225$; $16^2 = 256$; $17^2 = 289$; $18^2 = 324$; $19^2 = 361$; $20^2 = 400$

page 146 • Goofy Gardener

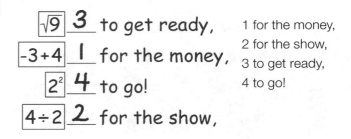

T O G E T
S Q U A R E
R O O T S

page 147 • A Radical Sign

$\sqrt{9} = 3$; $\sqrt{16} = 4$; $\sqrt{25} = 5$; $\sqrt{49} = 7$; $\sqrt{64} = 8$; $\sqrt{81} = 9$; $\sqrt{100} = 10$.

page 148 • On Your Mark!

$\boxed{\sqrt{9}}$ **3** to get ready,

$\boxed{-3+4}$ **1** for the money,

$\boxed{2^2}$ **4** to go!

$\boxed{4 \div 2}$ **2** for the show,

1 for the money,
2 for the show,
3 to get ready,
4 to go!

page 149 • How Four Can You Go?

$2 = (4 \times 4 \div 4) \div \sqrt{4}$

$3 = (4 + 4 + 4) \div 4$

$4 = \sqrt{(4 \times 4 \times 4)} - 4$

$5 = (4 \times 4 + 4) \div 4$

$6 = (4 + 4 + 4) \div \sqrt{4}$

$7 = 4 + [(4 + \sqrt{4}) \div \sqrt{4}]$

$8 = 4 \times 4 \div 4 + 4$

$9 = 4 + 4 + (4 \div 4)$

$10 = 4 \times 4 - 4 - \sqrt{4}$

$11 = 44 \div (\sqrt{4} + \sqrt{4})$

$12 = \sqrt{(4 \times 4 \times 4)} + 4$

$13 = (44 \div 4) + \sqrt{4}$

$14 = 4 + 4 + 4 + \sqrt{4}$

$15 = (4 \times 4) - (4 \div 4)$

puzzle answers

page 150 • Your Number's Up

1. ONE STEP AT A TIME / HOLE IN ONE / A LONELY NUMBER
2. TEA FOR TWO / DICE IN A MONOPOLY GAME
3. LITTLE PIGS / THREE MUSKETEERS
4. QUARTERS IN A DOLLAR / 4 PRIVET DRIVE (The Dursleys' address in Harry Potter)
5. POINTS ON A STAR / OLYMPIC RINGS / SCHOOL DAYS IN A WEEK
6. HALF A DOZEN / LEGS ON AN INSECT
7. DWARVES WITH SNOW WHITE / DAYS IN A WEEK
8. ARMS ON AN OCTOPUS / OUNCES IN A CUP / FIGURE 8 IN ICE SKATING / EIGHT SIDES ON A STOP SIGN
9. CAT LIVES / PLANETS IN OUR SOLAR SYSTEM
10. FINGERS OR TOES / COMMANDMENTS
11. PLAYERS ON A FOOTBALL OR SOCCER TEAM / POLLO 11 MISSION TO THE MOON
12. MONTHS IN A YEAR / NUMBERS ON A CLOCK FACE
13. AN UNLUCKY NUMBER / STRIPES ON THE U.S. FLAG
14. FEBRUARY 14 IS VALENTINE'S DAY
15. MINUTES IN A QUARTER OF AN HOUR
16. OUNCES IN A POUND
17. TITLE OF A TEEN MAGAZINE / AMERICAN REVOLUTION STARTED IN 1776
18. HOLES ON A GOLF COURSE / AN AGE WHEN YOU ARE OLD ENOUGH TO VOTE
19. 1984 (title of a book) / BUILDING 19 (a discount store)
20. FINGERS AND TOES (all together) / 20 THOUSAND LEAGUES UNDER THE SEA (title of a book)
21. ANOTHER NAME FOR THE GAME OF BLACK JACK/ THE CENTURY WE ARE IN
22. FEBRUARY 22 IS GEORGE WASHINGTON'S BIRTHDAY
23. MICHAEL JORDAN'S NUMBER / CHROMOSOMES IN A HUMAN BEING
24. HOURS IN A DAY / TWO DOZEN
25. DECEMBER 25 IS CHRISTMAS DAY / A SILVER ANNIVERSARY
50. U.S. STATES / STARS ON THE U.S. FLAG
100 "ONE HUNDRED BOTTLES OF BEER ON THE WALL" SONG / PERFECT SCORE ON A TEST

page 152 • Shape Changers

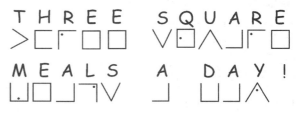

page 153 • Six-Sided Math

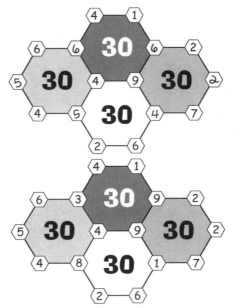

page 154 • Hide in Plain Sight

puzzle answers

page 155 • Life of the Party

1	2	3	4	5	6	7	8	9
P	O	I	N	T	L	E	S	S

page 156 • Going Around in Circles

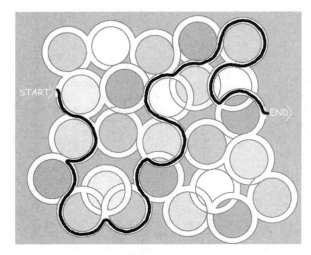

page 158 • The Last Straw

Tape the tips of three straws together to form a triangle that lies flat on the table. Now, take the remaining three straws and tape them so that one stands upright from each of the three corners. Finally, lean the three straws toward the center and tape all three tips together so that you have an open pyramid. This is called a "tetrahedron," and it is made up of one triangle lying flat on the table plus three more triangles for the upright side.

page 159 • Get to the Point!

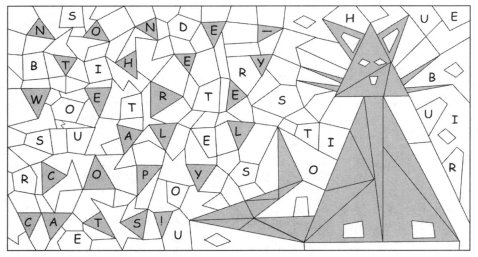

Answer: None — they were all copy cats!

puzzle answers

pages 160–161 • On a Treasure Hunt

The Windy Hill

1. Her father was afraid of ghosts and wouldn't want his money close to the cemetery. Cross out the cemetery.

2. Cash Steele did not like small dark places either. Cross out mine shaft, well, and cave.

3. If he buried the money, it would be to the north of his cabin. There are no underground hiding places left north of the cabin, so he must not have buried his money. Cross out dino bones.

4. If he hid it aboveground, it would be south of the cabin. Both the barn and the Lone Pine are north of the cabin, so cross those out.

5. If he didn't hide it in the well, then he didn't hide it in the windmill, either. He didn't hide it in the well (you've already crossed it out), so you can cross out the windmill as well. Now, the only other hiding place left is Windy Hill, which is the answer.

page 163 • A Square Deal

```
4 2 4 3 1 3 4 2 4
2 1 2 4 3 4 2 1 2
1 2 4 3 2 3 4 2 3
3 4 3 2 1 2 3 4 1
4 3 2 1 4 1 2 1 2
3 4 3 2 1 2 3 4 1
1 2 4 3 2 3 4 2 3
2 1 2 4 1 4 2 1 2
4 2 4 1 3 1 4 2 4
```

page 163 • The Domino Effect

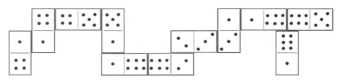

Dominoes work by matching the open numbers, so that a 1 goes next to a 1, a 2 next to a 2, and so on.

page 166 •

A Giraffe

page 164 • Picture This

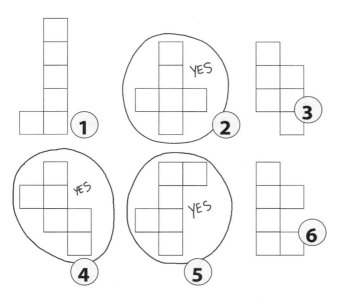

page 167 • Hink Pinks

1. Pile of games that weighs 2,000 lbs. — FUN TON
2. 5,280 foot grin — MILE SMILE
3. Two pastries that are each 12 inches long — SWEET FEET
4. Very difficult 3 feet — HARD YARD
5. Rubber ball that weighs 16 ounces — ROUND POUND
6. 28.4 grams that jumps quickly — OUNCE POUNCE
7. Urgent message that weighs 2.2 pounds — KILOGRAM TELEGRAM

puzzle answers

page 168 •
Star Power

page 171 • Measuring Your ZZZs

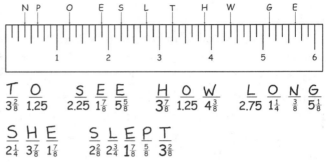

$\underset{3\frac{2}{8}}{T}\ \underset{1.25}{O}$ $\underset{2.25}{S}\ \underset{1\frac{7}{8}}{E}\ \underset{5\frac{5}{8}}{E}$ $\underset{3\frac{7}{8}}{H}\ \underset{1.25}{O}\ \underset{4\frac{3}{8}}{W}$ $\underset{2.75}{L}\ \underset{1\frac{1}{4}}{O}\ \underset{\frac{3}{8}}{N}\ \underset{5\frac{1}{8}}{G}$

$\underset{2\frac{1}{4}}{S}\ \underset{3\frac{7}{8}}{H}\ \underset{1\frac{7}{8}}{E}$ $\underset{2\frac{2}{8}}{S}\ \underset{2\frac{3}{4}}{L}\ \underset{1\frac{7}{8}}{E}\ \underset{\frac{5}{8}}{P}\ \underset{3\frac{2}{8}}{T}$

---

pages 169–170 • A Weighty Matter

Blue whale

page 172 •
Lost Billions

```
B I L L I O N N S B B I
B I L S B S N O I L B
I B S S N B I L L O N S
L N N B O B I L L N O
L N I O I I B B O B I
L O O I L B O L I B I L
I I L L O B S I L O B I
O L L L O N L B O I S L
N L I B I L I O B B I I
S I B L I B O B I L I B
I B L B B I L O O N S I
O B B I L I O O N S O L
```

page 173 • Googols of Fun

$\underset{A}{1}$ $\underset{G}{7}\cdot\underset{O}{15}\cdot\underset{O}{15}\cdot\underset{G}{7}\cdot\underset{O}{15}\cdot\underset{L}{12}$ $\underset{H}{8}\cdot\underset{A}{1}\cdot\underset{S}{19}$

A G O O G O L   H A S

$\underset{O}{15}\cdot\underset{N}{14}\cdot\underset{E}{5}$ $\underset{H}{8}\cdot\underset{U}{21}\cdot\underset{N}{14}\cdot\underset{D}{4}\cdot\underset{R}{18}\cdot\underset{E}{5}\cdot\underset{D}{4}$

O N E   H U N D R E D

$\underset{Z}{26}\cdot\underset{E}{5}\cdot\underset{R}{18}\cdot\underset{O}{15}\cdot\underset{S}{19}$

Z E R O S

---

page 174 • On Your Toes

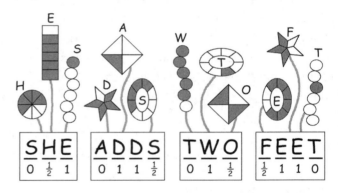

SHE 0 ½ 1   **ADDS** 0 1 1 ½   **TWO** 0 1 ½   **FEET** ½ 1 1 0

pages 176–177 • Logical Math

1. The other one is a nickel!
2. 99 + (9 ÷ 9) = 100
3. 30 ÷ 15 = 2 and 2 + 10 = 12. Note: 30 divided by half is not the same as 30 divided in half.
4. You have the three apples you took away.
5. "A pie in the face."
6. "One in a million."
7. "Six of one, half a dozen of another."
8. He weighs meat!

page 178 • Moving Around

Gary is moving to Boston, Harry is moving to Dallas, Larry is moving to Chicago, Mary is moving to Atlanta.

puzzle answers

page 179 • Taming Dragons

	Day 1	Day 2	Day 3	Day 4
Ruby	Smokey	Spitfire	Forktail	Blaze
Jade	Forktail	Smokey	Blaze	Spitfire
Sapphire	Blaze	Forktail	Spitfire	Smokey
Topaz	Spitfire	Blaze	Smokey	Forktail

page 179 • The Marriage Proposal

Ruby can take out one pebble and "accidentally" drop it into the river. Then, she'll insist that the pebble was white. Since the other pebble in the purse is black, everyone has to assume that she dropped the white pebble—and she won't have to marry the sneaky prince!

page 182 • Simple Symbols

```
  6 2 1        2 1 6
- 4 1 1      - 1 1 2
_____      _____
  2 1 0        1 0 4
```

page 182 • Buying Numbers

The customer was buying numbers for her front door.

page 183 • I Can't Find It!

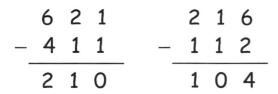

pages 180–181 • In the Land of Confusion

Can you figure out who is a sage and who is a jester? Xavier and Zachary are sages, and Yale is a jester. Here is the explanation: Xavier must be a sage because if he were a jester, he would lie about it. Since Xavier is a sage, Yale is a jester—his claim that Xavier is lying is untrue. In turn, that means Zachary is telling the truth, so he is a sage.

Are the boy and girl sages and/or jesters, and what color hair does each one have? They are both jesters; the boy has red hair and the girl has black hair. If the third statement is true, then either the first or the second statement must be untrue; but that's impossible—either they are both true or both untrue, since one is a boy and the other is a girl. That means the boy is a jester, which means that he is the one who said, "I'm a girl." Therefore, the girl is also a jester, because she said, "I'm a boy."

What can you tell about him or his son? They are both sages. Let's look at it this way:

1. If the statement is true, then they are either both sages or jesters; since the father is telling the truth, they are both sages.

2. If the statement is false and the father is a jester, his son must be a sage, in which case the statement is not a lie, which means that the father cannot be a jester.

That means the only possible outcome is that they are both sages.

Immediately, the sages cried: "Imposter! Arrest that man!" Why? If the King were a sage, he would say the truth, "I'm a sage." If the King were a jester, he would lie and say, "I'm a sage." Since the King said, "I'm a jester," he is neither a sage nor a jester, and is not a citizen of the Land of Confusion.

puzzle answers

page 183 • I Found It!

Students	# of books each student found
Jasmine	3
Katlyn	1
Josh	4
Ethan	5
TOTAL number of puzzle books found	13

page 188 • Who Owns That Car?

Look at the license plate upside down, and you'll see that the numbers spell out OLLIE LEE.

page 191 • An Average Day

One of the averages above is a mode. Which one is it? Average ice-cream flavor

page 194 • Spellulator

9,645 / 3 = (small, medium, or large) — 3215, SIZE

142 × 5 = (petroleum) — 710, OIL

1,879 × 3 = (what you walk on) — 5637, LEGS

10,000 − 4,662 = (honey makers) — 5338, BEES

50,029 − 15,023 = (barnyard animal) — 35006, GOOSE

206 + 206 + 206 = (the opposite of tiny) — 618, BIG

188,308 + 188,308 = (laugh in a silly way) — 376616, GIGGLE

10 + 13 = (not hard) — 23, EZ

926 × 2 × 2 = (an empty space) — 3704, HOLE

page 195 • Calling Code

1. IMA NUTT
2. FRANK N STEIN
3. TED E BEAR
4. TAFFY PULL
5. DREW A BOAT
6. SUMMER TIME
7. SANTA CLAUS

page 189 • Even and Odd

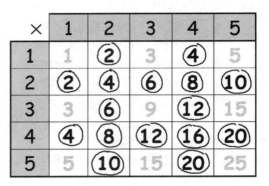

page 190 • Get Out of Here

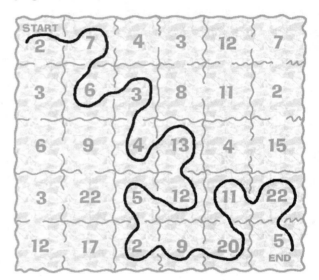

page 197 • Practice Solving Networks

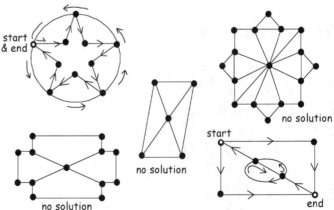

puzzle answers

page 198 • Color My World

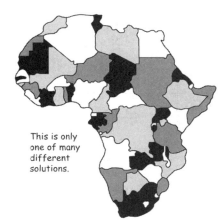

This is only one of many different solutions.

page 198 • Crazy Quilting

There are several ways you can color this pattern—this is just one way of doing it.

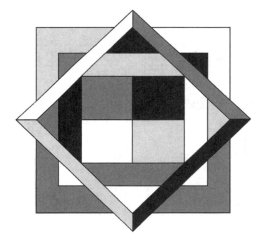

page 199 • An Unsolved Mystery

12 = 5 + 7	34 = 31 + 3
14 = 11 + 3	46 = 23 + 23
16 = 11 + 5	58 = 53 + 5
20 = 13 + 7	60 = 53 + 7
24 = 11 + 13	

page 200 • Around, and Around, and Around We Go

page 201 • The Very Last Cross-Number Puzzle

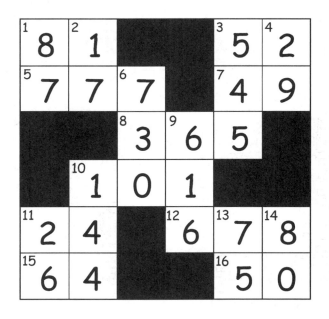

puzzle answers

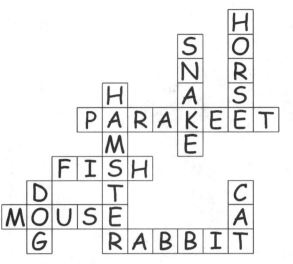

page 206 • Pet Groupie

page 206 • Mouse Maze

page 207 • Kitty Compounds

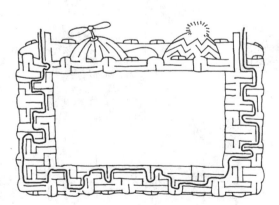

page 208 • Hamper Maze

344

puzzle answers

page 209 • Capitol Maze

page 211 • Lost Lemons

page 210 • Presidential Quotable Quote

---

page 209 •
Hidden Presidents

1. George Washington
2. Abraham Lincoln
3. Theodore Roosevelt
4. John F. Kennedy
5. Richard M. Nixon
6. Bill Clinton

---

page 209 • Capitol
Confusion

Correct answers: 1.2. and 3.

---

page 210 •
Rebus for President!

1. Dwight D. Eisenhower
2. George Bush

---

page 210 •
Presidential Quotable
Quote
Answers:

A. Person, place, or thing = NOUN

B. To fasten = LOCK

C. To hurry = RUSH

D What a cow chews = CUD

E. Adult male human = MAN

F. Caterpillar case = CO-COON

G. Building in which people live = HOUSE

H. Opposite of night = DAY

I. To move through the air with wings = FLY

J. A plaything = TOY

K. Pull Suddenly = YANK

L. A large number = MANY

M. Sound a dog makes = WOOF

N. To attempt = TRY

O. Abrupt = CURT

P. Unhappy = SAD

Q. In another direction = AWAY

R. Part of plant that grows underground = ROOT

S. Person trained to care for the sick = NURSE

T. Twelve inches = FOOT

U. Mixture of gases surrounding the Earth = AIR

V. Armed fighting between people = WAR

puzzle answers

page 212 • Serve 'em Up
2 to 4

page 212 • Positively Peachy

page 212 • Tropical Maze

penny — Ulysses S. Grant
nickel — Thomas Jefferson
dime — George Washington
quarter — Alexander Hamilton
$1.00 — Abraham Lincoln
$2.00 — George Washington
$5.00 — Thomas Jefferson
$10.00 — Abraham Lincoln
$20.00 — Franklin D. Roosevelt
$50.00 — Benjamin Franklin
$100.00 — Andrew Jackson

page 213 • Money Match

Answer: ceNTs

page 213 • Loose Change

page 213 • Money Maze

346

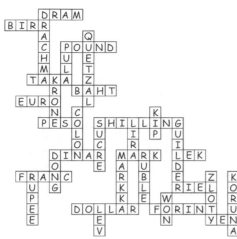

page 214 • Can I Borrow a Drachma?

page 215 • Space Maze

page 215 • Planet Groupie

● ● ◦ ●) (· ((●) (· (
A B O U T   T W E N T Y

))) · ● ●) · ● ● ◦) · ●))
N I N E   A N D   A   H A L F

● ● ◦ (
D A Y S

page 216 • Moon Phase decoder

KNEEL   ARM   STRONG

(Neil Armstrong)

page 216 • One Small Step

Answer:
In art the best is good enough.

page 221 • Color-a-Message

Answers:
Frames 1 and 5 are a pair.
Frames 2 and 6 are a pair.
Frames 3 and 4 are a pair.

page 222 • Same Frames?

page 221 • Color-a-Message

ROD = RED
GLUE = BLUE
BLOCK = BLACK
GRANGE = ORANGE
MELLOW = YELLOW
GREET = GREEN
WINK = PINK
CROWN = BROWN
WHINE = WHITE
MOLD = GOLD

page 221 • Mixing Colors

1. Pablo Picasso
2. Claude Monet
3. Mary Cassatt
4. Georgia O'Keefe
5. Leonardo da Vinci
6. Vincent van Gogh

page 222 • Famous Artists

puzzle answers

page 223 • Strike Up the Band

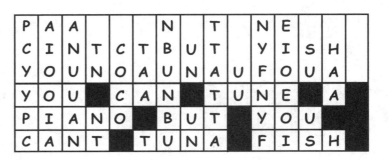

page 223 • Off Key Riddle

1. Johann Brahms
2. Peter Ilyich Tchaikovsky
3. Franz Joseph Haydn
4. Wolfgang Amadeus Mozart
5. Johann Sebastian Bach
6. Ludwig van Beethoven

page 224 • Classical Composers

1. Go In and Out the Window
2. It's a Small World

page 224 • Name That Tune

Read the Music
Answer:
He who sings drives away sorrow.

page 224 • Read the Music

1. shark (By the way, did you know that sharks can have as many as 24,000 teeth in their lifetime? When one falls out they just grow another one!)
2. child
3. beaver
4. grandma or grandpa!
5. dog
6. Marvin the mouse!
7. snake
8. vampire

page 225 • Whose Teeth Are These?

Answer: A buck-toothed clam!

page 225 • Tiny Teeth

page 226 • Brace Yourself!

Brush your teeth after every meal.
Floss often to clean between teeth.
Limit sweets to avoid getting cavities.
Visit your dentist for regular checkups.
The circled letters spell the word SMILE

page 226 • Mystery Words

page 227 • Many Mammals

page 227 • Many Mammals

The note reads "Dear Robin, Can you play baseball later? Would Chuck (woodchuck) lend you his bat (bat)? We'll go for (gopher) pizza, too. Tell your mom we ought to (otter) be home by six. Later, Martin (marten)."

Extra Info: Are you familiar with the animal called a "marten"? It is a sleek and furry mammal that looks like a very large weasle.

page 228 • Practice Your Paw-menship

1. Armadillo
2. Bat
3. Beaver
4. Deer
5. Dolphin
6. Mole
7. Opossum
8. Porcupine
9. Rabbit
10. Walrus

page 228 • What Are These?

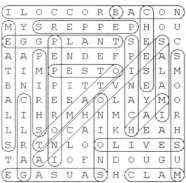

page 229 • The Works

page 229 • Pizza Maze

1. buzz
2. jazz
3. dizzy
4. fuzzy
5. puzzle
6. buzzard
7. blizzard
8. quizzes

page 230 • Extra ZZZ's, Please

puzzle answers

page 231 • Surprising Seven

page 231 • Where Are The Babies?

page 232 • What Do You Call a Baby?

1. BOOKEND
2. BOOKLET
3. BOOKCASE
4. BOOKMARK
5. BOOKWORM
6. BOOKPLATE
7. BOOKKEEPER
8. BOOKMOBILE
9. BOOKSELLER

page 233 • Book-ish Words

1. Charlotte's Web
2. Goodnight Moon
3. Little House in the Big Woods
4. Curious George
5. Number the Stars
6. Harry Potter
7. Winnie-the-Pooh
8. Cat in the Hat
9. Hatchet
10. Three Little Pigs
11. Pinocchio

page 233 • Reading Rebuses

puzzle answers

1. A "book crook"
2. On a "book hook"
3. A "book cook"

page 234 • The Book Nook

THE STINKY CHEESE MAN

page 234 • Oops!

A BOOK IS A FRIEND

page 234 • A Good Mystery

---

1. Nevada
2. Idaho
3. Connecticut
4. Virginia
5. South Dakota
6. Louisiana
7. Illinois
8. New Mexico

Circled letters spell out:
VACATION.

page 235 • State Scramble

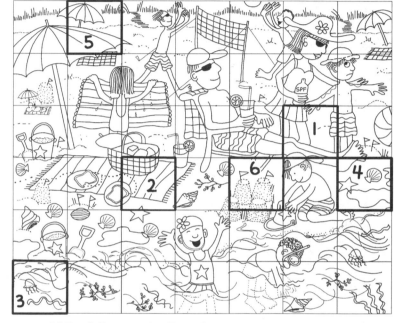

page 237 • A Day at the Beach

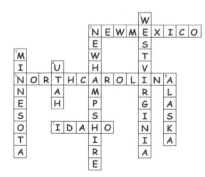

page 235 • License Plate Lottery

page 236 • Cross-Country Trip

START			
SEA	SHELL	FISH	HOOK
HORSE	BACK	HAND	BALL
FLY	YARD	OUT	GAME
PAPER	STICK	BREAK	DOWN
BACK	FIRE	FAST	TOWN

page 238 • Heading Home

puzzle answers

page 238 • Building Project

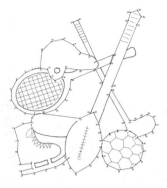

page 239 • Race to the Finish

Skate — Michelle Kwan
Golf Club — Tiger Woods
Tennis Racket — Pete Sampras
Batting Helmet — Mark McGwire
Hockey Stick — Wayne Gretzky
Football — John Elway
Soccer Ball — Mia Hamm

page 239 • Who?

page 240 • Take Me Out to the Ball Game

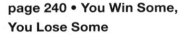

page 240 • You Win Some, You Lose Some

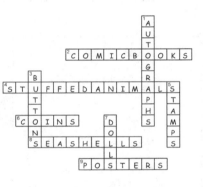

page 241 • Cool Collections

Two of the train stamps are exactly the same. Look closely — they are the two trains that have the big letter "Y" on the engine.

page 241 • Similar Stamps

```
  1    7·15·15·7·15·12    8·1·19
  A    G  O  O  G  O  L    H A S

15·14·5      8·21·14·4·18·5·4
 O  N  E      H U N D  R E  D

26·5·18·15·19
 Z  E  R  O  S
```

page 243 • What's a Googol?

puzzle answers

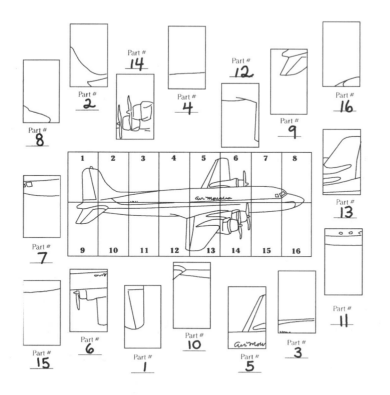

page 242 • Build a Model

page 243 • Roman Numerals

Guess who?

page 244 • Quick

1. I love my computer — when it **wo**rks!

2. Be**th ree**ked of smoke after sitting by the campfire.

3. My mother likes to **w**eigh **t**omatoes **on e**very scale in the store.

4. Annie wa**s even** early for school last week!

5. We can stuf**f our** dirty clothes in your backpack.

page 244 • Hidden Numbers

page 244 • Four Squares

353

puzzle answers

page 244 • Cross Sums

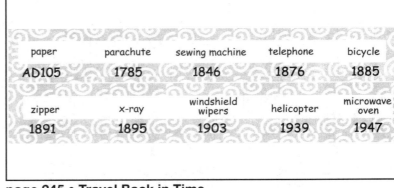

paper	parachute	sewing machine	telephone	bicycle
AD105	1785	1846	1876	1885

zipper	x-ray	windshield wipers	helicopter	microwave oven
1891	1895	1903	1939	1947

page 245 • Travel Back in Time

Page 4	L	Page 45	P
Page 6	I	Page 54	A
Page 9	Q	Page 79	P
Page 11	U	Page 97	E
Page 21	I	Page 114	R
Page 39	D		

page 245 • White Out!

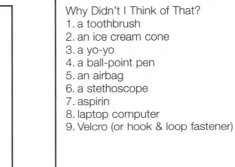

Why Didn't I Think of That?
1. a toothbrush
2. an ice cream cone
3. a yo-yo
4. a ball-point pen
5. an airbag
6. a stethoscope
7. aspirin
8. laptop computer
9. Velcro (or hook & loop fastener)

page 246 • Why Didn't I think of That?

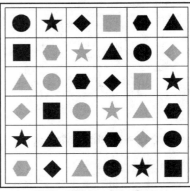

page 247 • Shape-ly Squares

page 247 • Fast Signs

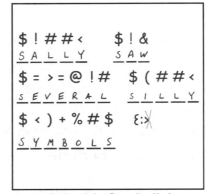

$! # #‹ $! &
S A L L Y   S A W

$ = › = @ ! # $ (# #‹
S E V E R A L   S I L L Y

$ ‹) + % # $ Ɛ:✗
S Y M B O L S

page 247 • It's Symbolic!

puzzle answers

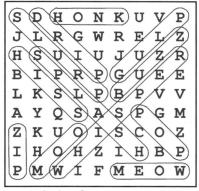

page 248 • Onomatopoeia

1. happy boy = glad lad
2. not real reptile = fake snake
3. splendid group of musicians = grand band
4. a group yell = team scream
5. a skinny female ruler = lean queen
6. a large branch = big twig
7. a cold swimming place = cool pool
8. a drink at noon = lunch punch
9. a made smaller black & white animal = shrunk skunk
10. a ditch in Paris = French trench

Answer to Teeny Weeny Hink Pink: Mervin is dreaming about a "mouse house," of course!

page 248 • Hink Pinks

1. Breakfast + Lunch = BRUNCH
2. Flutter + Hurry = FLURRY
3. Motor + Hotel = MOTEL
4. Smack + Mash = SMASH
5. Smoke + Fog = SMOG
6. Squirm + Wiggle = SQUIGGLE
7. Twist + Whirl = TWIRL
8. Chuckle + Snort = CHORTLE

page 250 • Blended Words

LITTLE =	SMALL	TINY	SKIMPY	SLIGHT
WALK =	HIKE	PLOD	STROLL	STEP
FUNNY =	STRANGE	WEIRD	CURIOUS	ODD
POKE =	STAB	STICK	JAB	PROD
GROUP =	BUNCH	CLUSTER	BATCH	CROWD
STAY =	WAIT	REMAIN	STOP	LINGER
BEND =	WIND	TWIST	TURN	CURV

page 249 • Simply Synonyms

puzzle answers

Perfect Palindromes
Answers:
1. We sew
2. Nurses run
3. Step on no pets
4. Never odd or even

In balloon: "Was it a rat I saw?"

page 250 • Perfect Palindromes

BLT = Bacon, Lettuce, and Tomato
RIP = Rest In Peace
SOS = Save Our Ship
SWAK = Sealed With A Kiss
TLC = Tender Loving Care
VIP = Very Important Person
UFO = Unidentified Flying Object
DJ = Disc Jockey
MYOB = Mind Your Own Business
ASAP = As Soon As Possible
TGIF = Thank Goodness It's Friday
SCUBA = Self-Contained
    Underwater Breathing Apparatus

page 251 • Short 'n' Sweet

1. PIG - BIG - BEG - LEG
2. FOOD - FOOL - COOL - COOK
3. HAND - SAND - SEND - SEED
4. CAN - MAN - MAT - MET - BET
5. JUNK - HUNK - HONK - BONK – BANK

page 252 • Recycled Words

Answers:
The things that could be recycled are: newspaper, glass juice bottle, plastic milk carton, cereal box, wire coat hanger, motor oil, plastic grocery bag, magazine, tin can, cereal box, paper towel tube.
"Junk" that could be reused: clothing could be cleaned and donated, glass could be replaced in window, apple cores and dead plant could be put in compost dirt and plastic pot from plant could be used for a new plant.
Hazardous materials: oil based paint or paint with lead in it, batteries, motor oil.

page 252 • Don't Throw It Out!

page 254 • Kriss Kross

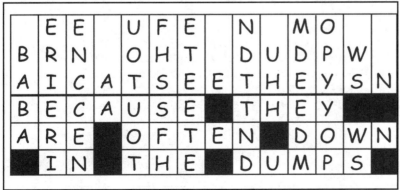

page 253 • New Life for an Old Joke

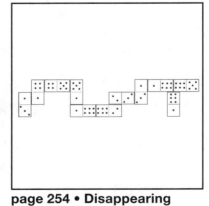

page 254 • Disappearing Dots

puzzle answers

1. Left over after a dark brown breakfast drink is brewed. (c)offee grounds
2. What is left after you burn logs in the fireplace. w(o)od ashes
3. Waste matter from farm animals. (m)anure
4. The vegetable skins that are removed before cooking. (p)eels
5. These creatures are good for the soil. w(o)rms
6. These fall off trees in the fall. leave(s)
7. Apples, bananas, cherries, etc. fru(i)t

Mystery Word: Compost

page 253 • Back to Nature

Turn One = 98 points
Turn Two = 96 points
Turn Three = 94 points
Turn Four = 92 points
Add all four turns together to get 380.

page 254 • Hopscotch Addition

Answer:
Sandy = 8
Peter = 10
Flo = 12

page 255 • How many Marbles?

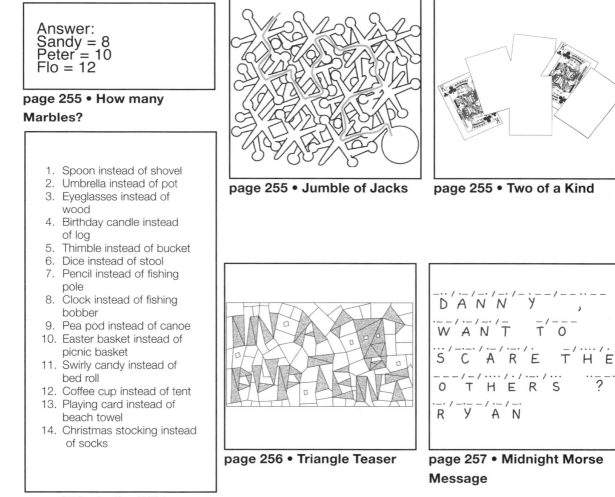

page 255 • Jumble of Jacks

page 255 • Two of a Kind

1. Spoon instead of shovel
2. Umbrella instead of pot
3. Eyeglasses instead of wood
4. Birthday candle instead of log
5. Thimble instead of bucket
6. Dice instead of stool
7. Pencil instead of fishing pole
8. Clock instead of fishing bobber
9. Pea pod instead of canoe
10. Easter basket instead of picnic basket
11. Swirly candy instead of bed roll
12. Coffee cup instead of tent
13. Playing card instead of beach towel
14. Christmas stocking instead of socks

page 256 • In the Wild

page 256 • Triangle Teaser

DANNY, WANT TO SCARE THE OTHERS? RYAN

page 257 • Midnight Morse Message

puzzle answers

page 258 • **Quotable Quote**

Answer: "on cloud nine"

page 258 • **How Do you Feel?**

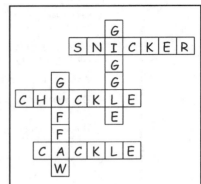

page 258 • **Love to Laugh**

"No one can make you feel inferior without your consent."

A. Sing without words = HUM
B. Seven days = WEEK
C. To touch = FEEL
D. Not me = YOU
E. In a little while = SOON
F. Midday = NOON
G. Not skinny = FAT
H. Larger than a town = CITY
I. Faster than a walk = RUN
J. More pleasant = NICER
K. Not far = NEAR
L. Towards the inside = INTO

page 258 • **Quotable Quote**

Answers:
1. Mrs. Katie Car-Pool
2. Mrs. Franny Foot-Ball
3. Mrs. Paula Pan-Cake
4. Mrs. Julie Jelly-Fish
5. Mrs. Rita Rattle-Snake
6. Mrs. Tammy Turtle-Neck

page 259 • **The Newlywed Name**

A Flurry of Families
Answers:
1. FISH live in a SCHOOL
2. LIONS live in a PRIDE
3. OXEN live in a YOKE
4. BEES live in a SWARM
5. SHEEP live in a FLOCK
6. ANTS live in a COLONY
7. GEESE live in a GAGGLE
8. DUCKS live in a BRACE
9. DOGS live in a PACK
10. CHICKS live in a CLUTCH
11. DOVES live in a COVEY
12. MONKeys live in a TROOP
13. CLAMS live in a BED
14. RABBITS live in a DOWN
15. SWANS live in a BEVY
16. WHALES live in a POD

page 260 • **A Flurry of Families**

Oh, Brother!
Answer:
Jennifer has three brothers (Billy, Tom, and Jim) and three sisters (Kathy, Therese, and Mary).

page 259 • **Oh, Brother!**

page 260 • **Just Like Your Mom!**

page 261 • Quotable Quote

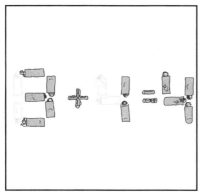

page 262 • Stephanie's Sleepover

1. HOUSEFLY
2. HOUSEBOAT
3. HOUSEHOLD
4. HOUSEWORK
5. HOUSEPLANT
6. HOUSEKEEPER

page 263 •
Household Words

Nope, they are a little short of the $4.50 they would need to each get double scoops. Together the boys only have $4.35. However, they could get two double scoops, one single scoop, and have a dime leftover if they wanted to. If they were really good friends, they would figure out a way to share the extra two scoops between the three of them!

page 261 • One Scoop—
Or Two?

Nina
Blair
Lauren
DYLAN
Maple Street
Pine Street
Pine Street
Maple Street

page 262 • Nice Neigghbors

1. SNAIL
2. HERMIT CRAB
3. TURTLE
4. BACKPACKER

page 263 • At Home
Wherever They Go

The boys decide to make applesauce!

page 261 • Share & Share Alike

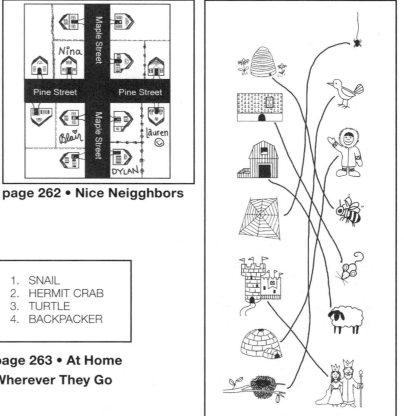

page 263 • A House for Me

puzzle answers

page 264 • Habitat Is Where It's At

---

1. Left over after a dark brown breakfast drink is brewed.
   (c)o ffee g rounds

2. What is left after you burn logs in the fireplace.
   w(o)o d ashes

3. Waste matter from farm animals.
   (m)anure

4. The vegetable skins that are removed before cooking.
   (p)eels

5. These creatures are good for the soil.
   w(o)r m s

6. These fall off trees in the fall.
   leave(s)

7. Apples, bananas, cherries, etc.
   fru i(t)

page 265 • Can You Speak the Language?

Find each letter and number of the secret message on the keyboard. Now for each one, locate the key in the next row down and slightly to the right. When you do this you will find that Charles Babbage's nickname is "THE FATHER OF COMPUTERS."

page 265 • Keyboard Code

Dumb Deletions
Answers:
1. Virtual Virus
2. Double Data
3. Perfect Password

page 266 • Dumb Deletions

:-o _____ ! My :X< _____ ate
Uh oh!   cat

something _____ :-*
                    sour

and is very _____ :-c .
                  unhappy

What a little _____ >:)
                    devil

he is!

page 266 • Smiley E-Mail

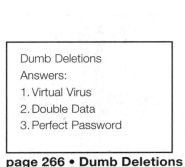

page 266 • Micro Maze

Answers to scrambled words:
1. READING
2. SCIENCE
3. MATHEMATICS
4. PHYS. ED.
5. SOCIAL STUDIES

Answer to circled letters:
  RECESS

page 267 • Subject Scramble

page 267 • It's in My Backpack

360

puzzle answers

page 268 • Whose Is Whose?

Answer:
Pizza and water.

page 268 • Hot Lunch

Answer:
There are 82 fish in the school that stretches across both pages. Actually, there are 83 if you add the one little fish which is scared of the submarine!

page 271 • School of Fish

page 268 • Bus Stop

Answer:
The letter reads: Hi! My name is Rudolpho. I have 10 years** and live in Brazil. I like to sing and to play guitar. What do you like to do? Please write to me SOON! Your new friend, Rudolpho.

**In many countries, people say that they "have" a certain number of years instead of they "are" a certain number of years old.

page 269 • Hello Friend

Uruguay

Malaysia

Liberia

page 269 • Stars & Stripes

Answer:
There is a lot to see under the sea!

page 270 • Shell Talk

Both a submarine and an octopus travel under the sea.

page 271 • What's Dot?

page 270 • Under the Sea

puzzle answers

1. WIZARD
2. KNIGHT
3. UNICORN
4. TROLL
5. FAIRIES
6. GNOME
7. DRAGON
8. PRINCESS

page 272 • Missing Parts

There are 65 basic squares and rectangles that make up this castle. However, if you start to count the outline of squares and rectangles of the same size that are next to each other as an additional shape, the total is MUCH higher! For example: If you count the right-hand tower the "basic" way, you get 20 rectangles; if you count it the "overlapping" way, you get 39. Try it and see!

page 272 • A Corner Castle

page 273 • Help!

T H E R E   I S N ' T   M U S H R O O M !

page 272 • Elf Talk

page 274 • Cookies

page 274 • Serve It Up!

Flour = 32 Tbsp.
Sugar = 24 Tbsp.
Cocoa = 4 Tbsp.

page 274 • Totally Tablespoons

The recipes (from top to bottom on the page) are for chocolate chip cookies, green salad, macaroni and cheese, French toast.

page 275 • Mystery Meals

1. AARDVARK
2. KANGAROO
3. MONGOOSE
4. RABBIT
5. OPOSSUM
6. GIRAFFE
7. GIBBON
8. HIPPO
9. PARROT

page 276 • Seeing Double

puzzle answers

page 276 • Color-a-Message

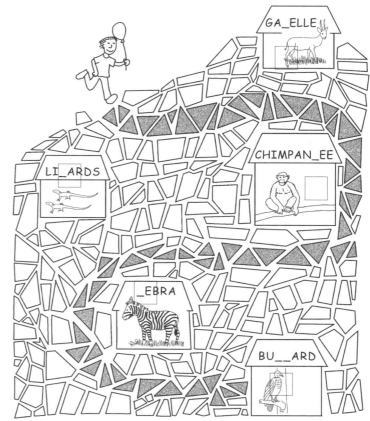

page 277 • Zack's Favorite

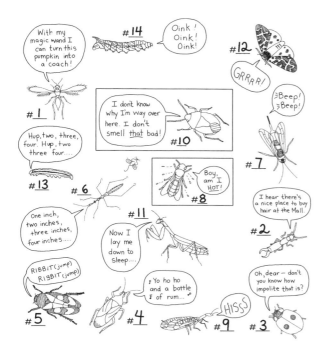

page 278 • A Bundle of Bugs

Ant, bee, beetle, fly, flea, ladybug

page 279 • Hiding in a Honeycomb

Itsy Bitsy

Answer:
A spider walking on a mirror!

page 279

Charlotte's Riddle

Answer:
Their webbing day!

page 279

BUTTERFLY to

FLY PAPER to

PAPERBACK to

BACKFIRE to

FIREFLY

page 279 • Mixed-Up Metamorphosis

Hiding in the garden are a teakettle, a plate of bacon and eggs, a pizza slice, needle and thread, a spool of thread, a blender, a chair, and a kite.

page 280 • Tools of the Trade

Answer: Stare at the dark line between the bee and the flower for several seconds. Now, keep staring at the line and slowly bring the picture close to your face. See what happens?

page 280 • Bee to Flower

DINVEE — ENDIVE

CREUUBCM — CUCUMBER

NTELPGGA — EGGPLANT

EANB — BEAN

OAPTOT — POTATO

ARROCT — CARROT

LOCIBCOR — BROCCOLI

LUTETCE — LETTUCE

PPERPE — PEPPER

PNHCASI — SPINACH

page 281 • Mixed-Up Garden

puzzle answers

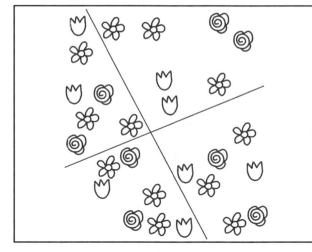

page 280 • Pick a Bouquet

page 281 • Herbal Seed Packets

page 283 • It All Makes Sense

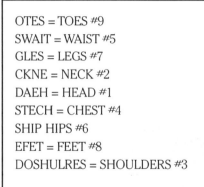

OTES = TOES #9

SWAIT = WAIST #5

GLES = LEGS #7

CKNE = NECK #2

DAEH = HEAD #1

STECH = CHEST #4

SHIP HIPS #6

EFET = FEET #8

DOSHULRES = SHOULDERS #3

page 283 • Body Scramble

5 Drop books at library.
4 Pick up pie at bakery.
2 Get mail at post office.
1 Pick up paper at computer store.
3 Buy flea soap at pet store.
6 Get milk at grocery store.
Thanks!
♡♡♡MoM   Do this last!

page 285 • All Over Town

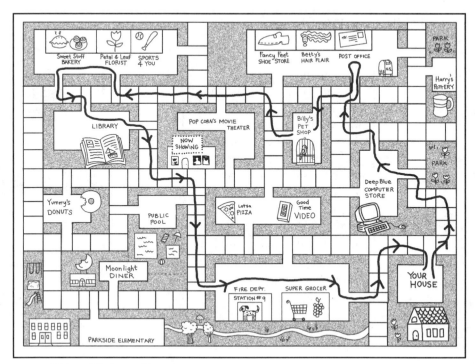

page 285 • All Over Town

365

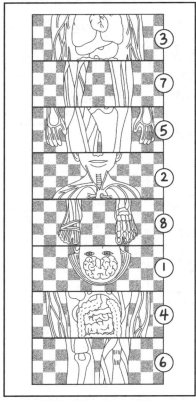

page 282 • The Inner You

page 284 • New Neighbors

The three tiny bones deep inside your ear are the smallest in your body. All three of them could fit on the nail of your pinky finger with room to spare! These tiny bones have an important job to do—they pass sound vibrations from your eardrum to a special nerve that goes to your brain. Then your brain makes sense out of all the noises you are hearing.

page 283 • Say What?

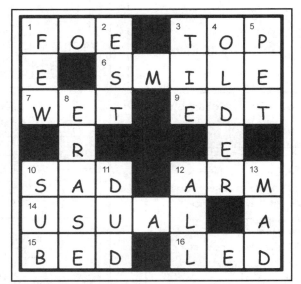

page 286 • Opposites Crossword

puzzle answers

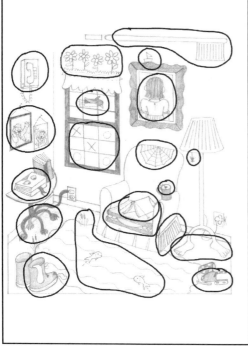

page 287 • What's Wrong?

"What's Wrong"?
1. Phone is too high
2. Two pictures are talking to each other
3. Book on table has eyes and tongue
4. Table has animal feet and tail
5. Boot is a dog
6. Rug is a pond
7. Slipper is a snowmobile
8. Floor lamp has bare feet
9. Spider is the chain for the lamp
10. Spider web is the lace doily on the chair
11. Mug has an eye
12. Magazine on the chair is a tent

13. Chair cushion is a sandwich
14. Ruffle on side of chair is a comb
15. Portrait of girl shows the back of her head
16. Small boat is sailing on the picture frame
17. Toothbrush is molding and air conditioning vent
18. Flowers are growing out of the curtains
19. Tic-tac-toe game on the window panes
20. Penguin is flying past the window

page 287

page 288 • Cut the Cake

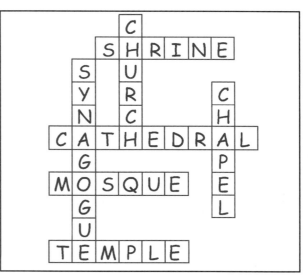

page 293 • Places of Worship

puzzle answers

I Can't Believe My Eyes!

Answers:

1. You see a number 13 or a capital letter B depending on which way you read, left to right, or top to bottom. Visually, the letters and numbers are so similar that the figure in the middle tricks your eyes and can be read either way.

2. The long black lines are parallel to each other. Take a ruler and measure to see that this is true. The short lines that go in different directions fool your eyes into thinking that the long lines are crooked.

3. This is perhaps one of the most famous optical puzzles. It is called the "Rubin Vase." You can see either two dark faces or a white vase depending on which color and shape you concentrate.

4. All the girls are exactly the same height! The perspective lines in the background fool your eye into thinking the girl on the right is the tallest.

5. This is an "impossible" drawing! There are either four planks or three planks depending on which end of the pile you are looking at.

6. Between the three bunnies they only have three ears!

7. Both lines are the same length. Measure them to see that this is true. The short, slanting lines at the end of the longer lines fools your eyes into thinking the top line is longer.

8. Try tilting the book so this page is at eye level, as if you were looking across the top of a table. The secret message is "HELLO!" Once you see the message with the page tilted, it is easy to figure out how the squares and lines make up the letters. Can you figure out how to write other secret messages this way?

9. You might have to twist your vision a little, but this hexagon can also be seen as a transparent cube. Try lightly shading two of the triangles that are right next to each other. This will help you to see one of the "sides" of the cube.

10. You should see flashing grey dots where the white lines cross. What's really interesting is that if you look directly at a grey spot, it disappears!

11. Even though the white triangle is not really there, your mind fills in the space between the three dots so that you "see" the triangle.

pages 289–290

Calling Code

Answers:

1. IMA NUTT
2. FRANK N STEIN
3. TED E BEAR
4. TAFFY PULL
5. DREW A BOAT
6. SUMMER TIME
7. SANTA CLAUS

page 288

Dividing the Booty

Captain Jack gets 25 coins

One-Eyed Pete gets 10 coins

Barnacle Bill gets 5 coins

Peg-Leg Larry gets 10 coins

page 292

puzzle answers

Household Chores

1. SWEEP floor
2. WASH dishes
3. SET table
4. VACUUM rugs
5. DUST furniture
6. RECYCLE newspapers
7. EMPTY trash cans
8. FOLD laundry
9. SCRUB sink
10. WATER plants
11. COOK meals
12. FEED pets

page 293

Walk the Plank

Answers:

1. A pirate would probably not deposit his money in a <u>BANK</u>.
2. Stealing a pirate's wooden leg and replacing it with an umbrella might be considered a <u>PRANK</u>.
3. Pirates probably <u>STANK</u> because they couldn't bathe very often.
4. On board a pirate ship they might use a <u>CRANK</u> to turn a wheel.
5. If pirates <u>DRANK</u> sea water they would get really sick.
6. Many pirate ships <u>SANK</u> during a bad storm or after a battle.

page 292

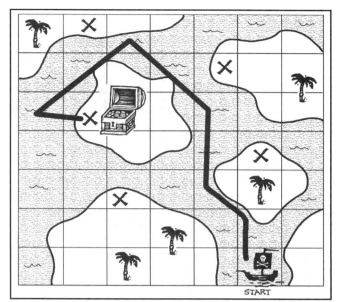

page 291 • X Marks the Spot

Having Fun

1. FLY KITE
2. EAT FOOD
3. READ BOOK
4. TAKE NAP
5. WALK DOG
6. CLIMB TREE
7. THROW BALL
8. PLAY CARDS

page 297

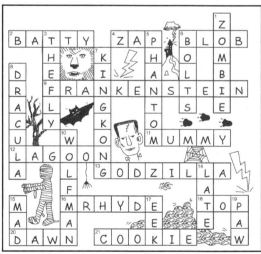

page 296 • Late at Night

page 295 • An Ugly Crowd

369

puzzle answers

page 294 • Weekly Maze/After-School Activities

Monday	Tuesday	Wednesday	Thursday	Friday
library	scouts	swim	piano	movies
baseball				

page 296 • Way to Grow

page 295 • Scared?

TERETOPHOBIA

1. B L A N K E T
2. S A N D W I C H E S
3. C H I P S
4. N A P K I N S
5. L E M O N A D E
6. F R U I T

Answer: P I C N I C
        B A S K E T

page 297 • Ready to Go

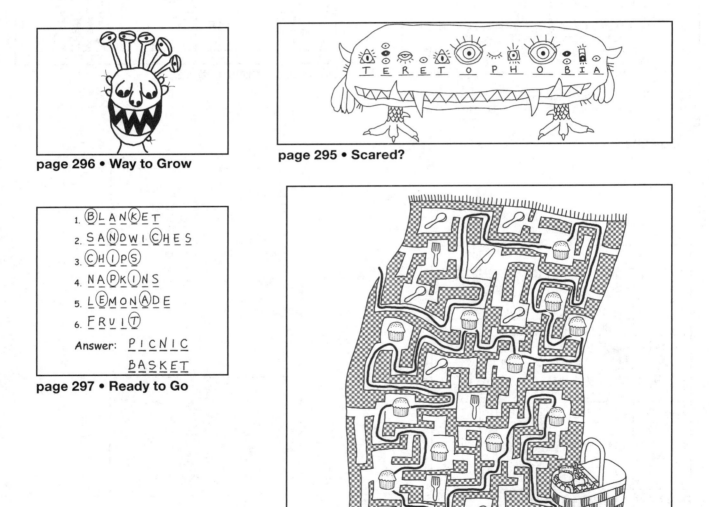

page 298 • Ants

puzzle answers

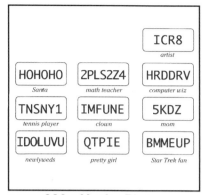

page 299 • Vanity Plates

ICR8	artist
HOHOHO	Santa
2PLS2Z4	math teacher
HRDDRV	computer wiz
TNSNY1	tennis player
IMFUNE	clown
5KDZ	mom
IDOLUVU	newlyweds
QTPIE	pretty girl
BMMEUP	Star Trek fan

Tallest Tree

Answer: It is a giant Sequoia that stands three hundred and sixty five feet tall — wow! That's tall!

page 300

Properly Pronounced

Answers:
1. MAPLE
2. BEECH
3. OAK
4. SPRUCE
5. BIRCH
6. PALM
7. WILLOW
8. FIR
9. Juniper
10. mahogany
11. poplar
12. cedAr
13. balsam
14. hickory

page 300

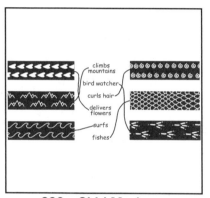

page 299 • Skid Marks

climbs mountains
bird watcher
curls hair
delivers flowers
surfs
fishes

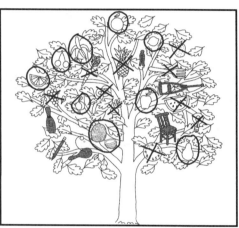

page 301 • Good Things Grow on Trees

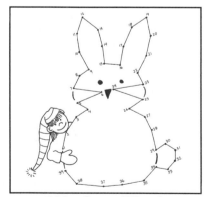

page 302 • Snow What?

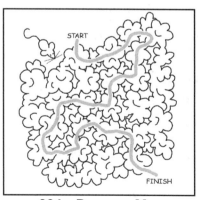

page 304 • Popcorn Maze

puzzle answers

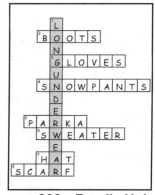

page 302 • Bundle Up!

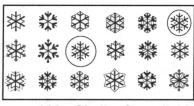

page 303 • Similar Snowflakes

Hot Chocolate

Answer:

Jon = 0, Keith = 6, and Adam = 3

page 302

Merry Poppin'

Answers:
1. Popeye
2. Poplar
3. Poppy
4. Popular
5. Popsicle

page 304

Mystery Menu

Answer:

Read all the capital letters in the menu to find the following hidden message —

TWO SODAS FOR THE PRICE OF ONE

page 304

Snowy Words

Answers:
1. snowball
2. snowflake
3. snowman
4. snowmobile
5. snowshoes
6. snowplow
7. snowstorm

page 303

page 307 • Tasty Endings

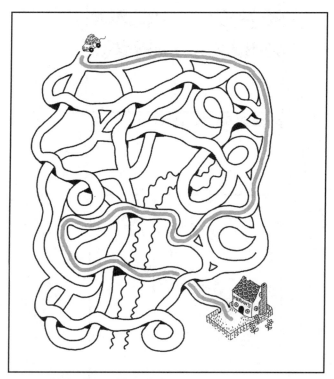

page 307 • Bye, Mervin!

372

page 305 • Now Showing

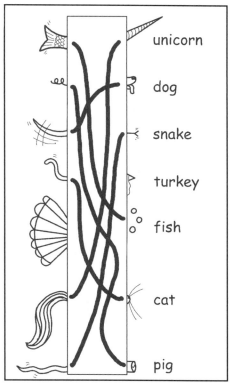

page 306 • The Tail End

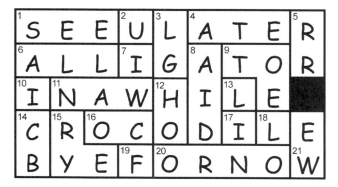

page 306 • The Last Word

373